*Education in Social
and Cultural Perspectives*

TO MY FAMILY AND FRIENDS

ACKNOWLEDGMENTS

Although the final responsibility for the ideas in this book must rest with the author, many people have assisted in their formulation. Morris Cogan, George Goethals, and Neal Gross, of the Faculty of the Harvard Graduate School of Education, read portions of the manuscript in an earlier form. Donald Dunbar and Tilden Edelstein of the Simmons College Faculty have read and commented upon certain sections. Teaching a course jointly with Frederick Anderson of Simmons College helped to formulate many thoughts, as did the opportunity of assisting Dean Francis Keppel of the Harvard Graduate School of Education in his summer school course for two years. Mrs. Barbara Sapin of Simmons College discussed many of the issues relating to teaching. Marilyn Mason typed the manuscript in its final form. Perhaps my greatest debt is to my students, particularly those in my seminar on the sociology of education, from whom I learned much.

Education in Social and Cultural Perspectives

HAROLD L. HODGKINSON
Dean, Bard College
Annandale-on-Hudson, N. Y.

Englewood Cliffs, N. J.
PRENTICE-HALL, INC.

Introduction

One of the great difficulties of the teaching profession is the problem of retaining a freshness of outlook. Like everything else, a continuous experience in one school in one community, working with children who are quite like each other, can inhibit our perspective of the world and our place in it. When, in our daily existence, we fail to apply new modes of thought and new interpretations of the familiar sense-data around us, we stultify.

The purpose of this book is to provide some new ways of looking at the schoolhouse, teachers, administrators, and children which we often take for granted. The perspectives of several areas of social science research are translated into the realities of specific educational situations in the hope that teachers and prospective teachers may deepen their understanding and insight into the nature of the social system which we call American public education.

Most teachers possess little awareness of the insights into teaching which could be gained from knowledge of behavioral science research. On the other hand, most behavioral scientists are unaware of the real problems which the teacher faces in the course of a typical day. Some merging of interests is clearly needed. It is the hope of the author that the reader may come to see that within the social sciences are many exciting controversies and findings which are directly related to the problems of education, and which may be used by the reader in studying some of these problems. To that end, technical terminology has been reduced to a minimum necessary for understanding the issues. Because the author feels that the content of the social sciences should be exciting to educators (and to anyone else, for that matter), notes have been designed to serve as a source for extra material if the reader is interested in the particular idea being discussed.

This is a book with which the reader should argue. It is *not* objective; it states a point of view, and the reader is cordially invited to disagree with the positions taken in dealing with educational issues. The author has found that the material discussed here provides a good vehicle for forcing students to come to their own positions on certain crucial educational questions.

A final caution must be added. This book is in no way intended to be a *complete* coverage of the behavioral science research which is related to education. There is much left to be done in terms of illuminating the social problems of schools; the present endeavor represents only a small fraction of the material in the behavioral sciences which could be used for this purpose.

Table of Contents

CHAPTER ONE

Perspectives

In this first chapter, it may be helpful to establish certain frames of reference which will be used throughout the rest of the book. These perspectives are very familiar to the social scientist, but may not be so to the practicing educator.

Many thinkers have considered a society as an organism consisting of specialized parts, each of which performs a specialized function necessary for the successful operation of the whole "creature." Just as an animal has eyes, ears, legs, and a digestive system, each of which performs a necessary function, so does a society have parts which must function together. Plato, for example, believed that a society (and a man) consisted of three major "subassemblies." The lowest component consisted of the physical appetites; the middle component consisted of the spirited elements which give men and societies their push and drive; and at the top (of both the man and the society) governing the other two parts could be found the intellect, the rational spirit, which could transcend physical drives and could provide a source of direction for the use of the energy in the system. If one does not mind biological analogies, the mind must govern the heart and the stomach.

This parallel of man and society has a certain superficial appeal. Perhaps people enjoy thinking that the virtuous society is similar in structure to the virtuous man. However, the organismic conception of *society* is a dangerous one in that it postulates a living, thinking being called *society* which has an existence of its own, apart from the individual people who are members of it. If one believes in this conception, one may soon feel that he is not responsible for his actions and that things are determined by *society,* a separate entity of which he is not a part. The organismic conception of society would seem to lead often to a completely fatalistic or deterministic position which allows for *no* individual freedom or will. The analogy breaks down when we consider a political revolution, which has no biological counterpart. The cells in one's left thumb are stuck there; they cannot escape as people sometimes can.

Another point of view states that a society is simply the sum total or output of all the activities of every member of that society, that there is no larger organism which dictates to the parts. This approach seems reasonable, but it neglects one vital factor: Although human behavior varies widely as one moves from society to society, it is generally true that *within* any particular society there is a great degree of consistency, conformity, and homogeneity. Children tend to be brought up in the same way; family structure is usually about the same, adults work for the same things and tend to agree on what behavior is good and what is bad. How can we explain this consistency of behavior without postulating a supercreature which dictates behavior to each individual?

It is here that we must add the concept of culture to our

discussion. So far, we have gotten along with the term society, referring to a group of people living together. However, when we find people living together, we generally find a degree of homogeneous behavior which is very great, a homogeneity in which even the *deviants* are usually aware of the rules and norms from which they are deviating. There must be some sort of "social cement" in operation here which binds people together and limits their actions. For want of a better term, we shall call this social cement *culture*. As the term society expresses the *organizational* characteristics of a group of people living together, so the term culture represents the shared and agreed-upon values, attitudes, and behavior norms which control the *selection of appropriate behavior*. It is possible to explain briefly the workings of culture without resorting to the organismic model.

Because individuals differ in their hereditary composition, some will be more able to perform certain tasks than others (e.g., it is impossible for men to bear children). Within every society there are smaller units with more specialized functions, to which each individual refers for norms and behavior. Because the individual *refers* to these subgroups for cues to acceptable action, they can be called reference groups. Just as an actor learns a given role which he will perform, so each individual acquires a role for each reference group to which he refers. This role represents the desired norms and performances of the reference group. Each individual may have a large number of reference groups from which he takes his cues and acts out his roles. For example, an American living in the Puritan era may have had to play the roles of father, husband, son, farmer, carpenter, hunter, politician, religious leader, and soldier. Today, that same person might find a different set of roles to play. The roles of husband, father, and son have undoubtedly changed in quality and nature, while other roles have supplanted the farmer and carpenter roles. Occupational roles are now more specific. The consumer role is one role of tremendous importance today; and as people become more interdependent we will become, to an even larger extent, buyers of the services of other people.

It should be pointed out here that the norms of various reference groups may differ; therefore, the role *expectations* for a given individual from two or more differing reference groups may be incompatible. When an individual gets rewarded by one group and rejected by another group for the *same* behavior, we may say that he is in a role conflict situation.

It would seem logical to contend that there is a relationship between the quality and quantity of role conflict and the consistency of the personality; that a great deal of role conflict may lead to emotional instabilities. One component of a well-adjusted personality, in terms of this analysis, is a person whose roles are relatively consistent with each other, a person who has developed a basic personality which changes in only minor respects as he switches from role to role. The schizophrenic falls at the other extreme.

Certain roles are simply given to the individual at birth. He has nothing to say about them. These roles (sex, family, age ranking with other children in the family) are said to be *ascribed*. Other roles develop *after* birth are based on various abilities—intellectual, manual, athletic, etc.—and therefore involve *achievement* of one sort or another. For each type of role, there are appropriate levels of reward usually in the form of social approval. This social reward we will call status, and we can therefore speak of ascribed (birth) and achieved (performance) statuses. By definition, ascribed statuses cannot be altered, whereas achieved statuses can be. Status as seen here is the social coinage through which we pay people for services rendered.

The concepts which have been developed here all point in the same direction—toward a *multidimensional* approach to personality. That is to say, we are committed to a view which cannot deal with culture or personality along only one line of analysis. The idea of a person, as developed here, is that of a kaleidoscope of shifting drives, needs, and attitudes. The conception of culture is also made in terms of smaller subcomponents, some of which change through time, while others remain stable. Instead of the person being one integrated unit of energy, he is considered as a bundle of smaller energy units, sometimes working together, sometimes not. We cannot, therefore, be satisfied by describing personality or culture in terms of only one variable. The personality develops, in large part, through the cues and actions of other people, both acting as individuals and as groups.

Our framework is that of interaction—people behaving as individuals, but keeping a wary eye on what the others are doing. Viewed from this perspective, personality and culture are simply two sides of the same coin, as are other supposed dichotomies such as the individual versus the group, the mind versus the body, and performance versus expectations. Man is a reciprocal animal, both with his fellow men and with the various and differing aspects *of his own being.*

An important caution must be added here. If one wishes to investigate a system of interacting objects, one is forced to select certain aspects of the system, "freeze" these elements somehow for analysis, and then insert them back into the system. Whether we are investigating molecules, cells of animals and plants, or a political party, we have distorted the system by removing certain parts of it. Therefore, when we talk of stratification or acculturation, we are speaking of only *selected* areas of the totality of behavior we call a culture. The play continues, even as we stop to analyze the meaning of a single line of dialogue.

CHAPTER TWO

Ranking and Rewards—

For Whom?

What Is Social Stratification, and How Does It Occur?

For reasons which are perhaps obvious, Americans are frequently uncertain and evasive when social stratification (and particularly "social class") comes up for discussion. In a nation which professes a belief in equality of opportunity for all men everywhere, any talk of ranking, stratification, or social classes means to many people that the democratic ideology must have failed in practice, and therefore ranking people on any basis is something to which not everyone will admit. This uneasiness which people feel about ranking others and making these rankings *public* is one of the major reasons why research on this topic of stratification is so difficult.

There is, however, fairly definite evidence that some pattern of social stratification is present in every human society, and in many animal societies as well. Several social theorists have been led to conclude that since this process goes on in all societies, it must be of some functional importance for the continued existence of the group. However, there are differing points of view on precisely what the function of the ranking system *is*.

Kingsley Davis conceives of society as an integrated unit (but not an organism) with many jobs which must be carried out if the unit is to perpetuate itself.[1] Some sort of "insurance" must be provided to make certain that those who are capable of performing the tasks essential to the society actually *do* perform them. Some motivation or reward must be present in the social structure to entice the right person into the right task. This reward is generally high status, which may also mean the possession of power and influence. However, the jobs to be done can be ranked on at least two criteria: (1) The functional importance of the job to the society as a whole, and (2) the scarcity of people available who are competent to do the job. Therefore, the *most* status is given to those jobs which are of immediate and vital importance to the society, and for which there are relatively few competent people. Many people have objected to this argument, stating that in contemporary America, at least, the entertainer may make more money than the professor or the judge. This objection may be met by pointing out that *social* status need not necessarily be entirely consistent with *economic* reward; that the over-all status of the judge is still higher. The other possibility is, of course, that as we move into a leisure time economy in which people have more and more free time, the job of the entertainer may have as much, or more, functional importance as that of the judge. This is at present sheer conjecture, however.

Talcott Parsons agrees with Davis on the necessity of a stratification system, although he emphasizes the individual in the social situation, and the individual's perception of the system. Just as we can rank various activities in terms of their social worth, we can also rank the *performance* of this activity by an individual.[2] Practically everything which can be done can be done well or poorly, and therefore evaluation of action is a natural corollary of activity itself. This means that evaluation of performance will occur at *all* levels of the activity scale, and not just at the top levels of ranked actions. Even if a person is doing a menial task which could be performed by virtually any member of the society, his performance is nevertheless potentially subject to evaluation by others.

It is worth pointing out here that we are dealing with two different types of societal reward—the evaluation of the worth of a particular activity, and the evaluation of a particular individual's performance in that activity. The first we shall call *prestige;* the second, *esteem.* More will be said about those variables later.

Davis and Parsons are both making virtually the same point, although they approach it from different directions. Davis is saying that any society, to be efficient, must motivate the ablest people to carry out the most difficult jobs by rewarding them maximally. Looking at the individual within society, Parsons says that any performance is subject to evaluation, and therefore the performing *individual* is also subject to ranking. These points of view are complementary, not antagonistic, just as prestige and esteem are not necessarily conflicting types of social reward.

It would seem reasonable to assume that social stratification of some sort is a typical pattern in societies. When men live together with their fellows, their needs can be satisfied far more efficiently by using and rewarding the special attributes of various members, thus resulting in a stratification pattern. This stratification pattern will tend to be expanded through time to include future generations as well as present. Therefore, by assuming that the son of a man with certain achieved and ascribed statuses will tend to inherit those statuses we have a way of perpetuating the behavior patterns of the society. The achieved and ascribed categories of status *overlap* —that is, the son of a great runner or baseball player may inherit from birth (ascribed status) the status for which his father worked (achieved status). As a matter of fact, it could be said that here we are dealing with a major source of motivation for people in many societies. Just as a rat or squirrel stores up food, internally and externally, for protection against the severity of the oncoming winter, so the human stores up status by his achievements, on the assumption that by doing so, he is protecting his children and other members of his family against the hardships of life by ascribing, or transmitting, his status to them.

We can easily see the benefits that arise from the existence of a stratification system, both in terms of the perpetuation and reward of the behaviors of the members of the society, and in terms of the promotion of a stable culture with consistent, easily learned patterns. However, there are many dangers in praising stratification systems as an unmixed blessing. Perhaps most important is the conservative bias which may result from such thinking. If we are convinced that stratification systems are necessary and are consistently present in societies, then it is fairly easy to assume that the stratification system in operation at the moment, regardless of what it does to people, is both justifiable and incapable of being changed. Thus the acceptance of stratification can easily lead to an acceptance of the *status quo.* Many religions have consciously striven to promote an acceptance of the present social and economic stratification hierarchy on the grounds that it originated as an act of the deity. There is an old English hymn which makes this point clearly:

> The rich man in his castle,
> The poor man at his gate,
> God made them high and lowly,
> And ordered their estate.

It is perhaps feasible that those in power, at the top of the stratification hierarchy, have often tried to impress upon their followers that the system simply cannot be changed, that "this is the way things were meant to be." Particularly in earlier Oriental societies, the stable stratification systems were considered to be a part of the all-embracing religious power. Religious and secular systems of stratification were one and the same. Whether it be right or wrong, the acceptance of stratification can lead to the acceptance of tyranny and injustice, and to the notion that the present order is unchangeable. We shall see that education has often been used to preserve the *status quo*.

In What Ways Are People Stratified?

Proceeding from Parson's position, we can say that *any* action is capable of being evaluated; therefore the number of possible bases of stratification is limited only by the number of activities which are performed by the individuals who comprise the society. An individual can be evaluated both by the behaviors which he shares with others and by behaviors which he does not share with others. As a subcategory of the latter, he can be evaluated by his *lack* of behavior in a behavior-provoking situation. (In many circles in contemporary America, one may be evaluated if he does *not* buy a new car every so often, or if he does not laugh at the right times and at the right jokes.)

Each reference group which influences a given individual will provide him with some stratification criteria. This means that the individual is involved in many differing, and perhaps contradictory, stratification patterns. A given action on his part may increase his status in one reference group and lower it in another. There is no reason to assume that stratification systems which originate in different reference groups are necessarily complementary. Our general answer to the question, then, is that people can be stratified according to any behavior which is recognized by members of the society. However, we would logically suspect that the most powerful and pervasive stratification systems would be developed around those activities which were of the most vital importance to the functioning of that society. For example, if a tribe existed only by the skill of its hunters who provided the only source of food, then one would suspect (1) that hun*ting* as an activity would rank high on the stratification order (prestige), and (2) that hun*ters* as they perform the activities of their trade would be exposed to a rather complex and sophisticated evaluation of their worth, both by fellow hunters and by members of the tribe who were not hunters (esteem). We would suspect, therefore, that the major stratification systems found in any society would reflect in a direct way the major interests or needs of that society.

One Dimension or Many?

Now that we have agreed that a wide variety of activities can originate stratification systems, we must decide which of these systems are worth further investigation. There are two major approaches to the problem. The first is to select a single dimension of action which appears to be of importance, investigate that area thoroughly, and establish conclusions for that area alone. The second involves developing an over-all view of the many stratifications systems and their functional interrelationships. Our earlier preference for the multidimensional approach to social analysis means that the second should be preferable.

Although many writers have given lip service to the multidimensional model of stratification, the two major tendencies among those who write on the topic represent distortions of the model. The first of these tendencies is to develop a number of stratification criteria, such as economic, social, occupational, and educational factors, then lump these together and call the *composite* "social class." [3] The opposite tendency occurs when a writer selects *one* criterion for stratification, such as economic factors, and then generalizes on the basis of this one factor to build up an all-inclusive stratification system, overlooking other relevant variables. If we use cooking as a metaphor, the first group has thrown all the ingredients into the pot indiscriminately, without measuring to get the right proportions, while the second group has tried to make the product using only one ingredient. There are many pleas in the sociological literature for more work on the interrelationships of the various dimensions of stratification;[4] however, there are few investigations, either theoretical or empirical, which consider the problem in depth.[5]

Much of this confusion in approaches to stratification may be due to the complexity of the society being considered—the society in which we live. Present-day America probably has a greater number and variety of status-producing characteristics than any other society, either contemporary or in the past. Also, because our society and our culture are in a state of constant change, it is hard indeed to keep up with the system of awarding status which must also be changing rapidly. This complexity presents a great temptation to *simplify*, to consider what may be many different status systems as one fundamental system. When we read of *the* social class system in America, we must be extremely careful to discover exactly how the terms *social* and *class* are being used. It is quite easy to overgeneralize conclusions about social class, as we shall see.

What Is a Social Class?

This is both a very complex and a very simple question. The simple answer would be something like this: Any group of people who feel socially involved with one another—who feel that in some sense, in some ways, they are different from others who are not members of the group—can be called a social class. We have already mentioned that each individual has many reference groups, and that these groups are not necessarily harmonious and complementary in their "pull" on the individual. It could be said, therefore, that an individual belongs to as many "social classes" as he has reference groups

—a rather large number. This definition of social class is certainly acceptable, but if used in this way, the term has such wide coverage as to be virtually meaningless. If the term is to have any utility, it must be clarified and applied to a limited range of social groups, not to the totality.

American social thinkers became interested in social class as an empirical problem largely at the time of the Depression of 1929, when many thoughtful persons were forced to revise their notions of the fluidity and adaptability of the capitalistic system. However, European thought had long accepted social class as a part of cultural tradition, stemming from feudal times and before. The European class structure was rigid, and ascription was as important as achievement in awarding status.

Karl Marx represents the epitome of a genre of social thought which put great emphasis on the conflicts between social classes, particularly conflicts of economic position. Marx saw these classes acting on a grand scale, a scale large enough to include the entire European population. Many American writers have simply transplanted an economically loaded Marxian perspective to the contemporary scene in the United States. They may be justified in doing this; however, it should be said that America has not had the *tradition* of rigid social barriers which have been present in Europe. Americans as a result may not be able to think in *social* class terms as easily and realistically as can the European, and it may be dangerous to apply concepts which emphasize economic and class determinism to a nation which does not emphasize these concepts. At any rate, the concept of class transplanted from European thought is that of an entire nation, not that of the reference groups of an individual. The stratification systems which can be found in a small town are seen simply as a direct reflection of this larger system which included everyone. A major debate in America has evolved around the question of whether or not these all-transcendent social classes exist in fact.[6]

The Measurement of Social Class

Probably the most widely used index of social class is that
of Warner, who attempted to isolate a "typical" American
community for study.[7] It is clear that what Warner meant by
typical is in some sense a subjective judgment about the central tendencies in American society—that is, the selection of
a typical community is as interesting in its insights into the
frame of reference of the *selector* as it is into the community
itself. At any rate, once the community had been selected,
two instruments were used to measure the social class system.
The first is the Index of Status Characteristics which measures
occupation, amount and source of income, house type, and
dwelling area. The second instrument is a measure of Evalua-
tive Participation which represents the individual's interaction
with other members of the community. These instruments are
usually referred to as the ISC and EP, respectively.[8]

There are many difficulties with this approach. First, in a
large city, the greater anonymity of individuals might mean
that the ISC is a more productive and realistic index than the
EP. When people do not even know the names of the families
who share their apartment house, it is difficult to see the
validity of the EP, which is also frightfully expensive to
administer. On the other hand, in a semi-rural small town,
the EP may be *more* important than the ISC. If it is true (and
it is) that one index may be more useful in community A, and
the other in community B, then cross-community studies which
check the findings in one community on another are of little
value, unless the two communities are virtually identical. If
cross-community studies cannot be accomplished successfully,
it is hard to see how generalizations about the *American* social
class system can be made.

Increasingly, the pattern of American life is that of working
in one place and living in another. This means that at least the
father may be involved in two different communities and two

different stratification systems. The regional high school has meant that in many areas the children are also taken out of the community to join an entirely different "community"—that of the school itself. Our tremendous geographical mobility allows us to take part in the activities of many communities, and Parsons has told us that any activity is capable of being evaluated. This ability to move great distances in a short time must change our ideas of the nature of *community* itself. The local community, which Warner saw as a microcosm of the United States, may not be the key to social class in contemporary America.

Regardless of these and other objections, the Warner studies have had a major impact in shaping our thinking about American social classes. In general, these studies postulate a typical American community as a six-class affair, ranging from lower-lower to upper-upper. Each class (or at least the major divisions of lower, middle, and upper) was a group of people with *personality* characteristics held in common, as well as the ISC and EP items. The lower class tended to be involved with basic physical needs, were much more uninhibited than members of other classes, and had little interest in politics and education. The middle class (a smaller group than the lower class) was very interested in getting ahead and making a good impression. Very inhibited in impulse gratification, these people valued education as a way of moving up the social ladder. Members of the upper class, whose families had been in the community for generations, were much more concerned with the past and with holding on to things which they had acquired.

These personality characteristics have been described in several publications by Warner and his colleagues at the University of Chicago.[9] These publications have had a great influence in certain areas of education, for example, in testing. This influence has often been commendable in pointing out certain differences in environmental background which have worked to the disadvantage of the lower group, for example,

in the taking of intelligence tests.[10] However, these biases have
to some extent been corrected in the tests themselves. Also,
there are many factors at work today which are making the
population increasingly homogeneous. The minimum wage
laws, the graduated income tax, the mass media, the migration
to suburbia and exurbia, all tend to suggest that we are becoming part of a more uniform environment, perhaps too uniform. If nothing else, the American pattern of installment
buying has virtually eliminated class patterns of consumption.
Anyone can own a highly valued article if he is willing to pay
for it over an extended period.

Another important attempt at developing social class indexes
was done by Centers. While the widely used ISC of Warner's
procedure measured objective, visible indications of status,
Centers attacked the problem from the subjective frame of
reference and attempted to study the status *perceptions* of
people. Warner concentrated on a single community, while
Centers studied perceptions of a more diffuse group of people
in many sections of the country. By simply asking people what
social class they belonged to, Centers tried to get at what he
thought was most important—not the objective signs and symbols of status, but the way in which people ranked *themselves*
in relation to visible evidence of status. However, because he
had to rely exclusively on the techniques of interview and
questionnaire, Centers had to accept the position people assigned themselves in the class structure without correlating
this information with what others thought of them, or with
objective data such as that produced by the ISC. In this connection, it should be pointed out that many studies indicate
that an individual will answer differently to an open-ended
class question in which he is allowed to choose the names for
the class categories than he will to a question like the one
Centers used, in which the person *must* choose between upper,
middle, working, and lower class. For example, Kahl and Davis
found that many who spontaneously rated themselves middle
class changed to working class on the forced-choice question

used by Centers.[11] It seems clear that when you ask a person what social class he belongs to, you may get a fairly objective evaluation of where he thinks he really does belong, and you may get where he thinks he *should* be placed. Thus this question is measuring aspiration as well as present placement.

Clearly, a more specific way of measuring status perceptions would be an improvement over the simple forced-choice question used by Centers. One interesting refinement was developed by Hyman, who listed a number of status dimensions, such as economic, intellectual, cultural, social, physical attractiveness, and general.[12] He then asked his subects to check their status on each of these dimensions, in the context of each of the following groups: (1) total adult population of the United States, (2) friends and acquaintances, and (3) occupational group. He found that within each status dimension, the individual's judgment of his status shifts *when the reference group is changed*. This is entirely consistent with our earlier statement that an individual's status perceptions come from (and will vary with) his reference groups. It would seem from this discussion that unless the subject is asked to specify the reference group he is using in the question, his answer regarding his class placement is of little use.

An interesting conjecture, in relation to the studies of Warner and Centers, is that the investigations themselves may not only be *describing* people's attitudes about social class, they may also be *producing* attitudes through the way in which questions are asked. If a person is not accustomed to thinking in class terms, the task of ranking himself in one of four classes may have a pronounced educational effect on him, and he may change his attitudes in the process of answering the question. The Kinsey studies are open to the same criticism. However, the researcher is in a dilemma here. How can he ask a question which will be so innocuous as to alter no one's frame of reference and still ask a question which will yield significant information? One of the major difficulties with social research is that the object being investigated is a human being who has the ability to be influenced by the measuring devices themselves. The neutron does not alter its structure simply because a scientist has a hypothesis, nor does it talk back. People (and this is both fortunate and unfortunate) do. The layman who wishes to understand and use social research must understand that there are certain situations in which measuring techniques used to measure a social phenomenon may, in the process of measurement, alter the very nature of the phenomenon itself.

We may now consider a third alternative to the approaches of Warner and Centers, an approach which attempts to avoid the pitfall we have just mentioned. The most widely used method of measuring social class is simply to take one variable —occupation—and generalize the results into a social class system. Occupation as a factor has some big advantages in being easy and inexpensive to obtain; however, it is subject to many difficulties. When a person evaluates occupations according to their relative social status, he may think of the *duties* of a person in that occupation, or the *prerequisites* needed to enter the occupation, or the economic *rewards* one gains from the occupation, or the non-economic rewards, such as increased power and influence.[13] (In relation to the latter, many teachers may be willing to take a low economic ranking as a trade for the high degree of power conferred upon the teacher in the self-contained classroom.) It is also possible that when a person ranks an occupation, he is doing it by thinking of the people he knows who are members of that occupational group, not necessarily by objective occupational characteristics. Measures such as occupation are fixed in time, whereas people are not—their occupational patterns change quickly. We are therefore justified in questioning the validity of occupation as an index of social class. A young man just starting out might be rated very low, whereas in a few years he might surpass an older person who had reached the limit of his achievement. It is also likely that people differ in their occupational ranking on the basis of the reference group which comprises their *own* occupation; that is, the farmer may rank occupations using a different set of criteria from those used by a banker.

An even more fundamental criticism of occupation as a measure of stratification is that some people may simply not consider it as an important index of class or status. They will do the ranking because they are asked to do it, but that does not mean that they are *ego-involved* in occupational stratification, nor does it mean that social classes are formed on the basis of occupational characteristics alone.[14] No one has shown that occupation is the sole factor which determines an individual's place in a social system. We have already mentioned the difference between prestige and esteem. Unless the ranker can actually watch a person performing a certain job, and unless he is competent to judge the merits of the occupational *performance,* he is only capable of assigning prestige to the job itself. Esteem, which is at least as important as prestige, is completely excluded from the occupational ranking scale. Perhaps part of the appeal of occupation as an index of social class is the fact that occupations can be broken down into at least three major groups: blue collar or manual jobs, white collar or non-manual jobs, and jobs which represent executive and professional skills. These three groups represent the essence of the three major social classes to many minds. Yet, what are our assumptions when we classify a skilled tool and die maker as a member of the lower class because he is a manual worker? His economic status is probably far superior to that of many white collar workers, and his intellectual and social status can be just as high as theirs. In general, it would seem that occupational rank is one important indication of social status, but we cannot say that a single nation-wide system of social classes has been built around occupation.

Another approach to the problem of finding a satisfactory stratification index involves the more recent attempt to investigate the consistency of an individual's ranking on several status criteria. The assumption here is that a person at a given level on one status criterion will be expected by his peers to have other competencies and status positions on other dimensions, which are in some way comparable to his position on the initial dimension. Status evaluations, then, tend to cluster or crystallize around a certain level for each individual, and some individuals have a much more consistent pattern than do others. Certain studies indicate that a person's status consistency may be related to his desire for change in the power structure, his political tendencies, and the quality and quantity of his social participation.[15]

Although this approach tends to avoid the pitfalls of some of the other methods of measuring social class or status in that it attempts to evaluate the interrelationships *between* status dimensions for individuals, it does have limitations which should be mentioned. Consistency *per se* does not tell us much about the relative position in the hierarchy. A person with consistent positions on occupational, economic, intellectual, and political dimensions could be at the top of the ranking or at the bottom. This device is therefore more useful in describing what happens *within* certain major status categories than it is in isolating the categories themselves. Another problem concerns the development of a scale which will weight the various dimensions of status in terms of their importance. Here again, individuals may, and undoubtedly do, differ in whether economic factors are more or less important than occupational ones in their over-all judgments of status position. It seems likely that each individual's system of status evaluation will be a highly personal thing, not necessarily comparable to the system of his next-door neighbor.

One of the assumptions in this sort of thinking is that to get a judgment of a person's over-all social status, one adds up the person's score in each of the status categories used, then divides by the number of categories to get the total. This "averaging" of the various status factors may *not* be the way in which people make status judgments. It may be that many people, instead of making a composite, simply take the most obvious or unusual aspect of the person being evaluated and leave it at that. The question of *how* people make status judgments has been explored more thoroughly by novelists than by social scientists, although the field of motivation research has recently become a center for this kind of study. The search for a single set of status evaluations for a given person or for a group seems doomed to perennial failure, as each person has as many sets of status evaluations as he has reference groups. This makes it logically impossible for an individual to give a single, definitive ranking either to himself or to others, which would take into account *all* of the status criteria used by the individual and which would be compatible with all of his reference groups. Certainly the status judgments of an individual are affected by the *personalities* of those whom he is ranking, and personality measures are notoriously complex and ambiguous.

Thus far we have considered four types of research which have attempted to isolate social class phenomena, and have found that no type is completely acceptable. There is at present no single empirical measure of social status, and we have discovered no proof that in the United States there is a single system of social classes which includes all citizens. However, it is true that people at different levels on the constantly shifting and amorphous continuum of social status do behave differently. The banker and the carpenter do have many behaviors in common, but there may be important differences also. Now if the banker and carpenter *do* behave differently, how can this differential behavior be explained without resorting to a rigid system of social classes which forces different people into different behavior patterns?

Social Class and Differential Behavior Patterns

Although in Warner's research six social classes were usually used, other experimenters have used as few as two [16] and as many as ten.[17] The major reason for this variety is that the investigator selects the number of classes which will yield the maximum amount of differential behavior in his results. For example, if one were looking for a fairly broad and easily identified differentiation in behavior such as whether or not a given group attends sporting events or not, one would need but two categories. However, if one wished to refine this data to determine what *kind* of sporting events were preferred by certain members of the group, a larger number of categories might be used. Kinsey's data, full of nuances and small differentiations, needed a large number of categories, while that used by Hicks did not. Notice, however, that these are *statistical* classes, imposed *on* the data by the experimenter.

The leap of faith necessary here is the assumption that these statistical classes or categories are also *social* classes, simply because they isolate differences in behavior. For example, we would have to assume that an analysis of people according to occupation which produces differences in their behavior is therefore isolating *social* differences as well. However, in what sense can we be sure that behavior differences are necessarily an indication of social differences? Unless the individuals involved *recognize* these differences in behavior and unless they feel that these differences are important socially, we cannot say with any assurance that we are dealing with a social difference, only with a statistical one.

Nevertheless, certain differences in behavior have been related experimentally to different "social" classes. If these classes have stability through time, as Warner and others have asserted, then the behaviors which are supposed to be class-linked must be passed on to each new generation. The most likely unit for accomplishing this transmission is of course the family, and many investigations have been made of the ways in which families train their young. If these investigations of child training procedures reveal a continuity within each social class, then the argument for the existence of a rigid, semi-closed system of social classes in America has been strengthened. On the other hand, if the behavior of training children fluctuates *within* the social class, then the argument for a single system of social classes loses much of its force.

The evidence on child training practices seems at first glance to be very contradictory. The contention of the earlier studies of Warner, Havighurst, and others at the University of Chicago was that the lower class mothers were much more permissive and relaxed about such things as toilet training and weaning, while the middle class mothers were much more strict.[18] On the other hand, a more recent study done in Massachusetts reported contradictory findings.[19] One of the major reasons for the claim that middle class people are more anxious and insecure than lower class people, as was contended by the Chicago group, was that the strictness and severity of the middle class child training patterns produced a child with severe inner conflicts, while the lower class parents' leniency with weaning and toilet trailing produced a more relaxed child who could enjoy physical pleasures without worrying too much about his conduct. Now if the middle class child training patterns are as permissive as the lower class patterns, as was indicated in the Massachusetts study, then it is impossible to make generalizations about class behavior in child training activities producing class-linked personalities. The authors of the Chicago study have explained the differences between their results and those of the Massachusetts study by pointing out possible differences in the two samples used. For example, the Chicago study took 47 per cent of its sample from the bottom two occupational categories, while the Massachusetts study took only 27 per cent from these categories.[20]

We may, however, use other interpretations for this divergence as well as those of the social class theorists. For example, it is very likely that the mass media have produced a much more uniform set of child behavior codes, and these codes are available to virtually everyone. The "family" dramas on radio, television, in movies, and in the popular magazines all seem to support the same point of view as to how children should be trained. Cheap editions of child training handbooks,

such as those of Gesell and Spock, have filtered into all levels
of our society, leading us to suspect that child training practices are becoming more and more homogeneous throughout
America. There is considerable recent evidence which supports this contention.[21] We are therefore justified in stating
that the stereotypes of the strict middle class mother and
father, and the lenient, relaxed lower class parents do not exist
in contemporary American society. This statement should not
be interpreted to mean that there are no longer any strict
parents in America. It simply means that these people are
spread out over a wide range of social and economic groups
and are not concentrated in the smaller range which is called
the middle class.

On the basis of the evidence presented, it seems that the
existence of class-linked patterns of child training, a necessary
argument for those who contend that there is a single social
class system in America, cannot be substantiated. We are left,
at present, in a rather confused state, as the phenomenon of
differential behavior is still with us, even though we cannot
explain the phenomenon as a function of social class. However, there may be other approaches and explanations which
will clarify the problem.

The Value Orientation Hypothesis

This is a totally different area of social research which may
shed new light on the problem of developing a satisfactory
explanation of differential behavior. This research area is not
concerned with social classes as such, but with values which
people hold, regardless of their placement on occupational or
economic criteria. The major assumption behind this theory
is that for each culture there is a central tendency of values,
a "core" which represents the major goals of that culture.
There may be subsystems of values which deviate, but the
central value system is continually pulling in the deviating
groups, producing greater homogeneity. Just as whirling physi-

cal objects are gripped by centrifugal *and* centripetal forces, so societies are propelled both toward heterogeneity and homogeneity, the deviant value systems tending to pull the culture apart, and the core system pulling the whole system together. Remember that we are speaking here of a system of *values*, not an economic or political system, although these will certainly be influenced by the value system.

The advocates of this type of analysis have determined the central value tendencies in American society in the following way.[22] There are five basic questions which every person answers through being a member of his culture:

1. What are the innate predispositions of man?
2. What is the relationship of man to nature?
3. What is the most significant time dimension?
4. What is the most valued kind of person?
5. What is the major type of kinship organization?

The answers group themselves into three major categories:

I	II	III
1. Evil	1. Neither good nor bad	1. Good
2. Nature over man	2. Man in nature	2. Man over nature
3. Past	3. Present	3. Future
4. Being	4. Being-in-becoming	4. Doing
5. Lineal (*All* hereditary members in the family group)	5. Collateral (Individual *in* family)	5. Individualistic

For the value analyst, the dominant value orientation in American society is contained in the third column. Americans tend to be optimistic, feeling that man is basically good and that he can triumph over nature and himself to shape his own ends. They also feel, accordingly, that activities are important, that one's goodness is measured by achievements, that the future will be superior to the present and is therefore more important. Because of the importance of individual achievement, the American sees himself as an *individual* first and foremost, and does not wish to become encumbered and tied down with a large number of kinship responsibilities which might limit his future achievements.[23]

There are, of course, many limitations to this kind of analysis. There is no reason to believe that a combination of values from all three categories might not become a "central" value core—that is, a culture could be found in which people believe that man is basically evil, that the present is the most important time dimension, and that doing is more important than being. Also, people undoubtedly are inconsistent in their application of these categories to the problems of everyday experience—for instance, in dealing with children, the future may be the dominant time dimension, while the present may be dominant in terms of the purchase of consumer goods. To a degree, past, present *and* future are all used by most people, and to pick out one variable as being the crucial one is difficult. Any scheme of this sort must be limited by the subjectivity of the person devising it.

Even with these limitations, however, people like Florence Kluckhohn would contend that this central core of values in American society (which can be held by anyone at any social or economic level) may be as useful in predicting differential behavior as are objective measures of occupation or income. There is some relatively recent support for this contention in the research of McArthur, who was interested in predicting achievement in college work. He found that the usual socioeconomic criteria did not explain why some students were successful and others were not.[24] He did find, however, that those boys who came from public schools (representing presumably the core culture) were superior in academic achievement to the private school boys, who held a deviant value pattern. This case illustrated that performance was to some degree explained by value criteria when the socioeconomic measurements failed. Additional support comes from research done with boys from the so-called lower-middle or "common man" class.[25] Although these boys were very similar in terms of father's occupation and income level, they varied greatly in their aspirations, in their self-confidence, and in their academic achievements. The boys differed primarily in the *values* which they held. The usual tests of socioeconomic status do not indicate a person's level of need for some kind of achievement, nor do they indicate the most likely sources of fulfillment of this need. Yet, if we want to know *how* people behave we must find out *why* they behave, what their goals and needs are.

The need for this kind of information is seen in another educational issue. In many instances, schools are evaluated according to the amount of money spent per student, the assumption being that the higher the amount spent, the better the education. However, there is very little relationship between the amount spent per child and the extent to which the child uses his abilities; the child in the wealthy system is seldom much closer to working at his maximum level than his less fortunate counterparts. The difficulty is, of course, that the statistics do not indicate whether or not education is of value *to the child*, specifically in terms of whether or not school achievement is an important achievement area for him. The conviction that school achievement is important is a difficult thing for a parent to buy. A parallel situation is that of the parent who gives his child $50 for every A on his report card, then wonders why the boy never reads for recreational purposes on his own time. Those workers in social theory and research who are interested in value orientations believe that we must determine the antecedents of achievement motivation in order to understand future behavior, that we cannot say that because a given family has a given income level their children will or will not want to do well in school. If we assume that behavior is not random but is purposeful, then it seems reasonable to expect that by investigating motives and the values which germinate motives, we can learn a great deal about what kind of behavior to expect from individuals in the future, more than we could from objective measurements of physical objects, as was done in Warner's ISC score.[26]

The value orientation hypothesis is also useful in explaining a recent social phenomenon in America—the fact that people are becoming remarkably similar in all aspects of their being. If we assume that there is a system of rigid, semi-closed social classes in this country, then it is practically impossible to explain this homogenization. On the other hand, if we postulate a central core of values, acting like a magnet to pull all deviations toward it, then the explanation of how people become as identical as the interchangeable parts in a production line is reasonably clear. However, a caution should be added, in that the value orientation hypothesis does not allow for changes in the central value system as time progresses. Various factors may be altering the nature of the system; for example, the prevalence of installment buying as an American style of life undoubtedly has the effect of emphasizing the present (Buy Today—why wait until tomorrow?) even though the future is supposed to be the central time dimension. Therefore the value orientation hypothesis should not be taken as a permanent, definitive statement of the dominant values in American society, but should be understood as an analysis of one aspect of the process of social change. As such, it has considerable utility, if we remember that certain aspects of the core culture may be changing through time.

Summary

We have seen thus far that some system of ranking people, both in terms of an *im*personal evaluation of the kinds of roles they play, and in terms of a *personal* evaluation of how well they perform these roles, is a component of society. High ranking roles are rewarded with prestige; high ranking performances are rewarded with esteem. The achieved status of one person may be passed on to his children as ascribed status. A system of stratification may be built up around *any* activity which is performed by some or all members of the society. Because each individual belongs to many reference groups (his family, those with whom he works, members of his religion, his political party, and his leisure activities, to name only a few), he may be subjected to a variety of stratification criteria, not necessarily complementary to each other.

Many writers have argued, on the basis of European theoretical formulations, that there is in America a central stratification system called the "social class" system which can be found in virtually every American community. Although called social, these classes are usually determined by direct measurements of objective factors such as occupation, income, and type of house. Another approach involves establishing social class rankings by asking people to rank themselves in a predetermined list of classes, without consideration of the fact that people in America may *not* ordinarily use social class rankings in their everyday lives. Other studies have investigated social class by using only one variable, that of occupation, assuming that *social* classes are built around the occupational category alone. Although class personality types have been built up around this research, there is little evidence that today a single social class system serves as the basis for apportioning social status.

Several writers have attempted to get at the problem of stratification without assuming a single social class system, asserting (and correctly) that stratification is multidimensional, occurring in a wide variety of contexts and using a wide variety of criteria on which people rank themselves and others. These studies have investigated the interrelationships between the rankings of a given individual on many stratification criteria, looking for the relative consistency of his position. However, people may not "average" their status in their actual dealings with others. With all of this research, few investigations have been made of the *process* of status formation: How do people actually perceive social stratification systems, and how is status awarded? One thing that is clear is that the process is basically subjective:

> The variables of status are mediated through an individual who acts selectively in his choice of reference groups, who

strives selectively for status, whose personal values affect the
composition of status and the emotional composition of a given
status, whose conceptualization of a reference group may be
different from its actual character, who is not affected by all
aspects of the culture nor by all references in the environment.
This essentially personal aspect of status cannot be ignored.
We cannot deal with these variables independent of their
meaning to individuals.[27]

This means that we can expect individuals to differ in respect
to the situations in which they are conscious of status, as well
as in respect to the *intensity* of their feelings about status. A
person would not be concerned about his status in a given area
unless he was ego-involved in that area and considered it of
some importance to him; therefore the areas in which an individual is status-conscious are the areas which he *values* as
important. Because people differ in their values and goals, they
will behave differently. Some writers have suggested that people behave differently because of a central value orientation
which some possess and others do not. Even with its limitations, this explanation seems much more likely than that of
saying that people behave differently because they belong to
social classes. There is little evidence that at the present time
a *single,* all-pervasive social class system exists in America, although our society is highly stratified in *many* ways. The research on child training practices supports this contention.

EDUCATION AND STRATIFICATION

American education is an institution in American culture, and like all institutions has a reciprocal agreement with
the culture as a whole, in that to a degree education determines
the culture, and to a degree the culture determines the educational system. Many of the stratification systems which are
visible in education simply *reflect* patterns of stratification
present in the larger society, while other types of educational
stratification are in *opposition* to those which dominate Ameri-

can society. One of the major areas in educational debate today concerns whether the school's function should be to reflect American culture as it is, or to reconstruct it. However, it is not necessary to become committed on the question as stated, as the dichotomy is misleading. It seems reasonable to say that education should perpetuate those aspects of American society which those involved in the educational enterprise feel are worthwhile, and that education should not perpetuate those things which are disliked by those responsible for the educational system.

One major difficulty here is that the responsibility for American public education is divided between professional educators and the elected lay members of school boards who have the legally defined responsibility for the schools. Many ideas which might be seen as a step forward to one group may be seen as an evil by the other.[28] Nevertheless, it seems clear that by selecting certain things to be taught and rejecting other things, the school does in actuality reflect *and* alter the culture. The question here is: What are the criteria used for this selection? The first step in answering this question is to uncover some of the major stratification systems which exist in schools.

Cues to Status

Where does one look to find evidences of stratification? In almost any organization, those who are on the "inside" have developed a set of relatively sophisticated cues which indicate clearly the amount of status given to each member. These cues are (sometimes intentionally, sometimes unintentionally) not easily understandable to the "outsider." For example, the white collar bureaucrat is extremely sensitive to differences in size of office, view from the window or windows, texture of rug (if any), number of secretaries (if any), distance from office to the superior's office, and possession of a dictaphone. Spectorsky has written a very entertaining book concerning the status perceptions of the Exurbanites, who feel, for example, that a person seen driving a Jeep must be a man of very high status, as no one could get along with *just* a Jeep, thereby establishing unequivocally that the driver of the Jeep must own two cars.[29] A great deal of literature, from the novels of Marquand to the plays of Shaw, has dealt with the perception of cues to status. What would *My Fair Lady* be worth if it were not for the fact that when Britishers hear a Cockney accent they immediately make negative judgments about the social status of the speaker? Speech is one of the most pervasive cues to social status, yet we know little about how these cues are interpreted.

When we enter the world of the school, a whole new set of status cues appears. Although some of these cues are common throughout the educational institution, others are unique to one specific school or town. As an example of the latter, the writer recently visited a prominent experiment in the use of educational television to secondary schools. Two high school English classes were being broadcast, one to a large audience of college preparatory students, the other to all the other English students (the second was called, ambiguously enough, "General English"). In the college preparatory studio there were three cameras, while in the studio broadcasting to the non-college students there were only two. Staff competence also varied in the two studios, suggesting that school and TV studio operate on similar status cues.

Educational Status Systems

The example of the school and TV studio was selected because it points out nicely the ambiguities of many status systems. We think often that we are stratifying students by their *ability* when actually other factors form the basis of the system. In most high schools, and many junior high schools, students are stratified by curriculum—one selects from choices such as college preparatory, commercial, vocational, and general. A common assumption held by teachers, students, and parents is that the basis of this stratification is intelligence, that the college preparatory students are the most bright and the general students are the least bright. Undoubtedly the system works this way in many cases, but the essence of the system is not intellectual ability but *occupational choice.* One might object by saying that enrollment in a college preparatory course is not a matter of occupational choice; but ultimately it is, as certain occupational levels, such as professional, managerial, and executive, can only be entered through having a college background. The student in the college preparatory program may not have decided on a specific occupation, but he (and/or his parents) have decided on a high *level* of occupational status, whatever the job may be. The parents may be extremely influential in this decision. The child may feel that he is in the college preparatory program because (1) all his friends are in that program, or (2) because he never thought about any other possibilities, as "it was always assumed" that he would go to college.[30] More likely, however, is the students's admission that he wants to make a lot of money and must have enough education to get the job which will provide him with this money.

Although the curriculum stratification is not basically a stratification by ability, this is often accomplished through ability groupings *within* the curriculum division; that is, there may be three or more sections of the college preparatory group, the student being placed in one of the three on the basis of his test scores and previous academic record. We might point out here the general tendency to give more status to the students in the college preparatory program, with decreasing amounts to those in commercial, vocational, and "general" programs. The school is here reflecting the occupational status system in American society, which parallels the school curriculum in its status awards to members of various occupations.

Here we have approached one of the major dilemmas in the educational stratification system. Teachers and parents share the view that academic status is important and should be rewarded by the school. Yet for the egalitarian, *all* students are of equal worth, and stratifying by academic achievement is somehow "undemocratic." The environmentalist is quick to point out that the awarding of academic status is as much a measure of the student's cultural background as it is a measure of his innate ability. Many schools have given up the tradition of giving letter grades for academic achievement, and use broader and less distinct categories such as pass or fail, or satisfactory or unsatisfactory. The awarding of *social* status to those who demonstrate superior academic achievement is no longer the dominant mode of stratification in many schools. Many writers have pointed out that the contemporary school often selects activities in such a way that *every* student is rewarded,[31] regardless of his academic accomplishments. Games are picked in which everyone wins and no one loses, thereby allowing *no* differential status rewards.

Many teachers feel that by conferring social status on certain good students, they are perpetuating the academic aspect of the school's status system. However, the question of the allocation of status is more complicated than meets the eye. Let us assume that a certain boy has made the highest score on a test given by a teacher. The teacher commends the boy in class and congratulates his parents. Our inclination is to say that his social status has increased, but this statement is only partially true, as we are looking at the situation from the frames of reference of the teacher and parents. It may well be that the *boy's* principal reference group consists of his classmates, who may *not* include academic achievement as an area which they reward with status. In this situation, then, the boy's status was raised from the perspective of teacher and parent, but in terms of his peers it may have actually declined. Because his dominant reference group consists of his peers, *the boy himself* may feel that he has lost status [32] and may go out of his way to see that next time his marks are good but not spectacular.

This leveling process occurs in certain subject fields also. A boy may do well in science and still be socially acceptable, but the excellent English student who happens to be a male stands in considerable risk of being branded by his peers as effeminate. In similar fashion, the girl who tops the physics and chemistry classes may be considered a trifle odd. A revealing poster, advertising a recent dance at a college in Massachusetts, stated some of the reasons for attending. The major point was stated as a question: "Want to be friends with the gang, but can't help getting A's?"

There seems to be a principle of status *compensation* here which has not been carefully investigated. This means that if a person gains status in one area he must give up, or forfeit, something else. Consider, for example, the stereotype of the terribly bright boy of 8 to 12 years of age. What does he look like? There is general agreement that he is very scrawny in build, with thin arms and legs. His head is huge, almost hydrocephalous in size but perfectly round in shape. The eyes (which are very weak, blink constantly, and take up most of the head) are surrounded by huge thick glasses with heavy circular frames. Most of the research on gifted children indicates just the opposite—that they are superior physically as well as mentally;[33] yet the stereotype still exists. The explanation probably lies in some peculiar notion that in a society in which everyone is equal, no one should be superior in everything, and talented individuals must "pay the price" for their talent by being mediocre in other areas.

Thus far we have pointed out that academic achievement is one area of stratification in education, and that its importance in relation to other factors need not be held by all concerned. One recent study has reported that for a large sampling of students from a variety of schools, academic achievement was the *least* important status area,[34] falling far behind sports and extra-curricular social activities. Of course this may be only a stereotyped response, in that students know that they are not *supposed* to enjoy academic success as much as success in other activities.

Students are also stratified by grade level. We think of the grade system of kindergarten through high school as a ranking of increasing difficulty of academic accomplishment. However, as a result of the trend toward social promotion in many areas of the country, the entire group which entered kindergarten at the same time may move through the system simultaneously, with few staying behind to repeat one or more years. This means that the nature of the system of grades has changed from a set of *intellectual* barriers to a set of *chronological* barriers. Nevertheless, there is still a certain amount of status given to students in the older grades by teachers and the administration. There are typical behaviors for certain grade levels which interact with other stratification systems, such as that of sex. As one moves through the grade levels, the behavior which is expected concerning members of the opposite sex changes also. The third-grade boy may see girls as something to throw rocks at, while the junior in high school is expected to behave in a somewhat more gentlemanly fashion.

Within a grade level, there is often an amazing amount of tacit agreement among students as to what behavior is appropriate at each grade level. Status given a student by the grade level is usually prized, as the unit constitutes his peers, whose opinion he usually values. The class president is admired by both his teachers and his fellow students, while the class "brain" is often admired only by the former, and does not *represent* the group. The president can therefore enjoy status rewards from both groups without alienating anyone. The class unit also limits social interaction to a large extent, in that a student in the junior class will have little to do with members of the freshman class. At the same time it intensifies social interaction *within* a class.

One interesting aspect of the restrictions on student behavior in terms of social interaction is that students frequently impose the restrictions on themselves and yet are relatively unaware of them. The author once pointed out to a class of high school girls that *every* girl was wearing white bobby sox, and that *every* sock was rolled over exactly three times. Every sock was encased in a saddle shoe of identical description. When questioned as to how this agreement had come about, the girls seemed genuinely astonished at their conformity. Apparently many of the folkways and mores which are manifested in common everyday behavior exist at a preconscious level. It is probably true that if one asked a goldfish to write down all the things that were in his fish bowl, the last thing he would think of would be water. The high school senior, when asked why he does not date freshman girls, will seldom be able to give a more cogent answer than "I just couldn't." Before we condemn the American student too severely, however, we might ask how much of the behavior in the day of a typical American *adult* could be clearly and rationally explained, without resorting to conformity as the explanation.

Students are also involved in a stratification hierarchy based on special abilities. Not all special talents are included, however, as the school cannot provide enough activities to develop all the talents of every student. Nevertheless, there are certain activities which are almost universally rewarded in the secondary school, and which require special skills. The boy with high athletic ability is generally given high status by his classmates. One would think that *any* athletic performance of high calibre would be rewarded with high status for the performer, but such is not the case. The high status sports are almost without exception team sports, in which a group of boys represents the school in direct competition with teams from other schools. Football and basketball are generally considered to be the most important team sports. We speak of track and swimming *teams,* but the basis of competition here is individual, and there is no time in which the whole team is working together simultaneously toward a common goal, which is the basis of the football and basketball competition. When the track man wins, he wins primarily as an individual. Every second of the football competition, however, is *group* competition. Regardless of what sportswriters say, no individual player can win a football game by himself. Track and swimming are only team sports in that the individuals' points are totaled to give a team score. The football team has a group *identity,* and this identity is, to the spectator, the identity of the school. The football team from Middletown High represents, in a very real sense, Middletown High itself.

To some extent, chorus and band competitions also provide this sense of school identity, except that the identity in an athletic contest comes from winning, from beating an organization from another community, and the music competitions generally allow everyone to perform before awarding prizes or ratings. Unless there are only two schools entered, no chorus is singing against *one* other organization, and therefore the school is not establishing its identity. There are many examples of a student winning a state or national contest in an individual sport such as golf or tennis without his classmates knowing anything about it. The scholar is in somewhat the same position, in that when he wins a scholarship he does so as an individual. It would be hard indeed to say that Middletown High won a four-year scholarship to Yale.

We have been suggesting that it is the activities which define the *identity of the school* to the outside world which are given the highest status, by students and faculty alike. In the noncompetitive area of class activities, such as the junior class play and the senior yearbook, we find a group serving to give identity to a larger group. The senior class yearbook *is* the senior class; and it identifies the senior class to the rest of the student body and to the whole community as the books get passed around. The model airplane club, on the other hand, does not represent the school and does not represent a class, and so is relegated by teachers and students to minor status.

It is undoubtedly to the good that these activities are selected for high status according to the amount of identity they give to the school or class, for this means that the students *want* to have an identification with their school, which is a healthy thing. Parents and teachers may groan about the amount of energy consumed by spectators and players during a football game, but on the other hand, athletic competition does provide students with one of the only socially approved means of expressing their identity *as a school,* and this may be of considerable importance. Private schools, which do not generally participate as actively in such interscholastic competitions, are often known to have little "school spirit," and this loyalty to something bigger than the student may be a very healthy influence. Loyalty to school may lead to loyalty to a political party, to a nation, and ultimately to an organization of nations working for peace. However, it seems unfortunate that in a nation founded on the principles of individual initiative, individual achievement, and non-conformity, the educational system must confer its highest status awards on *groups* of students and not on individuals. The pinnacle of overconformity, in which the individual gives himself over completely to the wishes of the group, is reached in the performance of the football and basketball teams. The reader might well speculate here on the validity of the factors which lead to the awarding of high status to group athletics. Are these patterns (roughness, physical aggression, subverting the individual to the group) the ones we wish to reinforce in *adult* society? Should the football team represent the school?

This whole stratification system of athletic ability is one which has apparently just grown, like Topsy. Teachers and administrators have seldom, if ever, considered the assumptions *behind* the system, or its educational worth to the total school program, as we have attempted to do here. If the reader decides that the present system of allocating status to students is not all that it could be, then he might consider doing something about it. However, in the previous section we mentioned that stratification systems, if they continue to exist through time, must serve some significant function for those involved. Very little is known about how, if at all, such a system can be consciously altered. How, for example, would we go about *making* students reward the academic achievements of their peers with higher social status? How could we structure activities involving academic achievement so that the activities would produce in the student body as a whole a sense of loyalty and identity with the school? Everyone feels a need to be recognized, both as a member of a group and as an individual. How could intellectual activities be arranged to provide both types of recognition? How can we eliminate the idea that a student who gets good grades or is interested in the arts is a sissy? In most elementary schools, boys as well as girls are encouraged to give free reign to their creative powers through paint, crayons, musical instruments, and the spoken and written word. In most junior and senior high schools, such encouragement is no longer given to boys. Why not? Should we build *aesthetic* achievement into the status system of the students, and if so, how?

Stratification Systems Based on the Teacher

We have already mentioned that systems of awarding status overlap, that some status judgments made by students may be shared by teachers. The organization of student programs around college preparatory, commercial, vocational, and general curricula is one example of a shared status system. The college prep students are usually given an unusually high amount of social status by their peers, in that they are elected to positions of responsibility in school affairs far more often than they should be by chance. Just as membership in a college preparatory program means high status for the students, so also for the teachers of these groups. As a teacher continues through the years in a school system, she tends to acquire more status and more bargaining power. As a result, she (or he) is permitted to teach more desirable classes, which means almost without exception the brighter or "easier" sections in the college preparatory division.[35] Just as the college prep student is rewarded with high status from the students and teachers in the school, so the teacher of college preparatory classes is given higher status. In the majority of cases in which the teacher teaches classes in several of these curriculum divisions at the same time, a ratio of the number of college prep classes compared with the number of less desirable classes is used by the other teachers to determine the status of the teacher.

New teachers, because of their poor bargaining power, are seldom given superior classes, even though their college training may have emphasized the techniques and materials used in college preparatory classes. Even when a beginning teacher does get a good class, it may be counterbalanced by her being assigned a very difficult class. Though many superintendents and principals are sharply critical of this practice, it is still widespread. The graduate of a teacher education program whose student teaching experience was limited to the better students in a suburban school is at a real disadvantage in a large metropolitan school, working with students in the non-college preparatory curriculum programs.

This status system which revolves around the curriculum divisions of the school is really a system based on the future *occupational* goals of the students, as has been mentioned. In this way, the system is simply a reflection of the occupational status system used in the larger society. College preparatory, commercial, vocational, and general curricula can easily be translated into the occupational status levels: executive, professional, and white collar for college preparatory; minor white collar for commercial; skilled workers for vocational; and semi- or unskilled workers for the general. The teacher of college preparatory classes is given high status partially because his students are potential members of high status occupations. This is the teacher's vicarious reward. The system of teacher status is clearly not related to the difficulty of the task. Almost any teacher will admit that it would be hard to *prevent* a well-motivated, status-conscious college preparatory division from learning, that the real challenge comes with the non-college students whose academic studies do not relate to their personal goals, who are in school because they *have* to be. Yet the teachers who face up to this difficult task are not suitably rewarded with higher status. This sounds like a refutation of the

Davis-Moore argument that higher status was given to those who performed more difficult tasks. However, it is not, as they mentioned another criterion—*functional importance* to the society. It is definitely important that good students get through college to help satisfy the demand for increasingly large numbers of professionals, managers, and technicians. The high school education of the college preparatory student is thus *functionally* related to future occupational success. At the other extreme, the general student's education has little or no relation to career, and little functional importance to the society. It is of little importance to the future plumber *qua plumber* that he take American history.

Therefore, we could argue that although the teacher of "general" history is doing a very difficult and taxing job, the *functional importance* of the job for the operation of the society as a whole has not been established. If we add the elements of immediacy and intensity (when we need a doctor, dentist, or plumber, we need him *at once*), the teacher of the "general" students is even further behind. As evidence, it might be observed that except for contemporary "reform" movements, the college preparatory curricula are relatively uniform, while there is considerable latitude in the "general" curricula. Because we do not really know what the general program should do, there are few good justifications of the general curricula, further evidence for its lack of functional importance to the society as a whole. Because of this lack of functional importance, we can say that the Davis-Moore argument has not been refuted in the awarding of differential status to teachers of various curricula.

The functional importance of education can be seen to vary with the curriculum, and thus explains to some extent why the teacher of college preparatory classes is given higher status by teachers, students, administration, and the community. The occupational prestige system of American society has filtered into the school, to the benefit of the college preparatory teacher. The teacher of general students is not, in terms of the occupational prestige system of the society, performing as vital a function. Parsons has recently contended that the reason for the non-college student's apathy and negativism about academic work is that the student is *so* deeply involved in gaining academic success and is so plagued with his failures that in order to retain his self-confidence he must reject the academic values and standards of the school.[36] There are undoubtedly many students who do feel this way, but our analysis would suggest that the non-college student may not feel that academic achievement is related to his life goals *as he sees them.* At any rate, the teacher of non-college students suffers and loses status because of this reflection of the occupational prestige system in the school.

Teachers are also involved in a status system based on the age of their students. Clear evidence of this can be seen in communities which have several salary schedules, one for elementary school teachers, one for junior high, and one for high school. This salary differentiation is usually explained by saying that elementary teachers are usually unmarried women who can live on very little income; nevertheless the difference in economic status often leads to a decrease in *social* status for the elementary school teacher. The teacher's stock in trade is supposedly brains, and the conviction is widespread that elementary teachers need less of this commodity than do teachers at the higher levels. Many students in the beginning years of a teacher training program select elementary teaching simply because they do not feel that they are bright enough to teach junior or senior high students.

This admission of second-rate status for the elementary school teacher is one of the major problems in the professionalization of teaching and is an unfounded admission. The fundamental intellectual processes, and the assumptions behind them, are often difficult to grasp, and more difficult to convey. For example, every adult is probably aware that $100 - 99 = 1$, but how many *undertand* the processes involved and the assumptions behind these processes? We can all apply the rules of speech with some success, but do we understand how language functions? Understanding these fundamental concepts upon which all further work is based is a challenge to any intellect.

If we apply the functional analysis of stratification to the job of the elementary teacher, the difficulty of the job to be done might lead us to believe that the elementary teacher should have high status. However, the second criteria for status —scarcity of *highly trained* personnel—may provide us with an explanation of the lack of status for the elementary teacher. There is, of course, a teacher shortage in this country, and the public press is full of references to the need for more teachers. Yet the complaint is usually a quantitative complaint, not a qualitative one. It is much easier to say that we need more teachers than it is to say that we need better teachers, especially if what is meant by "better" must be clearly spelled out.

Teacher training programs do not generally substantiate the notion that the teaching role is difficult and requires long training. Many states are now recruiting new teachers through one session of summer school given to any college graduate who wishes to teach. Now if one can be a teacher with only six weeks of specific preparation, then the level of difficulty of the job may not be very high. Also, many non-teachers can see *themselves* performing the role of elementary school teaching, whereas they cannot see themselves arguing a case in court or performing an appendectomy. This means that the doctor and lawyer do things which are unfamiliar to the average person, while everyone has children around the house. The first-grade teacher simply has a few more children around. Looked at from this perspective, it may be easier to see why many people favor a lower salary for elementary teachers, and lower status as well. It is true that elementary teaching has a functional importance in American society. Healing people and collecting their garbage are functionally important too, but the latter can be done by practically anyone. The same comment is often made about elementary school teaching, so that its functional importance is overridden by the commonly held notion that *anyone* can be a grade school teacher.

Teaching *per se* is an occupation, and as such it can be considered in the context of the occupational status system of American society. It is, like farming, one of the "maverick" occupations that do not quite fit the prevailing patterns. Teaching is very low in terms of its economic rewards; yet it is always given a relatively high amount of prestige status, at least in occupational rating scales. Perhaps this is merely paying lip service to an ideal which we are supposed to hold, that teachers should be paragons of all virtue. It is certainly cheaper to rank teachers high up in a rating of occupations than it would be to *pay* them a salary that would be compatible with their apparently high position. Many parents may feel that the teacher should have high status because the teacher acts as a parental substitute, *in loco parentis*. In this case, the high status given to the teacher is simply a reflection of the parents' high opinion of themselves. However, there is another way of looking at teacher status which is more intriguing. The teacher is still considered, even in many enlightened communities, to be a *museum of virtue*, an exhibition of outworn moral codes. Now it is true that a teacher has a "moral responsibility for students," but this statement is virtually meaningless unless we clarify the nature of this responsibility.

One apparent trait of advancing age is a tendency toward conservatism—not only politically but also morally. Living is a process and requires some reorientation from the person. As a result of this reorientation, some compromise of moral principle seems inevitable, especially as the person moves into more complex areas of actual decision-making. The person may as a consequence develop a reverence for previous times in his life when right was right and wrong was wrong. He undoubtedly wants his children to possess this unequivocal, black-and-white morality, even though he himself has grown beyond it. What he needs is a standard-bearer for this moral code which is no longer part of his workaday world, just as Jeeves the butler bore the upper-class standards of dress and taste, allowing his master to lounge around in disreputable clothes and use intolerable language.

Because of the teacher's responsibility for youth he has taken over as the champion of an outmoded moral code, allowing the rest of the population to continue in their contemporary sophistication, secure in the knowledge that the older standards are being maintained. In this sense the teacher has been a museum of virtue, especially the female members of the profession. There are communities in America today in which no woman teacher is permitted to smoke or drink in public, and very few dates are allowed the single woman. Church on Sunday is a must, and the teacher's evening hours are carefully observed. Here is local control of education at its height. Although much of this restriction on the teacher's behavior seems ridiculous to us today, it is easily explained in terms of the "museum of virtue" aspect of the teacher's role. Part of the teacher's function *as teacher* was to act in the specified way, to provide a sense of stability for the populace in an era of change, to make them feel that their children would be trained in the old ways. Today, however, the teacher as museum of virtue is passing from the American scene, largely because the community has lost some of its control over its teachers.

When America was a nation of farms and small towns, the teacher lived in the community in which she taught, and could be directed in her activities by the community. The teacher today may live in one community and teach in another, twenty or more miles away. Urbanization and mass transportation have provided the teacher with a welcome cloak of anonymity during non-teaching hours. However, the teacher still serves as an image of adulthood for children, and this is a source of some of the teacher's status.

We see the virtuous man as being above petty grubbing for money, and we are therefore surprised when *teachers* organize and even strike to try to improve their economic status. Here is a basic status contradiction for the teacher, as he is supposed to live in the style of the upper-middle segment of the population on a salary which is surpassed by most skilled workmen. As a result the teacher claims that he must have more money to fulfill his role as teacher, while the community (which may see the teacher as virtue incarnate) may think that the teacher is being somewhat unfaithful to his role just by being *interested* in money. The citizen sees nothing incompatible in giving the teacher high *social* status and low *economic* status; these are consistent with the teacher's role. It may be that as teachers exert more and more pressure for higher economic status they are altering the community's perception of the teacher's role in the community, finally resulting in decreased social status. From the perspective of the citizen, if teachers strike they are just like any other occupational group, and the uniqueness of the teacher's role has vanished. This is not to say that teachers should not strike, but that teachers should be aware that by demanding *economic* status they may be destroying the image which gave them relatively high *social* status.[37]

This analysis has raised some questions concerning the occupational status of teachers. Should elementary teachers be given lower economic and social status than junior and senior high school teachers? Should women teachers have lower status than men? Should the teacher of college preparatory students be given more social and intellectual status than teachers working with non-college students? How (if at all) can the public image of the teacher be altered? Is social status more or less important to the teacher than economic status, and are there any ways in which he can increase both kinds of status *at the same time?* How have other occupational groups managed to raise their status, and could any of these techniques be used by teachers? Many have suggested that the use of force or pressure is "unprofessional"; how does the "professional" get what he wants?

Stratification Systems Based on the Entire School

Our concern in this section will be with those systems of
awarding status which relate the school as a whole to the community in which it exists. The "Little Red Schoolhouse" con-
jures up happy and euphoric memories to those who knew it,
because there was one school in the community, and this school
served a vital function. It was the source of all knowledge, and
made geographically isolated people feel that they too had
culture, that they were just as good as the city folk. The teacher
and the parents were a team working in harmony. If the
teacher wanted to use physical punishment on a child, it was
perfectly all right as far as the parents were concerned. The
school was the meeting house and the social hall, and town
life revolved around it. There are still many one-room schools,
more than most people would suspect,[38] but the Little Red
Schoolhouse as a social force is dead. Radio and television now
supply the small towns with an abundance of "current" patterns of behavior, and the automobile has made the farmer
and small-town resident a participant in big-city activities. The
small towns which are left have been engaged in pooling their
efforts to produce consolidated schools, so that there are few
examples left of a single school for a single rural community.

It is a commonplace to say that America is becoming a nation
of large cities and related suburbs, but the educational changes
that have come about as a result of this development are far
from commonplace. One characteristic of a large urban unit is
that certain parts of the unit develop very specific functions.
One section of the city becomes the manufacturing section,
another section becomes the business district, and so on. There
is some argument as to whether these sections are in the form
of concentric circles spreading out from the center like waves
from a pebble thrown in water, or whether they occur in ir-
regular shapes;[39] but there is general agreement that there is a
consistent pattern of *function* of areas of a city as one moves
out from the center. This function concerns both those who do

their business in an area, and those who reside in the area.

The exact number of areas may vary with the city, but the *sequence* is generally as follows: At the center can be found a district of large stores and offices, theatres, and other sources of entertainment. There is no residential housing in this district.[40] Outside the business district can be found a manufacturing area, containing factories and tenement housing. Turnover in the tenements is very rapid, as recent arrivals to the city, from other American cities and from foreign countries, often land in this area first. A wide variety of ethnic groups is present. Moving out from the manufacturing area, we find for the first time an area where the housing function is predominant. There is some light industry here, but most space is taken by multiple family dwellings—apartment buildings, duplexes, and triplexes. The immigrant is not seen so often here, and people stay in their housing for longer periods of time than in the manufacturing zone. Moving out, we find an area of higher-status housing, composed of single family units and duplexes. Small plots of land go with some dwellings. Outside this zone can be found the independently governed suburbs which are nevertheless regarded as being completely dependent on the metropolis, although the metropolis may be just as dependent on the suburb. Commuting into the big city is still possible by car and by metropolitan transportation systems. Housing is nicer; yards are bigger; people are well established in the community and move less frequently. Well past the suburbs one can, by peering carefully through the trees, discover semi-rural areas in which can be found a great deal of high-powered affluence. The twentieth century version of the Gentleman Farmer lives in an area known as the exurbs. Here one takes the train to work, not the streetcar, and a small farm may go with the property.

This is an overly brief and sketchy description of a very complex system, but the development of characteristics as one moves out from the center is all that is needed for our purposes. If we now consider the schools of a great metropolis, we find that they *also* reflect the kinds of development we have mentioned. As one goes out from the center, the school buildings get bigger, nicer looking, and more expensive. In the suburbs the schools have grass play areas, and in the exurbs the schools, like the houses, are often carefully placed in the middle of a large forest. Now we can compare the schools of these areas with the characteristics already noted.

When we meet a stranger, we often assess his status by using the most obvious of symbols—the clothes he wears, the car he drives, the house he lives in. Schools are also judged on the same kind of criteria, such as whether the building is new or old, whether there is only one building or many (and the campus style of architecture with many small buildings instead of one big one is very high in status), and whether the building is landscaped well, if at all. The school is indeed the showpiece of the community, and a great deal of care is taken to make the exterior as lavish as possible. In the exurbs, where people drive older model cars and would never be seen in a new Cadillac, the school building will carefully avoid any façade which might suggest conspicuousness or ostentation. It is, of course, very easy to assign status to a school on this basis. This is a judgment using criteria similar to those used in Warner's ISC. As we move out from the center of a large metropolis, the school exteriors will become steadily more expensive looking, and we can establish a status ranking of the various schools with little trouble.

Even by walking in the door of a school, we can rank by the objects we see around us. The size of the auditorium, the quality of the seats, the number of stoves and refrigerators in the home economics offices, the number of basketball courts in the gymnasium, the facilities in the science laboratories, the kind of lighting fixtures and floor surface used all reflect the community's *ability* to pay as well as an interest in education. However, if one wishes to look for status symbols inside a school, one of the best places to do so is in the central office. This is where the public officially encounters the school. The administrative offices are nearby, and important things seem to be going on. Close to the center of the metropolis, there may be one harried woman who handles the office alone, and often the principal will be helping out with absence reports. Those who wish to wait sit on hard benches. The principal's office is small; the desk is smaller; there is little chance of seeing a rug on the floor. As we move out through the suburbs, the central office gets larger; the seats get softer; the wood paneling gets more obvious, and the principal gets more inaccessible and must be seen by appointment. The exurban central office is a picture of quiet efficiency, and the principal's quarters resemble those of a middle-range corporation executive with dark wood paneling, contemporary furniture, and a quiet, dignified rug on the floor. Instead of containing a desk and chairs, the principal's office in the exurbs is big enough to allow for a large table, enabling the principal to hold large conferences right in his office. The values of Madison Avenue (and every metropolis has its version of Madison Avenue) are easily visible.

However, these are only the trappings and superficialities of the school. We can also trace lines of development which are more closely related to the educational function of the school.[41] As we move out, we find that the amount of money spent per child increases. The quality and quantity of audio-visual services also increases. Significantly, the proportion of those *going on to higher education* also increases, until we arrive at the exurban school which may resemble the private preparatory school in the numbers going to college. We have already pointed out that the college preparatory curriculum has more status than the others, and we have offered some reasons as to why this is so. The proportion of the graduating class which goes on to college is a statistic of the greatest importance in the status of a school. If one asks a principal or superintendent for some figures on the school, this figure will appear early in the interview. At the suburban and exurban level, there is often an open competition to see who has the highest percentage Sometimes the percentage is broken down to exploit the num-

ber admitted to "good" private colleges, as this figure is more
impressive than the number going to state colleges or universities. Adding those who enroll in two-year colleges, technical, and secretarial schools often makes the total even more
impressive.

Along with this increase in the numbers of college-bound
students can be found other factors which perhaps suggest that
the school may actually be serving different *functions* in different areas of a metropolis. The time and effort devoted to
educational research increases as we move out from the metropolitan center, partly because of increasing financial support
from foundations in the suburban and exurban schools, and
because affiliation with a research program can in itself be a
mark of high status. Part of this status may come from a connection with a good college or university which is also involved
in the research. Because of the interest of a college in attract-
ing better-qualified students, it is perhaps understandable that
colleges have become involved with suburban and exurban
schools, where a majority of the graduates apply for college.
The function of these schools is directly related to the function
of the colleges. Foundations are also interested in the suburban
and exurban systems, often since spectacular new programs
will be successful there because of the cooperative attitude of
students, teachers, administrators, and the community.

These research programs are undoubtedly important (although the suburban schools could get along very well, even
without help from the colleges and foundations). However, it
seems a shame that more money and *intellectual* effort does
not go into the problems of a slum school which serves an
economically depressed area of a metropolis. Colleges absolve
themselves from responsibility by claiming that they are not
competent to deal with the problems in this type of school—
but if not the colleges, then who? Being acutely status-conscious, colleges and foundations would rather associate themselves with high status schools in high status communities than
with low status schools in economically poor areas.

If we wished to investigate the different functions served by schools in various sections of a metropolis, we could begin with the increased interest in the college preparatory program in the areas far from the center. To a degree, the function of the school will have to change as the expectations of parents and students change. In a school near the center, there may be children of immigrants and transients, representing a wide variety of ethnic groups, each with its own set of behavioral norms. Cleanliness, obedience, and intellectual achievement may be totally absent from the actions of these children, so that before the school can impart the formal curriculum to the child it must *re-socialize* him. This taking of an individual from one culture and placing him in another is called acculturation, which is undoubtedly one of the major goals or functions of the school in this area. On the other hand, socialization in the dominant American mores is taken for granted in the suburban and exurban schools. These schools need not concern themselves with this function, but can proceed to gratify the college-oriented expectations of students and parents. Naturally one earns more status as a teacher by teaching Milton than by showing someone how to use a toothbrush, and the school which can devote all of its energies to teaching the formal curriculum will have higher status than the school which must acculturate its children—perhaps even teach them the English language—before it can even *begin* the task of imparting the formal curriculum.

There is another way in which schools differ and which may give another clue to the differing purposes and functions of schools, and this concerns family structure. Those who have investigated the family structure of cities have noticed that as one moves out, the family is less and less dominated by the father (patriarchal), moves into an egalitarian pattern in which father and mother share responsibility as a team, and may develop into a mother-dominated (matriarchal) family in the exurbs.[42] The stereotyped patriarchal pattern requires strict obedience from the children and constant, unwavering standards from the father, who sits in judgment and gives out punishments when deserved. Children are treated as imperfect adults, not as children. This picture of the patriarchal father figure is not a popular one in contemporary America. Patriarchal family life is seen as "undemocratic" and devoid of warmth and sympathy, but it has its advantages. The children are presented with a strong, consistent code of behavior which gives them a certain amount of security. We must remember that in Clarence Day's perceptive picture of Father there was a great deal of warmth and understanding. Father was a man who said that he would not *allow* the newly installed telephone to ring if he would be disturbed by it, and he was also the one who got up in the middle of the night to make sure that the stray puppy the boys had found was sleeping well. He never told his children that he loved them (they would have been horribly embarrassed if he had) but there is no doubt that he *did*. Patriarchs are often tyrants, but the authoritarian system, in which roles and positions are clearly specified, can be a very satisfactory system for the child if he is allowed to grow out of his subordinate role.

The "team" or egalitarian family structure is a phenomenon of great importance in American culture. Swanson and Miller have claimed that this type of family structure is now the dominant type in America,[43] and the research already mentioned indicating that "middle class" parents are becoming much more permissive about child training supports this position. This bureaucratic or egalitarian structure emphasizes cooperation in family endeavors and promotes the famous spirit of "togetherness." An after-dinner drive through suburbia will reveal hundreds of families sitting in hundreds of family rooms making hundreds of decisions about where the family vacation should be taken, or how the family budget should be spent, with each member of the family unit, the forty-year-old father and the three-year-old, allowed one vote. The children are perceived as "junior partners in the firm," and are treated as such. Interpersonal relations within the family group are of critical importance. The parents tend to see success for their children in terms of joining the right groups and meeting the right people, not in terms of spectacular individual achievements as the entrepreneur did.

The matriarchal family is less clearly defined, and may exist in the exurbs only because the father leaves for work before the children arise, and returns from the city after they are asleep, thereby losing any chance he may have had of being a patriarch. We might speak of this pattern as "matriarchal-by-default." The matriarchal pattern of domination is very different from patriarchal control, in that the matriarch creates a situation in which her nurturance is in one way or another absolutely necessary for the individual. This type of family often exudes an atmosphere of love and euphoria which disguises perfectly the type of control which the mother possesses. It was hard, but a child could break away from Clarence Day's type of patriarch and become an autonomous adult. It is much more difficult to break away from the matriarchal figure, simply because she has become indispensable and refuses to allow the child to break away from her nurturance.[44] In the exurban matriarchy the mother may function as a child welfare agency, getting the child to the dancing lesson, then the piano lesson, then the riding academy. The children must often be transported several miles just to play with another child, and social interaction is restricted. As an example of this, one exurbanite mother watched her small son place a worm on a rock and cut it in two. She was going to interfere with this brutality when she heard him say to the worm, "There! Now *you've* got a friend."

These patterns of family composition, although overly simplified and not always distinct, probably represent major tendencies in American family structure. We have mentioned that each appears more frequently in certain areas of the metropolis than in others, and now we can consider whether or not the schools in various areas reflect these patterns. It should be pointed out that the following generalizations are purely subjective, as there is no research available which either supports or refutes them. They are the personal observations of the author, and should be compared with the reader's own.

In the lower social and economic areas of the metropolis, the family pattern is largely patriarchal. The teachers in schools in these areas also tend to manifest a patriarchal attitude. Discipline is definite and rigid. Permissive behavior on the part of the teacher is not often seen. Even women act like men in their authority and command. The principal is the Great Patriarch, and fear of him is a very useful device for the teacher in maintaining order. Group projects and group decisions are not frequent.

As we move out into the suburbs and exurbs we begin to see a combination of the egalitarian (or bureaucratic) and matriarchal patterns. The emphasis on the classroom group *as a group* becomes very strong, and activities are planned to encourage the team concept. Projects are selected to allow each individual a chance to participate. The students are allowed to vote on the type of material to be studied, and for student leaders who may do some of the teaching as well as organize the unit of study. Before we assert that this type of classroom is the ultimate in democratic action we should study the situation a little more closely.

There are only certain clearly defined areas where students have freedom of choice (no students have the power to select their own teacher), and even within these areas there may be a great deal of hidden control. The teacher often plans *in advance* what the students will decide to study, then manipulates the situation so that the students reach the "right" decision. We mentioned the process through which the matriarch comes to power, and the same sort of scheme can be seen in many suburban and exurban schools, perhaps most easily visible in the change in the principal's role. Where the principal in the lower status school uses fear and rigid discipline to instill obedience in his students, the suburban or exurban principal typifies the bureaucratic approach by being relatively permissive, seeking to understand the student, and by using very subtle psychological manipulation to coerce the student in the desired direction. By providing some sort of nurturance, teachers at *all* grade levels may exercise matriarchal control over the students. Women teachers in these schools seem much more feminine, and often achieve an incredible amount of control simply by being overwhelmingly "nice." An excellent description of the hidden controls and of the matriarchal domination which comes from "euphoric, oceanic love," has been written by Henry,[45] in describing a suburban elementary school.

This section has been purposely slanted to overcome certain preconceived notions about the superiority of "democratic" teaching. There are, of course, schools and classrooms in which students are really allowed to make important decisions; and if the students err, the teacher and administration grit their teeth and go along, seeing that the road to maturity must be traveled by allowing students to learn from mistakes. But many situations which *appear* to be democratic to the casual observer contain a much more subtle (and perhaps insidious) kind of teacher domination, all the more dangerous because the students, and perhaps even the teacher, are not consciously aware of its existence. The student can fight a tyrannical, overbearing person if necessary and learn something from it, but it is hard to fight a school or teacher in which everyone is completely warm and "good."

We have presented two or three impressions of variations in the way in which students are treated in different types of schools. These variations undoubtedly reflect a difference in school *function*, and also a difference in the kind of influence the school can have on its students. In the suburban and exurban communities where permissiveness is used by parents in dealing with their children, the school generally supports the parents' position. In lower status districts in which a certain amount of authoritarianism is used by the parents, the school follows suit. The suburban school, by teaching the values of participation, warmth, understanding, and group activity, is much more in the mainstream of contemporary American educational and philosophical thought than is the city school. This helps to explain why more experiments are conducted there, and why more foundation money is spent in suburban and exurban school systems. Both the *functions* of the college-oriented suburban and exurban schools and the *techniques* used in these schools are given high status by those outside, more than the schools in lower socio-economic areas. This differentiation in school status is a rather cynical commentary on the American dream of equality and mobility, in that we practically assume that the child of high-status parents living in a high-status community will become a high-status adult. This is one of the reasons we reward the child's school with high status.

This account of educational stratification systems should not be considered as complete; the reader may well add dimensions of his own, or quarrel with the material presented here. Nevertheless, there is one pervasive theme running through most of the systems of educational stratification we have presented. They tend to reflect, *more than they conflict with*, the patterns of stratification which dominate American society as a whole. It is undoubtedly true that occupational status is very important, but should *educators* accept the thesis that the only good man is the one who holds a good job? Is economic position necessarily a good criterion for *social* status? Should students learn in school that prestige (status for the position) is more important than esteem (the quality of performance in the position)? Is it right that a teacher should condemn a potentially able student because he speaks and dresses like a member of the "lower class"? Is it in the best interests of the school that a boy who is an excellent student of English literature is all too frequently branded by his classmates as a sissy? What can be done by the school to see that students give status to their peers on a wider variety of stratification dimensions than athletic ability and conformity to group norms?

Many of these same problems will be met again in the next chapter from a different but closely related perspective—that of social mobility.

NOTES

1. K. Davis and W. E. Moore, "Some Principles of Stratification," *American Sociological Review*, 10 (1945), 242-249. Also K. Davis, "A Conceptual Analysis of Stratification," *Am. Soc. Rev.*, 7 (1941), 309-321; and K. Davis, *Human Society*, (New York, 1949), esp. pp. 365-370. The validity of the Davis-Moore position has been challenged by a number of writers, and represents one of the most stimulating controversies in contemporary social thinking. For the other side, see: M. Tumin, "Some Principles of Stratification: A Critical Analysis," *ASR*, 18 (1953), 387-394; R. Schwartz, "Functional Alternatives to Inequality," *ASR*, 20 (1955), 424-430; R. Simpson, "A Modification of the Functional Theory of Social Stratification," *Social Forces*, 35 (1956); and W. Buckley, "Social Stratification and the Functional Theory of Social Differentiation," *ASR*, 23 (1958), 369-375.

2. T. Parsons, *The Social System*, (Glencoe, 1951), esp. pp. 69, 158-160. See also his *Essays in Sociological Theory*, (Glencoe, 1949), 173.

3. Noted by H. W. Pfautz, "The Current Literature on Social Stratification," *American J. of Sociology*, 58 (1953), 391-418. See also P. Sorokin, *Society, Culture, and Personality*, (New York 1947), 261-271.

4. E.g., K. Mayer, "The Theory of Social Classes," *Harvard Educational Review*, 23 (1953), 149-167; J. Montagu, "Class or Status Society," *Sociology and Social Research*, 40 (1956), 333-338; and S. Lipset and R. Bendix, "A Theory of Social Mobility," *Transactions of Third World Congress of Sociology*, v. 3 (Amsterdam, 1956), 155-177.

5. The problems in this kind of research are formidable. See W. Warner and P. Lunt, *The Status System of a Modern Community*, (New Haven, 1942); G. Lenski, "Status Crystallization," *ASR*, 19 (1950), 405-413; and E. Hughes, "Dilemmas and Contradictions of Status," *Am. J. Sociol.*, 50 (1945), 353-359.

6. This is another exciting controversy. See W. Goldschmidt, "America's Social Classes—Is Equality a Myth?" *Commentary*, 10 (1950), 175-181; A. Kornhauser, "Analysis of the 'Class' Structure of Contemporary American Society," in G. Hartman and T. Newcomb (eds.) *Industrial Conflict*, (New York, 1939); G. Lenski, "American Social Classes: Statistical Strata or Social Groups?" *Am. J. Sociol.*, 58 (1953), 139-144; A. Rose, "The Concept of Class and American Sociology," *Social Research*, 25 (1958), 53-69. The interest in the problem goes

back into the past. See G. Simmel, "Superiority and Subordination as Subject-Matter of Sociology," *Am. J. Sociol.*, 2 (1897), 392-415.

7. For a good summary of Warner's position, see W. Warner, *American Life: Dream or Reality?*, (Chicago, 1953); also J. Kahl, *The American Class Structure*, (New York, 1957), ch. 2. For a competent critique of Warner's position, see H. Pfautz and O. Duncan, "A Critical Evaluation of Warner's Work in Community Stratification," *ASR*, (1950), 205-215.

8. For a manual describing the use of these indexes, see W. Warner, M. Meeker, and K. Eells, *Social Class in America*, (Chicago, 1949).

9. E.g., A. Davis and R. Havighurst, *Father of the Man*, (Boston, 1947); W. Warner, R. Havighurst, and M. Loeb, *Who Shall Be Educated?*, (New York, 1944).

10. A. Davis, *Social-Class Influences upon Learning*, (Cambridge, 1951).

11. R. Centers, *The Psychology of Social Classes*, (Princeton, 1949), is Centers' major work on the subject. See J. Kahl and J. Davis, "A Comparison of Indexes of Socio-Economic Status," *ASR*, 20 (1955), 317-325. For another comparison of the two techniques, see J. Haer, "A Comparative Study of the Classification Techniques of Warner and Centers," *ASR*, 20 (1955), 689-692.

12. H. Hyman, "The Psychology of Status," *Archives of Psychology*, 1942, no. 269.

13. See P. Hatt, "Occupation and Social Stratification," *Am. J. Sociol.*, 55 (1950), 533-543.

14. See Anne Roe, *The Psychology of Occupations*, (New York, 1956), 39. There is no doubt that the formation of stratification systems is a much more complex process than the occupationally-based stratification research would have us believe. See O. Glantz, "Class Consciousness and Political Stability," *ASR*, 23 (1958), 375-383; T. Lasswell, "Social Class and Size of Community," *Am. J. Sociol.*, 64 (1959), 505-508; M. Kohn, "Social Class and Parental Values," *Am. J. Sociol.*, 64 (1959), 337-351; J. Bensman and A. Vidich, "Social Theory in Field Research," *Am. J. Sociol.*, 65 (1960), 577-584; T. Lasswell, "Orientations Toward Social Class," *Am. J. Sociol.*, 65 (1960), 585-587; and H. Blalock, "Status Consciousness," *Social Forces*, 37 (1959), 243-248. These readings represent some recent and perceptive analyses of some of the ways in which our thinking about stratification should be broadened.

15. G. Lenski, "Status Crystallization," *ASR*, 19 (1954), 405-413; J. Foskett, "Social Structure and Social Participation," *ASR*, 21 (1956), 431-438; and G. Lenski, "Social Participation and Status Crystallization," *ASR*, 21 (1956), 458-464.

16. G. Hicks, *Small Town*, (New York, 1947), 93-98.

17. A. Kinsey, W. Pomeroy, C. Martin, *Sexual Behavior in the American Male*, (Philadelphia, 1948), 331.

18. A. Davis, R. Havighurst, "Social Class and Color Differences in Child Rearing," *ASR*, (1946), 698-710.

19. R. Sears, E. Maccoby, H. Levin, *Patterns of Child Rearing*, (Evanston, Illinois, 1957), 446.

20. See R. Havighurst and A. Davis, "A Comparison of the Chicago and Harvard Studies of Social Class Differences in Child Rearing," *ASR*, 20 (1955), 438-442.

21. E.g., M. White, "Social Class, Child Rearing Practices, and Child Behavior," *ASR*, 22 (1957), 704-712; and the perceptive article by U. Bronfenbrenner, "Socialization and Social Class Through Time and Space," in E. Maccoby, T. Newcomb, and E. Hartley, *Readings in Social Psychology*, (New York, 1958), 400-425.

22. F. Kluckhohn, "Dominant and Variant Value Orientations," in C. Kluckhohn and H. Murray, (eds.) *Personality in Nature, Society, and Culture*, (New York, 1953), 343-357. Also, F. Kluckhohn, "Dominant and Substitute Profiles of Cultural Orientation," *Social Forces*, 28 (1950), 376-393; and C. Kluckhohn, "Values and Value Orientations," in T. Parsons and E. Shils (eds.) *Toward a General Theory of Action*, (Cambridge, 1951).

23. For the classic account of how this attitude evolved, see M. Weber, *The Protestant Ethic and the Spirit of Capitalism*, (New York, 1930).

24. C. McArthur, "Personalities of Public and Private School Boys," *Harvard Ed. Rev.*, 24 (1954), 256-262.

25. J. Kahl, "Educational and Occupational Aspirations of 'Common Man' Boys," *Harvard Ed. Rev.*, 24 (1953), 186-203.

26. For two of many examples see M. Winterbottom, "The Sources of Achievement Motivation," in D. McClelland, *Studies in Motivation*, (New York, 1955), 297-306; and F. Strodtbeck, "Family Interaction, Values, and Achievement," in D. McClelland, et al., *Talent and Society*, (New Jersey, 1958), 135-194.

27. H. Hyman, "The Psychology of Status," *op. cit.*, 80.

28. The most striking presentation of this problem is that of Myron Lieberman, *The Future of Public Education*, (Chicago, 1960).

29. *The Exurbanites*, (New York, 1958).

30. Many of the novels of John Marquand point out eloquently how, in the upper classes, no one ever considered *not* going to an ivy league school. Evidence for the favored position of the college preparatory student is seen in some schools which have an unwritten policy of never giving a student in the college preparatory program a grade lower than a B, while students in other curricula cannot earn anything higher than a C.

31. For a revealing portrait, see W. Whyte, "The Organization School," in *The Organization Man*, (New York, 1956).

32. Much work needs to be done on the deviations in expectations for different reference groups. See Jenkins and R. Lippett, *Interpersonal Perceptions of Teachers, Parents, and Students,* (Washington, 1957).

33. L. M. Terman and M. Oden, *Genetic Studies of Genius,* Vol. IV, (California, 1947), and L. Hollingworth, *Exceptional Children,* (New York, 1941).

34. J. Coleman, "The Adolescent Subculture and Academic Achievement," *Am. J. Sociol.,* 65 (1960), 337-347; also J. Coleman, "Academic Achievement and the Structure of Competition," *Harvard Ed. Rev.,* 29 (1960), 330-351.

35. H. Becker, "The Career of the Chicago Public Schoolteacher," *Am. J. Sociol.,* 57 (1952), 470-477.

36. T. Parsons, "The School as a Social System," *Harvard Ed. Rev.,* 29 (1960), 297-318.

37. On this issue, see M. Lieberman, *Education as a Profession,* (New York, 1956).

38. The Office of Education has asserted that in 1959, over 10 per cent of the elementary school population was in one-room schools.

39. See S. Green and D. Carpenter, *The American City,* (New York, 1953).

40. There is, of course, a trend to introduce in some cities very high status residential units right in this area, but not as a general rule.

41. These are only two of the many functions of the school—the *manifest* function of educating children, and the *latent* function of providing a centralized status symbol for the members of the community.

42. Park and Burgess, *op. cit.*

43. G. Swanson and D. Miller, *The Changing American Parent,* (New York, 1956).

44. For two excellent statements of the problem here, see A. Green, "The Middle-Class Male Child and Neurosis," *ASR,* 11 (1946), 31-41; and K. Horney, *The Neurotic Personality of Our Time,* (New York, 1937).

45. J. Henry, "Working Paper on Creativity," *Harvard Ed. Rev.,* 27 (1957), 148-155. On the same topic, see also E. Friedenberg, *The Vanishing Adolescent,* (Boston, 1959).

CHAPTER THREE

Social Mobility
and Education

What Is Social Mobility?

In a sense, stratification and mobility are two sides of the same coin: Stratification concerns a system of status ranks, and mobility concerns the movements of individuals or groups from one rank to another. We have already mentioned that statistical categories were often erroneously referred to in social research as *social* classes. In similar fashion, we cannot talk of *social* mobility unless we are referring to a change in the amount of social reward or status given to an individual or group by other individuals or groups. However, we have spoken of social stratification as if it were only a system of assigning social status; and we will see that it is also, by assigning *criteria* for the status award, a system of *barriers* through which the individual must pass if he wishes to increase the level of his social status. If he cannot meet the criteria for the status award, then he may move *down* through the system, or remain at the same level.

Societies differ in the amount of social mobility they allow, but every society, even a caste society, has some mobility.[1] At the other extreme, no society has anything near "perfect" mobility, which would be a condition in which ascribed (or birth-given) status did not exist. Here we have one quarrel with the functionalist theory of stratification put forth by Davis and Moore, as they state that the most qualified persons for the most difficult jobs *must* be allowed to perform those jobs. Clearly this position assumes complete social mobility if a society is to operate at maximum effectiveness, and it is doubtful whether a completely mobile society could exist for any time at all. Ascribed status inevitably forces us to waste certain talents, but this is simply the price we pay for the sense of continuity and stability which patterns of ascribed status can produce.

We have already mentioned that a person's status will vary with the reference group, and that often an action which increases the individual's social status with *one* reference group will simultaneously decrease his status in the eyes of another. As an example, remember the boy who got the top mark in a big exam, thereby increasing his social status in the eyes of his parents and his teacher, but decreasing his status with his peers. Or let us assume that individual A, who values occupational status, gets a promotion. His friend B also values occupational status, while his friend C does not. Clearly B and C will differ on whether or not A has been *socially* mobile, although there is no disputing that A has been occupationally mobile.[2]

We have been stressing, and justifiably so, the multidimensionality of social mobility, making the point that increased status in one dimension (occupation) does not necessarily mean increased status in another dimension (religion). Individuals strive *selectively* for status, and members of reference groups award status selectively. Even so, there are general patterns of consistency, in that changes in occupational status generally correspond with increases in economic status, which may lead to increased status in other dimensions, such as *political*.

The situation is further complicated by the fact that mobility can also be taken to mean geographical movement with no change in status. If I take a job which is identical to the one I now hold, but is in a different city, there is no necessary change in my social status as seen by the groups to which I refer. Unfortunately, these hard and fast distinctions are difficult to make, as many geographical moves are tied up with status changes simply by the change of area. If I work for a large corporation in a district office in a small town and am transferred to a district office in a large city, this may mean an increase in status in the eyes of the people who know me, even though I am doing exactly the same work that I was doing before. On the other hand, as a white collar worker I might have enjoyed a high position in the small town which would be lost in the big city where being a white collar worker may not have the same significance. The status assumptions involved in geographical motion are very complex, as we have to contend with the reference groups of the individual in his present location *and* the reference groups he will associate with when he moves. Clearly, if one is moving from Oshkosh to Philadelphia, one must consider the attitudes of people in both communities, although the greatest concern will generally be with the new environment with which he must deal.

Many social thinkers have attempted to set up categories to explain social mobility. The most frequently used distinction is between *vertical* (change of status) and *horizontal* (no change in status) mobility.[3] We have seen already that this type of explanation is much too simple to use with the complex questions of physical and social motion. For examples of this complexity, let us add another dimension to the problem. It seems logical that there are at least two ways in which one can increase his social status: first, by an out-standing *individual* performance, and second, simply by be-longing to a *group* which is in the process of increasing its status in relation to other groups. The latter (group mobility) is becoming a more widespread type of social mobility than the former (individual mobility) in bureaucratic societies, for reasons mentioned by Max Weber. Simply by being in the right group, one can rise in relation to other groups. But we may assume that there must be certain demonstrations of per-formance, or prerequisites, which must be completed before an individual will be allowed into the group, so that indi-vidual and group mobility can interact when individual per-formance leads to membership in a mobile group. We know very little about why some people see "success" as an individual thing while others see it as a matter of group membership, but we would certainly expect that the bureaucratic type of family organization, which emphasizes group responses, will produce more interest in group mobility while the older entre-preneur pattern would produce more interest in individual achievement.

Mobility can also occur through *formal* and *informal* chan-nels, if we agree that change on *any* dimension of status is social mobility. Imagine a drill press operator who becomes known and admired throughout the plant as the star pitcher of the plant baseball team. He is still a drill press operator; his place in the *formal* hierarchy of the plant is still the same. But his social status has unquestionably increased, due to his performance in an informal area of plant activity. Often a person increases his social status simply by being in a job *longer* than anyone else. There are many school systems in which the janitor has outlasted several principals and most of the teaching staff, so that he is often consulted by local politicians and reporters about the condition of the schools. In some factories seniority may bring economic benefits as well as the security which comes from being at the bottom of the list of those to be laid off. Others simply proceed to make themselves *indispensable* in a very quiet way, without changing their occupational status. This person can do small things that had been done by others until eventually all decisions must be cleared through her. The feminine pronoun is used here advisedly, as this is a particularly important mechanism for status-conscious women who are blocked in the *formal* promotional system because of their sex. We know far more about the formal systems of allowing people to increase their social status than we do about the informal systems, which may actually be more important to many people than the formal ones.[4] It may be possible to manipulate the informal systems so that they can drain off the conflict and anxiety produced by the formal systems, and later we will see how this might be done in the school.

The Measurement of Social Mobility

The research on social mobility is easier to deal with than the research on "social class," as there are fewer kinds of research on mobility. The one major index of social mobility is the factor we noted as being the major index of stratification—occupation. Occupational information is simple, easy to get, and correlates well with other indexes of position and status.[5] We have already noted, however, that occupation is not *one* variable but many, such as occupational prerequisites, occupational duties, economic occupational rewards, and psychic occupational rewards.

The typical measure of occupational mobility is a comparison of the occupational situations of one generation of fathers with those of their sons. In a completely mobile society one would expect a complete dispersion of the sons into the entire occupational range—that is, sons of bankers would be found in all occupations in equal numbers. They would become postmen, unskilled laborers, skilled machinists, and minor white collar workers *just as frequently* as they became bankers. Sons of farmers would become bankers just as often as they became farmers. Occupation of father would have no influence on occupation of son. We can therefore compare what occupations the sons *actually* enter to this "ideal" mobility pattern to discover how much mobility exists.

There are several problems in using this technique. First, all fathers are not selected from the same age range, and the same is true of their sons. One father may be at his peak while his son is just starting at his first job, while another father may be too old to hold a high status job at the same time that his son has just received a promotion. A more important problem is that we do not know whether or not sons compare themselves with their fathers in real life. It may be more likely that sons will compare their occupational status with others of their own age and not with their fathers. If so, the research will not be indicative of how mobile the sons actually *felt*, and thus will not be an indication of *social* mobility.

Nevertheless, this technique is the only one in common use at present. It is unfortunate that research has neglected *non*-occupational changes in status. Clearly, the occupational status system is changing rapidly. It is becoming more complex, and because of this, more symbolic. We *must* resort to superficial symbols of status such as house, car, and clothing if we find out that a man is a transistor rater. In simpler times, if we found that a man was a maker of shoes, we could evaluate both the job and the individual's performance in that job, as we knew something about shoes and their manufacture. It is difficult for us to set up standards for transistor raters when we do not understand what they do or what an excellent performance would be. Occupational status may be becoming less and less important as we become more ignorant of the functions of various complex occupations, and are forced to use general symbols which tell us little specifically about the occupational status of an individual. The Cadillac is owned by people from every occupational rank from farmer to unskilled worker to doctor, and therefore is no longer a symbol of *occupational* status. This trend will increase as we become more alike in

our consumption patterns of food, clothing, cars, housing, and
the objects with which we spend our leisure time. But even
with all these deficiencies, the occupational mobility research
can give us some useful information.

How Much Mobility Is There?

If we split the occupational system up into two groups,
manual or blue collar occupations and non-manual or white
collar occupations, the answer is simple. There is a great deal of
occupational mobility *within* each of the two groups, and much
less *between* the two. Crossing the "collar" line from the blue
to the white is certainly one of the most difficult moves to
make,[6] but the leap must be made if one is to reach the upper
levels of occupational status. It is probably an awareness of
this fact that has caused manual workers, realizing that their
chances of advancement through the formal structure of the
plant were not very good, to do everything they could to develop a small business of their own and get out of the factory.
Many of them will take a considerable financial loss to give up
their factory job and become a minor white collar worker.
The temporary loss is the price they pay for what they think
is an increase in their job potential, but many become disillusioned when they realize that the white collar is not a royal
road to status.

Unfortunately, many of these workers are not looking at
the situation objectively, for in terms of wages, hours, holidays,
skill, and prestige, the advantages of the white collar worker
over the blue collar worker are considerably weaker than they
once were, and in some instances do not exist at all.[7] Nevertheless, the American Dream persists in the minds of men, and
the white shirt-and-tie has become an overworked symbol of
success in our occupationally complex society. When people
give up higher financial rewards for the sake of a white collar,
it must be important to them. We have already pointed out
that status judgments do not always square with objective

judgments; but if enough people *feel* that wearing a white collar is important, then the white collar complex becomes a *social* reality, even though there may be no economic gain involved in getting a white collar job.

Thus far we have said that the amount of occupational mobility *within* the blue and white collar classes is far greater than the mobility *across* the collar barrier. There seems to be little disagreement on this point, but we might also be interested in finding out whether mobility rates are changing or not. This is a more complex question, as we must take into account the fact that the whole occupational structure is changing rapidly. The number of white collar jobs in the economy is constantly expanding, while the number of blue collar jobs is decreasing.[8] Instead of seeing the occupational structure as a pyramid with the majority of jobs at the bottom, we should picture a diamond of occupations, with the majority of positions in the middle (the lower white collar variety) surrounded by professional and executive positions above and skilled and unskilled manual work beneath.

Because of this rapid change in the nature of the occupational structure, it is extremely difficult to determine whether or not mobility rates are changing. When you compare fathers who entered the world of work in 1925 with sons who entered in 1945-1955, you are dealing with two different worlds, and comparisons are almost impossible to make. Also, we have been treating the occupational structure as a whole, attempting to derive an answer for the entire system, when perhaps we could look for variations *within* the system, such as the barrier between manual and non-manual jobs. For example, occupational mobility rates vary as you go from one section of the country to another. The rates are not uniform at all. Also, the chances for occupational mobility vary with the *size* of the community in which the person was raised, giving the person from a large metropolitan area a distinct advantage over the person who grew up in a small rural town. Because we set up the list of occupations with a top and bottom, it is impossible for those in the *top* levels to become upwardly mobile; and those in the bottom category cannot show downward mobility.

All the evidence available suggests that there is no major shift in over-all mobility rates, but there may be many changes in *parts* of the system which cancel each other out. For example, assume that upward mobility from the farm and unskilled worker categories has increased, and that downward mobility from the executive and professional categories has increased. The results would cancel out, and the net result would be the same, with no over-all change reported. However, the changes in the *lives* of people might be enormous, even though the statistics indicate no change. These studies of occupational mobility generally compare only *sons* with fathers and not daughters with fathers, which might be an even more interesting problem of the rapidly changing role of women in our culture. The chances of a career for a talented girl are probably greater today than they were thirty years ago, and women should certainly be included in occupational mobility studies.

Although the studies must be viewed with caution for the reasons we have given, it is safe to say that there has been no dramatic reduction of mobility rates, although those who believe in a rigid class structure have argued that as the class structure solidifies, occupational mobility will decrease. But the reader should remember that our instruments measure quantity of occupational mobility, not quality, and there may be many changes in the ways which people use to become occupationally mobile, and in their feelings about the criteria for mobility.

What Are the Psychological Results of Mobility?

The problem here has been beautifully phrased by Robert Lynd:

> The pattern of our culture is one of great individual mobility, both horizontal and vertical, and consequently one in which

human beings tend to put down shallow roots. This mobility involves positive gains in the access it gives to wider and more varied experience. But . . . the individual in our culture is tending increasingly to "travel light": he . . . moves his place of residence more quickly, commits himself irrevocably to fewer things, often avoids making friendships with those who may become liabilities, and he even seeks subtly to disencumber himself from in-laws and the now vanishing lateral kinship areas.[9]

Mobility (used here in a general sense) is something of a double-edged sword. It makes our behavior more flexible and adaptive; it allows for easy interchange of ideas and thereby increases intellectual and technological progress. On the other hand, it may present men with too many alternatives to a situation resulting in mental collapse; it increases the superficiality of personal contacts and the feeling of isolation; and it increases the suicide and alcoholism rates. People in a mobile culture become restless and seem to be looking for something which they cannot name, without realizing that this "something" is the price they must pay for the advantages of mobility.

Even greater problems are in store for the person who accepts the definition of success now in vogue (the accumulation of symbols which represent economic status) and who is then denied any *socially acceptable means* for achieving success. The boy from the tenement district watches the constant parade of high status objects parade across the television screen and across the pages of the newspaper or magazine. He is told that *good* people own these things, and that it is the *things* which make the people important, through a mystical process not clearly explained. Naturally he wants to play a part, become a member of this group whose norms apparently represent American culture (several studies have indicated that the faith people have in the mass media and the ability to believe everything they are subjected to is miraculous).[10] He therefore wants to possess those things which will make him respected and esteemed by his fellow men. He soon finds that if he is not good in the abstract skills desired by the school and does not have outstanding athletic ability, then the paths leading to these objects through schooling are closed to him. The culture has set up barriers which prevent him from gaining the prerequisites necessary for high status.

There seem to be two courses of action for our young man, and neither of them is very appealing. First, he can reject the norms and the objects which the mass media tell him he should desire. Second, he can continue to accept the norms and objects which he should desire, and use *socially disapproved means* (the only ones available to him) such as stealing, to obtain the things he desires. Many authorities on juvenile delinquency have contended that the delinquent has rejected the values of the society, while we have argued that it is because the delinquent *accepts* the dominant values of American society, but cannot gain the symbols of status through legitimate means, that he turns to unlawful activity which will get him what he wants. There is no reason for a youth to steal a Cadillac if he did not want that car and think it an important object. If he rejected the idea that owning a fine car is a good thing, he would not have stolen it.[11]

This explanation does not hold for all kinds of crime, of course, but it does indicate how pressure for mobility can put the person who *cannot* be mobile in a very damaging position psychologically. It is common knowledge that an animal can be driven to a condition closely resembling hysteria by allowing him to see and smell food but not allowing him any way to get to the food. If the acquisition of status acts as food to the human psyche, then we have done the same thing to our boy from the slums. The reader might well consider in this context the statement that *a society gets the crime rate that it deserves.* Part of the blame must be placed on the complexity of occupations in our society which forces us to give status to people by using symbols and prevents us from directly evaluating the performance on the job, as we cannot develop criteria for what a good performance is.

There is another way in which social mobility can cause damage to the individual. When we think of social mobility, we think of an increase in status on the part of an individual or group as seen by reference groups. This means that the individual does not change his reference group allegiances; he only increases his status in the eyes of the group. However, occupational, economic, or political mobility may result in a different kind of social mobility—a *change* in reference groups. An example may make the distinction clear. Assume that a person is the best table tennis player in his office or plant. This may increase his social status, but it will not necessarily add new reference groups. The people who know him may look at him with more respect, but that will be all. However, let us assume that his victory at the plant has given him new incentive, and he begins to play in state and finally national tournaments. He will soon develop a new reference group, consisting of top amateur and professional table tennis players. In the real world, almost every case of social mobility results in some change in the group alliances of the person. This change may involve developing new groups and rejecting (in a nice way, of course) older associations which might hinder the person in his new position. The table tennis player, for example, might want to avoid his old friends who are not good at the game, especially when he is in the company of professionals.

This process of giving up certain group memberships and individual friendships in order to move into higher status groups is a very difficult thing. There is often a considerable time lag between the performance which gets him in (paying the entry fee at the country club, getting the promotion, moving into the new house) and the social acceptance of the new group. This means that for a long period of time the individual is *formally* a member of the new group but does not have *social acceptance* from the new group—he is not one of them. On the other hand, he has made the move, and he must be careful not to be seen too often with his old friends.

For a long time, he really has no group membership, as he has divorced himself from his previous group memberships, and he does not yet have social acceptance from above.

A very poignant example of how uncomfortable it is to be "caught" can be seen on any college campus at graduation time. There is generally a social hour of some sort during which the seniors and their families meet the faculty. This is generally a painful occasion for all concerned, but especially so for the bright graduate whose parents come from lower social and economic origins, and know little about "correct" social behavior or intellectual problems. Nothing would make the student happier than to have his (or her) parents disappear into thin air, as they do not fit his new group alliances and in a sense "give him away." To avoid this problem, people tend to cut themselves adrift from their pasts, but this action carries them into unfriendly seas. A respect and love for the past can be a source of great emotional stability in time of stress, and this stability is lost to the person who must, in order keep up with the present and future, divorce the past.

There are, as we have seen, definite reasons for believing that both kinds of mobility—geographical moves and changes in status—can result in psychological damage, and research indicates that damage can result in schizophrenia, poor marital adjustment, increased prejudice, alcoholism, and crime. On the other hand, there is some evidence that for many people, mobility of any sort does not result in damage to the individual at all, but may actually increase his sense of satisfaction and well-being. Here we can ask a fascinating question which has not been investigated: Why is it that certain people thrive on mobility of any kind, while others find it a shattering experience?

There is no immediate experimental answer to this question, but some concepts from anthropology may help in speculating about it. The newborn child does not come equipped with the values, attitudes, and behaviors of his culture. These must be acquired. The process may occur in a formal didactic situation or simply through imitation of adult behavior, but every culture has mechanisms for indoctrinating its young. This process of indoctrination into the ways of a culture is called *enculturation*. Now consider the case of a person who has become indoctrinated into the culture, and then is moved to a different culture. He now must adapt to the new culture on the basis of the practices of his first culture. This process of adapting to a different culture is called *acculturation*. In some cases the process is very easy; in others it is extremely difficult. When acculturation is easy, it is because there is a basic compatibility in the values of the two cultures. There may be vast differences in behavior, but if the goals and directions of the two cultures are in agreement, the new behavior can be learned with little difficulty.

For example, we would expect that the Japanese who comes to America would have a difficult acculturation because members of the two cultures *behave* so differently. Such is not the case, as the Japanese and American cultures share many values which undercut the behavior differences, allowing the Nisei to accept and to be accepted by the segment of American society known as the "middle class." Assimilation into the culture is easy, and the Nisei quickly develops a loyalty to his new culture.[12] On the other hand, the Mexican who comes to America may have a very difficult acculturation, as the values of the two cultures are not easily reconciled. As a consequence, the Mexican may never become truly identified with American culture; he will simply be a Mexican living in the United States. When the cultures are compatible, people from one can merge completely into the other. When they are incompatible, people from one will not mix into the other but will remain as a minority group, associating only with their own kind.

This concept of acculturation is useful not only in movements *across* cultures, but in movements *within* a culture as well. If we take a six-year-old boy who was raised in the slums and put him into a wealthy aristocratic family, we are moving him from one *sub*culture to another, and the strain may be as great as or greater than the strain of moving from one culture to another. The slums may be only a few miles away from the mansion, but by moving the slum boy to the mansion we are moving him a great *social* distance, and his acculturation problem may be greater than that of the Japanese-American. This problem of subcultural acculturation and social distance has fascinated many novelists, particularly Dickens. See his *Great Expectations* and *David Copperfield.*

The individual who becomes socially mobile is also going through an acculturation process, in that he is moving from one subculture into another. We can apply the same arguments and say that the success of this adaptation will depend on the goodness of fit between the individual's value orientation and that of the new group which he wishes to enter. Here is one explanation of why it is that certain members of lower social and economic levels can fit in so well with the dominant value orientation supported by the middle classes, while others simply find the adaptation impossible. Social mobility will not cause difficulties if the individual can retain his values and his self-esteem in the new group or groups. The same move—geographical, economic, occupational, social, etc.—can be easy for one person and impossible for someone else.

What Is an Optimum Rate of Mobility?

Contrary to popular sentiments, any society can have *too much* social mobility, both for statistical and personal reasons. If we allow *everyone* to obtain the prerequisites necessary for high status positions, then there will not be enough high status positions to go around. We have already mentioned the dangers of selling someone on the mobile life, then barring him from the symbols of success. During America's Great Depression there were thousands of newly graduated college students who were unable to obtain the high status positions they felt were theirs by right. Many of the radical leaders of social movements at this time came from the ranks of disillusioned students who felt that the American culture had not fulfilled its promises. Strictly in terms of numbers, a society should not encourage people to work for high status positions if there are no high status positions available for them after they have completed the prerequisites.

On the personal level, a great truth was revealed by Gilbert and Sullivan when they said that *if everybody is somebody, then nobody is anybody.* As soon as a dimension of status is thrown open to everyone, and the requirements for status are so easy as to require little or no effort, then people will tend to stop building their status judgments around that dimension and will look for others. Some of the research done in World War II on army promotion rates corroborates this position. If only twenty per cent of a given rank were promoted to a higher rank, everyone was happy. Those who were promoted felt that the promotion meant something and was a distinct honor, while the eighty per cent who remained below could take refuge in numbers and retain their self-confidence. On the other hand, when the promotion rate was increased to fifty per cent, both factions were unhappy. So many were promoted that the award lost its significance for those who made it, while those who failed could not take refuge in numbers or blame the impersonality of the system.[13] We cannot assume that a high rate of occupational mobility would necessarily result in happier, more satisfied people, especially if the values of the individual were incompatible with those of the groups he would be associating with at the higher occupational and social level.

American culture seems to be pushing the egalitarian notion that everyone is entitled to a college education, on the grounds that this will increase equality of opportunity. It is easy to disagree with this notion for several reasons. First, the land grant colleges are now required to admit any graduate of an accredited high school in that state, but they are not required to *keep* them. As a result, between thirty to sixty per cent of the freshman class never achieves sophomore status. Is this increasing social mobility, or is it creating a bitter and disillusioned group of young adults?

The same fight was fought at the high school level, resulting in a victory for the forces of egalitarianism. The secondary school could not take the colleges' easy way out by eliminating the undesirables, as the schools had a legal responsibility for the child until a given age. Has the resulting system of "automatic" graduation from high school increased social mobility and equality of opportunity? Perhaps in some cases it has, but the over-all result has been to *lower* the amount of social status given to the high school graduate. It is no longer an achievement, no longer a way of *differentiating people,* and every status system is fundamentally a way of differentiating people. If a system is not selective, it will not attract the best people. As an example, consider a school which has a basketball team (high status) and a volleyball team (low status). The basketball team will probably consist of the *best* basketball players in the school, for the activity is rewarded with high status. The volleyball team will *not* contain the best volleyball players in the school, as it is not a high status activity and will not attract the best talent. The best volleyball players are probably on the basketball team.

As America becomes more and more of a single-minded homogeneous culture, we would suspect that the number of ways in which people can gain status would decrease. This is unfortunate, as it will mean that many people with special skills may not be able to practice them and receive social reward for their efforts. On the other hand, we cannot reward excellence in *everything,* because such things as brushing teeth and buttering bread are not designed to differentiate performance. But in every activity in which achievement requires effort and the exceptional performance differentiates the performer from the rest of the group, the performer should be rewarded with high status. There is a real danger for our culture here, as we are tending increasingly to adopt uniform standards for status. These standards (cars, houses, swimming pools, size of backyard barbecue) are *symbolic* and *vicarious,* and tell us very little about the real person behind the barbecue. The mass media are constantly trying to tell us who we are and who we should be, and too many people are shaping themselves around the status criteria forced on them.

In summary, we might say that increasing social mobility rates will be, at best, a mixed blessing. People will not exhibit feelings of happiness or personal fulfillment as a consequence. As the number of criteria for social mobility decreases, we might expect increasing dissatisfaction with them. Many individuals simply do not wish to be evaluated on the basis of their *occupational* advancement, and it seems unreasonable and ineffectual to force everyone to play the same game. If a pluralistic society is to thrive, it must have a wide variety of status and mobility criteria from which people may choose.

SOCIAL MOBILITY AND EDUCATION

The educational system is an institution operating within American society, and as such it will inevitably reflect to some extent the values of American culture. We found this to be true in examining some of the stratification systems which exist in schools. Because mobility and social stratification are but two sides of the same coin—differentiation—we would expect that the mobility systems found in schools would also mirror the cultural values of the larger society.

There is no doubt that the American school does not treat every student *equally,* if we consider equality to mean identity. To give every student identical treatment would mean that everyone would get the same grades; everyone would have the lead in the senior play; and the entire student body would belong to the National Honor Society. A better definition of equality might say that the school treats each student *according to his needs and abilities,* but this is the most optimistic and unrealistic statement imaginable. This definition suggests

that needs and abilities are innate, fixed in the genetic structure of the person. To a degree this is true, but no ability can
be developed unless the environment provides for the development of that ability. We can *never* know what this latent ability
is; we can only measure the performance level which the
environment allows. In similar fashion, higher needs develop
only after more basic needs have been satisfied by a friendly
environment. Many teachers make the mistake of assuming
that a score on an intelligence test or a spelling test is a measure of that student's *innate* capacity, while in reality it is
nothing of the kind. What the school actually does is to treat
each student *un*equally according to his *performances,* which
is exactly what American society does to the student when he
leaves school. However, the performances which are selected
by the school and society may be the wrong ones. Later in
this chapter we will defend this definition of equality as treating students unequally according to their performances.

Mobility Systems Based on the Students

We have already mentioned the importance of the curriculum division as a cue for status judgments; it is also a
criterion for occupational mobility, as a college degree is
mandatory for most high status occupations. It is worth men-
tioning that the two oldest American colleges, Harvard and
William and Mary, were both founded for occupational reasons. There was little concern for "training the mind"; there
were not enough ministers to go around, and these institutions
were founded to swell the ranks of an *occupational* group and
produce an American clergy. The "land grant" colleges, which
are required to maintain departments of agriculture, are a case
in point. Vocational education is certainly not a recent development in American life, as occupation and education have been
interrelated throughout our history.

The student in the college preparatory curriculum is given
high status by teachers and peers not only for his present level

of performance but also for what he may accomplish in the future. However, we must realize that the students themselves often tend to minimize their academic abilities in *all* curriculum divisions, and thus reflect an American goal of achievement without effort. Just as unions put rigid restrictions on the amount of work a man can do in a day, so the student subculture puts limitations on the amount of work the students can put into preparation of assignments.[14] The student who consistently excels in schoolwork is becoming socially mobile in his relationships with his teacher, but he may be losing status in the eyes of his peers, especially if he fails to observe the "rules" which govern study habits. If he wants to get into college, his relationships with his fellow students will play a considerable part in determining whether or not he is admitted; therefore he must often compromise and be a "good guy" if he wants to go to a good college.

Students are far more perceptive on the criteria for "nice guy" mobility than are their teachers or parents, in that they know which activities will best serve as evidence to the colleges of high social status. A sport for the boys, a position as an officer, either of student government or of a class (which will reflect both leadership ability and popularity) and membership in one or two clubs is the ideal activities profile toward which the college preparatory student strives. To see students selecting activities solely on the basis of how well they will look on the records is not a happy sight, yet the students' idea of the criteria for mobility (in terms of getting into a good college) are quite realistic and necessary. This is one reason why the college preparatory students dominate extra-curricular activities; participation in these activities is one of the necessary prerequisites for social mobility. The non-college students, however, see the same activities as meaningless and frivolous, because the activities are not seen as ways of gaining social status, both in the present and in the future. Because the extra-curricular program does have an impact on the school's ability to allow some students to become socially mobile through acquiring advanced education, we should examine it in some detail.

The extra-curricular activities program is a good example of how a school institution can simply *evolve*, with no one taking direct responsibility for the goals and implementation of the program. The children who already fit in with the prevailing value orientation of the school do not need these activities, but the student who comes with a deviant set of values could be helped a great deal in his social adjustment to the school. His acculturation could be made much easier. But when we look into a school, what do we find? It is usually those children who *already* fit in with the values of the school that are in the extra-curricular activities, while those who need the social confidence and the exposure to new values and new social customs do not participate.

Teachers and administrators generally try to be as permissive as possible about these activities because they believe that (1) students should be free to develop whatever outside interests they wish, and (2) that there are two types of activity—intellectual and social—and these two are like oil and water and cannot be mixed. Both of these assumptions are fallacious: the first, because people must be *exposed* to new activities before they can develop any interest in them; the second, because every learning situation has its social components. Even if we consider a student sitting alone reading a book, there is a communication process taking place, and this process is a unique interaction of the author and the reader—a *social* situation. Learning does not take place in a vacuum; it can occur any time one person interacts with others, either directly or vicariously.

Teachers who claim that Joe is incapable (and this means that he is *innately* incapable) of the act of memorization because he cannot memorize a list of American Presidents might be surprised to discover that he may know fifty very involved football plays and hundreds of cars, not only by sight but also by horsepower, year, piston displacement, and tire size. Is the list of Presidents more "intellectual" than the list of football plays? It may be more difficult to learn, but this is due primarily to a lack of immediate social context and ego-involvement with the list of Presidents. The college preparatory student may find an ego-involvement with the list of Presidents, as he can see a relationship of this list with future goals which he wishes to attain. This involvement need not be direct and immediate. A student may be willing to perform a very difficult task which he does not understand if he feels that the performance of this task is important for his future as he sees it.

The extra-curricular program could serve as an opening wedge for the student who finds the activities of the classroom (such as memorizing a list of Presidents) totally unrelated to his life. By allowing the student to develop a loyalty and involvement in an extra-curricular activity, the chances of his becoming involved in the classroom activities of the school are increased. One interesting thing about those who drop out of school and do not graduate is that they have taken little or no part in extra-curricular activities, and as a result have built up no personal loyalties to the school.[15] Many of these are potentially able students whose skills, if developed, could be of great value to others; yet the school does little to help these students who need help more than anyone. Even if the student did not wish to become mobile occupationally, the extra-curricular program could give him status in the form of *esteem* for the skills he has.

As an example of how this can work, there are several communities in which all of the maintenance of the school buses is done by the students in auto shop classes, working in their spare time. These students have become heroes, both in the school and in the community. Their responsibility for the safety of the children in their town has been pointed out in newspaper articles, and as a result these students have increased their social status enormously. Their grades have improved, and they have a real interest in school. Granted, they have not all decided to try to become bank presidents; as a matter of fact, some are happy in *not* being mobile occupationally because they have been given social status (esteem) for what they can do well.

This type of program will not necessarily increase occupational mobility, but it may help bring esteem up to the level of prestige as a way of awarding status to students. In this sense it allows many students to be *socially* mobile without having to move up on the occupational ladder. There are two kinds of aspirations which a student can have. One is for position (I want to be a lawyer); the other is for competence (I want to be the best carpenter in my town). They are not necessarily separate and distinct, since one could wish to be the best lawyer in a community; but in general the aspiration for a prestige position does not necessarily include the aspiration for esteemed performance, partly because the aspirant is more familiar with the position than with the performances that go with the position. The school tends to emphasize aspiration for position at the expense of aspiration for esteemed performance, at least in terms of *occupational* aspiration. This is unfortunate in that the school does little for the student who does not want a high status position. The program mentioned above is only one example of what could be done through a carefully conceived extra-curricular program.

In the world outside the school, one does not need to change occupations to increase his social status. If a person comes to be known as the *best* plumber in town, he has increased his status without changing jobs. The studies of occupational mobility have completely neglected this type of occupational mobility which does not involve moving into a high prestige job, and the schools tend to neglect it also. Yet the psychological rewards of knowing that you are an exceptional performer may be greater than knowing that you are perhaps a mediocre member of a high-prestige occupation.

We have already seen that the informal status system in a factory or office can serve the very useful function of providing social status for those who are, for one reason or another, unable to rise through the formal hierarchy. One would expect that the extra-curricular programs in schools could accomplish the same function, but at present they do not. Like the three-month summer vacation (which came into being long ago when children were needed on the farms to help with the crops, but which cannot possibly be justified in urban areas when teachers and students are working on double sessions), the extra-curricular program is difficult to justify in terms of its present role.

There is a considerable amount of evidence that the place of the child in the social hierarchy of the school reflects quite accurately the place of the parents in the social hierarchies outside the school. Friendship patterns, grades, and membership in school organizations tend to bear this out.[16] If you know the income and occupation of a student's father, you can predict whether or not he will go to college almost as well as you could by using intelligence test scores. This would indicate that the school is not serving its function of providing pathways for the able but underprivileged student to become occupationally mobile if he desires. The school program is geared largely to the needs of those who come from good environments and are *bound* to be successful. Some of the children from inferior background are allowed to enter this select group, but only if they manifest the correct values and required behavior.

It is worth pointing out here that the "required behavior" for mobility may vary as we move from school to school. We have already mentioned the way in which schools may differ as we move away from the center of a metropolitan area, and to a degree the required behavior may also vary in a similar fashion. In the patriarchal school, the student must show obedience to the wishes of the teacher and must meet fixed standards of accomplishment. As we move out to the matriarchal systems, we find much more emphasis placed on how the student relates to his peers in the classroom and outside. It is here in the suburbs and exurbs that the mental health movement has gained a great deal of influence both in the classroom and in the guidance office. Here, sociograms and other devices are used in profusion to determine how well the student is doing *socially,* and frequency of class participation has become *in itself* a standard of achievement, regardless of the intellectual quality of the participation. The author is familiar with several situations in which teachers grade largely on the basis of the number of contributions made by each student to the discussion. Sociograms are administered on a monthly basis and frequent conferences are held with each student to see how he is relating to the group. Frequently in these situations social interaction becomes the *curriculum* of the class, to the neglect of other kinds of learning. One's ability to get along with others may become a crucial factor in the *academic* grading system. In this way the school, which is to filter or "screen" students by their academic ability for entrance into higher education, may be producing more mobility by its *social* standards than by its academic standards.

Perhaps the greatest misunderstanding about the matriarchal school is that people feel that it encourages individual deviation from norms by allowing each child to express himself. In actuality, the pressures toward conformity may be much stronger in the matriarchal school than in the other varieties, although the pressures may not be easily seen by the casual observer. Because the exurban matriarchal school deals with students of *uniformly high* economic and social background, the pressures used by the school can be concentrated and selected just for this kind of student, while in a more heterogeneous area with a wider range of backgrounds this cannot be done as easily.

As we have indicated, the specific behaviors which will earn one the title of "good student" may vary from school to school. There may also be considerable variation in different classrooms within the *same* school. However, there is generally a tone or climate in each school which is rather consistently reproduced in the classrooms. The principal is generally the person who sets this tone, and the teachers who feel comfortable in this sort of climate stay, while others may move on. A change of principal is a vital matter to both faculty and students, as the tone which he conveys will in part determine what the students will have to do to be successful students, and what the teachers will have to do to be good teachers. Criteria for student and teacher mobility will depend in some degree on him.

Teachers generally pride themselves on their objectivity and lack of prejudice for minority groups, claiming that their students are all given the same chance to succeed. It may be true that on ethnic and religious grounds teachers are a very objective group, but that does not mean that they are open-minded in their treatment of all students. Teachers seem very ego-involved in what they consider to be "correct" standards of behavior, and the student who violates these standards is in for a difficult time, even though the violation has little connection with the intellectual tasks of the classrooom. These standards involve cleanliness, dress, speech, and control of aggression. They often override *academic* factors in selecting those who will be educationally mobile.

Why is it that the unwashed child, the boy in jeans and the girl in slacks, the student who yells and fights back when angered or threatened, and those who say "I ain't" and "He don't" represent such a threat for the teacher? Part of the answer is that teachers overemphasize distinctions of social status because they themselves have far more social status than economic status, and therefore must cherish their social graces as one of the few symbols of high status and mobility that they can afford. Also, the teacher (even the teacher who uses permissive techniques in the classroom) is basically an authoritarian figure with a legal responsibility for the children in the classroom; and these deviant behaviors are seen as a threat to the teacher's authority, ultimately leading to the danger of loss of control, which is probably the basic fear that all teachers feel at one time or another.

One of the major barriers to mobility which the school puts up is based on the fact that teachers add a *moral* connotation to these deviant behaviors, which is not really admissible. Teachers' behavior often suggests that the student who is un-washed, who uses slang, and who gets angry when hurt is not only incorrect but also immoral and evil. Social conventions (and language and dress are merely social conventions) may become the teacher's religion, and religion means morality. *Ain't* is not an innately evil word; it is simply not one of the language conventions of certain social groups. Actually it serves a perfectly valid linguistic function, and those who do not use the term are often forced into more complex patterns of language which have no particular advantage in either clarity or brevity.

However, when Johnny comes into the classroom and says "I ain't got no pencil," the teacher cannot be objective—her values and standards are being challenged. The teacher can-not talk of linguistic conventions. She must say "ain't" is *bad* and "I do not have" is *good*. She does not deny the tacit as-sumption that people who say "I do not have" are *better* than people who say "ain't." What the teacher does not realize in this case is that Johnny probably comes from a home and environment in which "ain't" is common and accepted usage. If the teacher says that "ain't" is used by ignorant, stupid peo-ple, Johnny is bound to recall that his own parents and rela-tives use the term. He is thus forced into either accepting the teacher's standards and rejecting those of his parents, or (and this seems more likely) denying the teacher's standards and retaining his allegiance to family and friends. Or let us as-sume that Johnny has been caught fighting and is told by the teacher or principal that it is only the scum of the earth who allow themselves to use physical violence, when Johnny knows that his mother and father sometimes throw things at each other. The student is again placed in an untenable position, as the school's values contradict what the student knows as his way of life.

The only possible alternative seems to be to convince the child that there are various standards of behavior and that he must behave in one way at school and another at home. This alternative is the one usually adopted by the school, but what are its consequences? Is it good for a child, perhaps of elementary school age, to feel that there is no such thing as right and wrong, and that you simply do what those around you are doing? Ethical standards and judgments are indeed relative, but this realization can be a shock to a college junior; and to a child in the formative years it could do considerable emotional damage. If the teacher is able to enforce her social conventions without adding this *moral* context, the child may be willing to play the teacher's game without getting hurt. However, as soon as the teacher says that this is the right way, the correct way, the *only* way, the child who knows other ways of behaving is immediately placed in a conflict situation.

In a suburban or exurban school, the teacher may be able to say that these are the only correct standards of behavior without conflict, as the students may be from nearly identical environments. In this case, no one will get hurt (although the students are getting a narrow-minded perspective on the human race). However, as racial and religious minority groups increase their economic status, they also move away from the center of the metropolis, bringing deviant behaviors and values to the outlying areas. Even when the children *share* some of the values advocated by the school, there can still be trouble. The most striking example of this occurs when a sizable Jewish population moves into a formerly Protestant area, for Jewish children often have a great desire for academic achievement and entry into high prestige occupations. As a matter of fact, Jewish children in contemporary American culture often exhibit more of what has come to be known as the Protestant Ethic than do the Protestant children whose bureaucratic upbringing has not emphasized individual achievement. One teacher in a suburban community, who happens to be a staunch Episcopalian, was recently accused of religious prejudice because all of his high marks were won by the Jewish children in his classes! In a school which practices the bureaucratic values of group achievement and social harmony, a few entrepreneur-minded students who push ahead to achieve high standards of intellectual accomplishment, ignoring the group in the process, can upset the program very rapidly.

There is little doubt that the school does serve a function in providing access to high prestige occupations. However, we have questioned whether or not the *criteria* used by school personnel for selecting the students for educational and occupational opportunities should reflect the student's background as much as they do. On the other hand, the school may be justified in using social conventions to select students for further opportunities, since adult society does the same thing. People are selected for high prestige jobs in part on what they say, how they are dressed, and how well they perform the social rites; so why should the school not do the same thing? The answer should be that the school selects on *intellectual* grounds, but clearly we are speaking of social rites even in the term intellectual, in that the intellectual is distinguished by having a distinct language and a set of social conventions, not necessarily by being better able to control his environment and get what he wants.

Perhaps teachers can be excused for confusing social conventions with a measure of intelligence, as even the Ph.D. candidate is evaluated on how well he follows the prescribed social norms.[17] Intelligence, however we wish to define it, can only assert itself in a given social context. What is needed is a measure of innate ability, a gene counter which could tell us exactly what the student's hereditary potential was, *regardless* of the environment, but this is an impossibility both for the practical reason that we cannot count genes and because the genetic capability is meaningless *without* the proper environment. If we really wanted to provide *intellectual* equality of opportunity, there would be only one way to do it. Because we cannot equalize the hereditary potential, we would have to equalize the *environment*. In order to do this, we would have to become a completely totalitarian state, and renounce our free system which allows people to live in different environments. In order to provide real equality of intellectual opportunity, we must give up our freedoms. Freedom and equality, which are so often produced as complementary, are seen here to be contradictory. This is why the school is justified in treating each student unequally according to his performances, because this is as close to equality as we can get without sacrificing other values, such as freedom. The idea of *unlimited* social mobility as a goal of the public schools is therefore a highly questionable notion.

Mobility Systems Based on the Teacher

The complications in the concept of occupational mobility are easily seen when we consider teachers. As usually defined, an occupationally mobile teacher would be one who left for another occupation of higher or lower prestige. Many teachers do this, of course, but teachers can also change their status by staying *within* the occupation of teacher. There are several ways in which this can be done. One is by changing grade level, such as going from elementary to secondary school, which will result in an increase in status. The other, and more popular way, is to join in the exodus to the suburbs and exurbs where salaries may be higher and the surroundings more pleasant.

The typical hiring pattern in a large metropolis is to send new teachers, who have absolutely no bargaining power, into the worst areas of the city where children are difficult to manage for reasons we have already mentioned. A few teachers become resigned to teaching in these areas and settle down there, but most yearn for the neat, orderly, docile children, the well-equipped classroom, and the sunlit teachers' lounge of the suburban school.[13] The teacher mobility pattern in a large city is generally away from the center of town, towards the suburbs and exurbs. There, teachers gain in pay, in status, and in community recognition. Also, the job is more in line with *their training*. New teachers, who see teaching as an intellectual mission, are often completely bewildered by children with deviant values and behavior. This is understandable, as there are few teacher education programs that do more than mention the problems of teaching in low social and economic areas. The new teacher's reaction to the problem is typified by the young lady who stayed in the city for only one year, then headed for the suburbs, saying, "I want some kids that I can *teach!*"

As a result of this movement, the city school has a very high turnover rate on the teaching staff, as well as among the student body. The teachers who stay are the truly dedicated and the dangerously incompetent. It is difficult for the administration to begin revising the program, for the teaching staff may change almost completely from year to year. Budgets are low, and teachers are often hired on a temporary basis and paid a daily wage so that minimum yearly wage laws can be avoided. Classes may hold as many as forty or fifty students, most of them rebellious. The threat of failing a course may strike deep into the hearts of suburban and exurban children who must pass their courses to get into college, but the threat of failure in school can do little to a student who sees no relationship between his school grades and his life. The city teacher must resort to more subtle threats. The easiest thing to do is to get out where children do not need to be shown how to behave. Here is a reversal of the functionalist approach. When the job to be done is the most difficult and complex, everything is done to see that the least competent and experienced people do the job. This, then, is one of the ways in which teachers may change their occupational status without even leaving the teaching profession—by moving from a low status area to the suburbs or exurbs.

The other most popular type of teacher mobility is leaving the classroom for an administrative position. Particularly for a man who must support a family, administration may be the only aspect of educational service which will allow him a living wage, as well as a reasonable amount of social status. One of the reasons for the increased number of men entering elementary school teaching is the knowledge that a principalship can be theirs in a very short time, whereas in a high school they might have to wait for many years. According to its advocates, one of the major advantages to the newly developed concept of "team teaching" is that it will develop a hierarchy of status *within* the teaching profession. This will mean that an experienced and competent teacher will not have to leave teaching in order to increase his social and economic status.

However, the mobility pattern of teachers is not as simple as it once was. Schools have adopted the same promotional policies that have been adopted in industry. In earlier time, the best drill press operator was made foreman, and the *best teacher* was made principal. The administrative position was awarded because of excellent performance in a non-administrative role. Business studies indicated that the best drill press operator did not necessarily make the best foreman, and as a result the foreman came to be chosen from those who had special competencies and training in the fine art of foremanship. In similar fashion, principals and superintendents have been seen to need special abilities and skills, not necessarily those used in the teaching situation. As a consequence, principals and superintendents, like managers and foremen, are frequently hired from *outside* the school or plant, on the basis of special training and experience. The worker can no longer assume that because he is the best worker he will be made foreman, and the teacher cannot assume that he will be elevated to a principalship.

Both the school and the factory have thus destroyed the continuity of a system of mobility. The worker no longer goes up through the ranks unless he takes a year or two off to get a Masters Degree in Business Administration. The teacher who wants an administrative position must also leave teaching and take academic work leading to an advanced degree in educational administration. Undoubtedly the present system advances those with the best skills for administrative tasks, but it also destroys something which may be of great importance. When a worker can no longer see a direct line of positions of increasing status in front of him, when he can no longer see his co-workers and friends in supervisory positions, he loses contact with the factory as a whole, and associates only with those who do his job. The others in the plant are strangers. The idea of interchangeable parts is a productive one, but the notion of interchangeable *workers* is a dangerous concept indeed.

Similarly, when a community promotes strangers to the administrative posts in the school system, teachers may also lose their feeling for the school system as a meaningful whole. There should be some way in which local communities could bring promising administrative talent up through the ranks, giving released time for obtaining the necessary training. In this way, the promotional system in the school could be a *community* affair, allowing the community to take justifiable pride in its own best people. Such a policy might represent another way in which a school system could establish its own community identity as an individual enterprise.

These are the formal mobility systems which exist in the schools. We can now look at a few of the *informal* ways of increasing status for those involved in the school system.

Informal Teacher Mobility Systems

As we have already mentioned, many people increase their social status without changing their occupational status by continually doing extra work and taking over responsibilities from others. These people become indispensable by gaining information and by performing tasks which they choose not to share with others. This type of mobility is particularly easy when those of higher status have too much to do and are willing to delegate some of their duties, and thereby some of their authority.

Another way to increase one's status is simply to stay in a given school system for a long time. Just as the factory worker with seniority gets certain privileges, so does the school staff member who knows the subtleties of local politics and knows "how things are to be done." Teachers and administrators are not the only people who can do this. In many schools the custodian may have considerable influence on the educational system by having outlasted the teaching staff and the administration. Being a local resident, he may have great influence with the school board and may know more about the ins and outs of local politics than anyone else in the school system. Particularly in a school system which has a rapid turnover of teachers and administrators, those who stay put are the ones the newcomers must consult to find out what the ground rules are.

These two ways of increasing social status, power, and influence are complementary and can often be seen in one person. For example, in almost any central office of a school (or college president or dean, for that matter) can be found a person whose status, power, and influence far exceed what one would expect. This person is usually a lady. Her formal title may vary, but she has been in the system a long time and has gradually gained a great deal of status and authority *within* the school by taking over certain functions which were formally delegated to others. Here we face one of the annoying complexities of social analysis, because school personnel may acknowledge her high status grudgingly, not willingly. There are positive and negative aspects of high social status, and the negative aspect is most clearly seen *when the actual amount of power and influence the person wields does not jibe with the amount one would expect from the job description.* As a result, the secretary in the Main Office may be thoroughly disliked, even though she has high social status. Power and status are generally intertwined, but status comes in a variety of sizes and shapes. We give high social status to some because we admire and respect them for their accomplishments, but their power usually squares with their formal position. Others *force* us to give them high status, but we resent it because their power and influence is not accompanied by the necessary position in the formal hierarchy.

Although we may dislike people who seize power in this way, it is difficult to criticize them, both for security reasons and because they are completely dedicated to the operation of the school. Their loyalty and devotion to duty cannot be questioned. Here is an example of an informal mobility pattern in which the person gains status and power without necessarily gaining *popularity*. High social status can cut both ways, toward admiration and esteem and toward notoriety and social rejection.

Another informal benefit of staying in the same system for a long time is that the teacher's bargaining power increases and she is able to get better classes with students who are more "intellectually stimulating" (this, loosely translated, often means easier to handle, fewer disciplinary problems). As the teacher becomes a senior member of a department, there may be a chairmanship available with some minor administrative duties, and this represents an increase in status. Also, as the teacher continues in a position, she acquires a reputation which is passed on to each succeeding class with remarkable accuracy. If she has been a strict disciplinarian the first few years, she can then relax her control considerably. Many new teachers cannot understand how the veteran teacher handles her classes so easily. They fail to realize that the students come to the veteran's classroom with a definite set of expectations as to how this person will play the role of teacher; students do not have these expectations for the new teacher. The self-fulfilling prophecy works again, in that if the students *think* that the veteran will be a stern taskmaster, they will behave obediently, regardless of what the teacher actually does in the classroom. The prophecy also works in reverse, in that if the teacher believes that a group of students will be hard to handle, she may easily communicate this to the class and they *will* be hard to control.

It is interesting to watch the same teacher work with a college preparatory class and with a general or commercial class. Often there is more disorder, talking out of turn, and general foolishness in the college preparatory class than there is in the "lower" group, yet the teacher is not at all bothered by it. This is because the teacher has a basic trust in the college preparatory class—they are "good" children who would not take advantage of the situation. But when the teacher enters the general class (and these students are sometimes spoken of as "My vegetables," or even "My leper colony," by the teacher), a wall seems to spring up between the teacher and the class, destroying any sense of rapport. Because the teacher *expects* the children to be bad, they often oblige. It would be interesting to see what would happen if a teacher were told in advance that her new class was a very good college group when actually the group was a non-college division.

Clearly the calibre of her classes is one index of the teacher's social status within the school. As she stays on and increases her status there will be other symbols of mobility—a classroom closer to the central office, new desks and equipment at more frequent intervals, perhaps a space closer to the building in the parking lot, if spaces are assigned. Another major step on the road to status is reached when the teacher is placed on tenure, in those systems which follow this practice. In the factory, seniority is rewarded with job security, and so it is in the school. For those whose route to occupational mobility is blocked, status systems develop *within* the occupational group and one of the criteria for social status within the group is *security*, especially in a fast-changing, uncertain culture like our own.

Those things to which we assign high status reflect our own basic needs. The unemployed worker wants a job which will bring him food and shelter; the worker who has satisfied these needs is interested in security, while the professional and executive worker has satisfied both these needs and sees a high status job as one that can satisfy his need for *stimulation* and challenge. But there is evidence that security is becoming a more pervasive need, reflected in virtually *every* occupation.[19] The increasing amount of family activity and "togetherness" may also be a manifestation of this quest for security; in fact, the large family, which used to be necessary to get the farm work done, may now be necessary again for psychological reasons in providing an island of stability in a sea of uncertainty and change. In similar fashion, the teacher on tenure may be able to find a certain stability and security in knowing that the job cannot be taken away except in drastic circumstances. Note that we have not been defending tenure against the merit system or any other system. We have simply described how the practice fits into the mobility system of the school by providing security.

Teachers may also increase their social status by performing certain extra functions in the school program, particularly in supervising student activities. In some schools teachers are paid for these extra services according to the hours involved; in other schools every teacher is expected to "volunteer" for such activities as part of the regular program, and no extra pay is given. It is interesting to observe that the status given to these activities by the teachers and by school boards reflects our discussion of the school in its search for identity. The "group-teams," especially football and basketball, *do* reflect the identity of the school, and coaches of these teams are highly paid and have considerable status in school and community. The "individual-teams," like track and swimming, do not establish the identity of the school as a social unit, and as a result the coaches of these teams often achieve little extra social or economic status for their efforts. Those activities which present an image of the school to the outside world—the plays, the yearbooks, the school paper—all tend to add to the social status of the teacher who is responsible for them. If, on the other hand, the participants in an activity never give a public performance of any kind, the teacher who guides that activity gains little.

Suggestions have been made recently to the effect that if the school could only make public performances of *intellectual* achievement, many of the school's problems would be solved, in that the students and teachers responsible would share in the high social status given now to the football coach. Unfortunately, not all kinds of intellectual ability and performance yield visible evidence of the achievement. The budding scientist may exhibit his homemade Geiger counter at a science fair and receive public acclaim, but what can the young philosopher, mathematician, or psychologist put up for public exhibition? Many of these activities are private and do not concern tangible objects, and thus cannot be demonstrated to an admiring public.

For example, consider a student who was brilliant enough to trace Einstein's reasoning process which allowed him to discover one of the basic rules of the nature of matter. How could the student *exhibit* what he had done? He could, of course, put $E = mc^2$ on a poster at the local science fair, but it is hard to believe that the applause would be deafening. Making models of things seems to be a particularly American approach to educational method, but contrary to popular sentiment we cannot always deduce from an excellent model any intellectual activity except what is needed to make the model. The existence of a model of the Globe Theatre (and there must be thousands of these in America) tells us little or nothing about the builder's knowledge of Shakespeare, his plays, or his time.

The acquisition of taste, of aesthetic appreciation, and of skill in abstract reasoning is essentially a lonely task both for the student and teacher, much more lonely than the production of a winning football team. The American culture has always rewarded cooperative activities which produce *tangible* evidence of achievement, and nothing could be further from this cultural value than the student who has gained a great deal of insight into the music of Bach or the subtleties of Othello. The students and teachers engaged in this type of activity can never expect to receive the social status of the football coach because (1) their activities do not project an image of the school to the outside community, (2) their work is individual and does not require extensive group cooperation, (3) there is no tangible evidence of achievement, and (4) there is no *opponent*, so there is no chance of winning, and winning is generally the most easily recognized and highly rewarded type of achievement in American culture.

Building social status into the intellectual achievements of students and teachers is a ponderous task, and by emphasizing models and contests to see who has the most knowledge, we are sacrificing the very essence of the individual's search for truth to *materialistic* concepts of achievement. The teacher who leads a small discussion group on Plato and Aristotle after school should realize that this activity will not always help him get a principalship. Here again the school is reflecting the dominant values of American culture in the school status system, and it is not clear that the school could set up a system which would *contradict* the criteria for social status which are used in our culture. The school, like the society, rewards producers more than thinkers.

Mobility Systems Based on the Entire School

One of the results of the tremendous increase in geographical mobility in America has been marked changes in the status of certain schools and school districts. The growth of the suburbs and exurbs has meant that many areas which only a few short years ago were largely rural and agricultural are now inundated by professionals who have the economic power to demand sweeping changes in the school system. As new communities have evolved, new schools and school systems have sprung up, many of them gaining high status because of their economic power. We have already mentioned that teachers are moving in a generally consistent pattern—away from the metropolitan center to the suburbs and exurbs.

All of this mobility of teachers, parents, and students has had one major result: the decline of the big-city school systems. Particularly along the eastern seaboard, every major city had at least one public school which was equal in status to the best private schools in the country. Today the situation has changed. The municipal government has had to provide increased social services, often for the very same people who have decreased the city's revenue by their exodus to the suburbs. City school budgets are woefully inadequate and cannot compete with the suburban and exurban salaries for teachers. In their efforts to keep teachers, metropolitan schools often resort to hiring people who do not meet certification requirements, as well as establishing a rule that prohibits a teacher from transferring from a "tough" school to a better one without being fired.

The suburban and exurban student population is reasonably constant and homogeneous, at least in comparison with metropolitan school changes in student population. Within a year, an area of a metropolis may change from five per cent Negro to fifty per cent. The average income for an area may change from $2800 to $1200 in one year. The population density may change drastically in one year. The effect of these changes on the schools is predictable. Consolidation is difficult within the city, so that a school which teems with children one year may be half full in three years. A racial or religious minority group can jump from a small percentage of the student body to virtually 100% composition in a year. Because of district regulations, many metropolitan schools are actually run on a segregated basis because of the composition of the population served by the school. Some classes have ten different teachers during a single year course, and many teachers find that the students with whom they begin in September are almost completely replaced by others before June. Continuity is lost for both students and teachers. Many of these students cannot square their values with those of the school, and a high degree of emotional instability results. The student body may be too heterogeneous for the teachers to cope with. Discipline is dependent on authority, and authority is dependent on *power*. When the teacher's sources of power are not recognized by the students as being of importance (failing the course, not getting into college, flunking out of school), then the teacher's authority decreases, and the ability to maintain discipline may vanish.

In the city schools these changes are usually for the worse, as the better students and parents are moving out constantly and leaving the city schools to be inundated by wave after wave of people. Thus, the schools constantly decrease in social and economic status as the more fortunate groups are able to move out. One of the greatest dangers here is that teachers tend to confuse racial attributes with social and subcultural values. The author is familiar with several cases in which a Negro group suddenly moved into a formerly white area. The teachers interpreted every behavior problem they encountered in terms of *racial* characteristics, when in actuality the most important aspect of the Negro group was their system of values which deviated sharply from that of the white group which had just moved out. The teachers would have had just as many disciplinary problems with *any* group which came from the same low social and economic level as did the Negro group, and which maintained a deviant value system.

These are just a few of the reasons for the decline in status of the city schools. Perhaps the most vital factor in the decline is the economic problem. To attract good teachers, the city schools must compensate for the social advantages of living in the suburbs. One way they can do this is by paying *higher* salaries than those paid in the suburbs and exurbs. With more money, the city school systems could hire top principals and superintendents who now are recruited by the suburban and exurban systems. With better leadership the city schools could begin to investigate the pressing problems of curriculum development and teacher training for a mobile, heterogeneous population, and the development of classroom procedures which would be effective, both in terms of learning and of discipline. Many of the difficulties of the city school could be eliminated if the class size were cut from forty to twenty, but this also takes money.

In the suburbs and exurbs a school system may increase its status by increasing the percentage of students going on to college, building spectacular new buildings, increasing the salary schedule, hiring a national figure as superintendent, affiliating with a high status college or university for a research program, or winning a large grant from a foundation. Most of these avenues for mobility are not as readily available to the city schools. We have already stated that the consequences of vertical (social distance) and horizontal (physical distance) mobility are not always favorable, either for individuals or for social institutions; and it would seem that this judgment has been substantiated by our analysis of the big-city school which must serve a highly transient population.

One avenue for increasing the status of a school or school system is available to virtually every school, at least at the secondary level, and this is the area of interscholastic athletics. The status lasts only as long as the team is winning, yet many schools spend as much on athletics as they do on school supplies, including textbook purchases. These schools get trapped in the same maze that many colleges are in if they become increasingly dependent on revenues brought in by athletic events. Sports-conscious school committees often put athletic status ahead of any other kind, and many community organizations, especially business and fraternal, exert pressure on the school to have a winning team. One such school committee is known to have issued, in a public meeting, an elaborately engraved award of merit to a winner of a state track meet, while a request for a commendation for a student who had won a national scholarship was referred for some unspecified reason to the Committee on Buildings and Grounds.

In most schools, the athletic arena represents one source of social status in which social norms and customs are not confused with performance. The football coach does not care if his quarterback says "ain't" or comes to school in sloppy clothes, as long as he performs well as a quarterback and stays out of trouble academically. For the truly gifted athlete, success in high school athletics can mean a scholarship to college and occupational mobility. But in many instances the boy is not so lucky. It is interesting to observe that the one avenue of social mobility in the school program which gives equal chance to those from deviant backgrounds has nothing to do with the intellectual function of the school. Also, unless the athlete is able to get a scholarship, the school has not helped the underprivileged boy toward *occupational* mobility. It has only given him a temporarily increased social status.

In this chapter, we have seen once again that the systems of stratification and mobility in the school generally reflect the systems at work in the larger society. The school also reflects the values of the local community in which it operates. There is little in the school program which would lead students or teachers to examine in a critical fashion the criteria for status and mobility which are used in the school or in American culture, as these criteria are generally accepted as given.

But why is occupational mobility *always* a worthwhile goal for *every* life? Why should prestige be emphasized in the school and in society more than esteem, when the psychological rewards of esteem may be higher than those of prestige? When the consequences are clearly going to be dangerous, why do we talk of increasing the amount of occupational mobility through education? What, if anything, can the school do for those who come to it with a deviant set of values?

Part of the difficulty here stems from the fact that Americans believe in many things which are inherently contradictory. We believe that all men are of equal worth, yet almost every aspect of our daily life is guided toward differentiating people, making them unequal in our eyes. A man should be agreeable and conform to the wishes of the group, but individuals should assert themselves and defend their rights. A person should desire the symbolic objects which stand for status, but he should see that a person's basic goodness is what is important, not the things he owns. All men are equal before the law, but a man is a fool not to hire the best lawyer he can afford.

The contemporary American conception of democracy has been dominated by a fear of anything authoritarian. When one individual gives orders to another, democracy has failed, at least according to the wide-eyed egalitarian. Americans must somehow come to terms with the fact that every society must have *some* authoritarian elements, that there must be some sort of enforced system of inequality. Even in present-day communistic and socialistic societies, as well as in earlier experimental communities such as Brook Farm, Oneida, and New Harmony, economic and social rewards have been distributed unequally. The *real* question to be asked is: What kind of system of inequality will best serve the needs of contemporary America? What should be the *criteria* which will be used as the basis for the unequal distribution of rewards? When a child becomes enculturated, he acquires the values and behaviors of his culture; he is not given perfectly free choice of the folkways and mores he will follow. This is basically an authoritarian, dictatorial sort of process, yet it is absolutely necessary for the preservation of society. Of course the authoritarian aspect of the process can be abused, but the fact remains that the enculturation process, even in democracies, is fundamentally opposed to the kind of egalitarianism advocated by social philosophers like Karl Popper.[20]

The systems of inequality we have seen in the schools are remarkably similar to those found in the rest of American culture. The criteria for increasing one's place in the hierarchy —docility, conformity, easy adjustment to any social group regardless of the conflicts in values the individual may have with the group—may not be the best criteria for the schools to use. In a democratic society, the people should be able to choose

the criteria for *in*equality which they think will be most beneficial, while in a dictatorship this is not possible. The democratic school, then, has a grave responsibility to develop in its
students the ability to evaluate status criteria in as intelligent a
fashion as possible, and to *reject* those mobility patterns and
status criteria which the students feel are not worth the risks
involved.

It should be clear that the American school is not performing
this function, and that it is not equipped to do this task. In a
culture which tends to limit its conception of democracy to
free enterprise capitalism, it is difficult to see how the school
could ever perform this function, without first declaring war
on the culture it is supposed to serve.

NOTES

1. See P. Sorokin, *Social Mobility*, (New York, 1927) for a competent theoretical discussion of social mobility. The empirical problems
are presented well in S. Lipset and R. Bendix, *Social Mobility in Industrial Society*, (California, 1960).

2. On this point, see R. Merton and A. Kitt, "Reference Group
Theory and Social Mobility," Merton and Lazarsfeld, eds., *Continuities
in Social Research*, (Glencoe, 1950), 84-95.

3. First introduced by Sorokin, *op. cit.*, 132-134.

4. To see how the formal and informal hierarchies of business operate, see D. Miller and W. Form, *Industrial Sociology*, (New York,
1951); and F. Roethlisberger and W. Dickson, *Management and the
Worker*, (Cambridge, 1939), esp. pp. 558-562.

5. See E. Chinoy, "Social Mobility Trends in the United States,"
American Sociological Review, 20 (1955), 180-186. However, some
recent studies indicate directions in which more fruitful research on
social class and mobility might move. See, for example, T. Lasswell,
"Orientations Toward Social Class," *American Journal of Sociology*, 65
(1960), 585-587; F. W. Terrien, "Too Much Room at the Top?" *Social
Forces*, 37 (1959), 298-305; H. Blalock, Jr., "Status Consciousness,"
Social Forces, 37 (1959), 243-248; G. Kolko, "Economic Mobility and
Social Stratification," *Am. J. Sociol.*, 63 (1958), 30-38; T. Lasswell,
"Social Class and Size of Community," *AJS*, 64 (1959), 505-508; M.
Kohn, "Social Class and Parental Values," *AJS*, 64 (1959), 337-351;
O. Glantz, "Class Consciousness and Political Stability," *ASR*, 23 (1958),
375-383; S. Lipset, "Social Mobility and Urbanization, *Rural Sociology*,

20 (1955), 220-228; G. Lenski and J. Leggett, "Caste, Class, and Deference in the Research Interview," *AJS*, 65 (1960), 463-467; E. Douvan and J. Adelson, "The Psychodynamics of Social Mobility in Adolescent Boys," *Journal of Abnormal and Social Psychology*, 56 (1958), 31-44; S. Boggs, "Family Size and Social Mobility in a California Suburb," *Eugenics Quarterly*, 4 (1957), 208-213; H. Beilin, "The Pattern of Postponability and Its Relation to Social Class Mobility," *Journal of Social Psychology*, 44 (1956), 33-48, as well as the articles by Kahl and McArthur mentioned in Chapter Two. The article by Kohn is of particular importance to any teacher who wants to understand his students.

6. This is substantiated by several studies, particularly N. Rogoff, *Recent Trends in Occupational Mobility*, (Glencoe, 1953), 50-55; S. Lipset and R. Bendix, "Social Mobility and Occupational Career Patterns," *Am. J. Sociol.*, 57 (1952), 494-504; and more recently by P. Blau, "Occupational Bias and Mobility," *ASR*, 22 (1957), 392-399. However, the representational quality of the samples used is questionable. Rogoff's study is based on data from Marion County, Indiana.

7. S. Miller, "The Concept and Measurement of Mobility," *Transactions of Third World Congress of Sociology*, (Amsterdam, 1956), vol. 3, 144-154. For a more recent study using a national sample, see G. Lenski, "Trends in Inter-Generational Occupational Mobility in the United States," *ASR*, 23 (1958), 514-523. This study indicates a significant increase in the number of white collar jobs in the American occupational structure, but does not indicate whether over-all mobility rates are increasing or decreasing.

8. G. Lenski, *op. cit.*, also P. Hatt, "Social Mobility and Economic Advancement," *American Economic Review*, 43 (1953), 370-376. For a brilliant analysis of the social impact of this phenomenon, see C. W. Mills, *White Collar*, (New York, 1951).

9. *Knowledge for What?*, (Princeton, 1939), 79.

10. See, for example, Hadley Cantril's study of the reaction to Orson Welles' famous radio broadcast in *The Invasion from Mars*, (Princeton, 1940).

11. For a thorough discussion of this problem, see R. Merton, "Social Structure and Anomie," *ASR*, 3 (1938), 672-682. See also E. Hughes, "Dilemmas and Contradictions of Status," *Am. J. Sociol.*, 50 (1945), 353-359.

12. W. Caudill has done a fascinating study of this problem. See his "Japanese-American Personality and Acculturation," *Genetic Psychology Monographs*, 45 (1952), 3-102.

13. See S. Stouffer, *The American Soldier*, (Princeton, 1949), vol. 1, 250-257. On the general question of whether or not increased social mobility is a good thing, see M. Tumin, "Some Unapplauded Consequences of Social Mobility in a Mass Society," *Social Forces*, 36 (1957),

32-37. It is interesting that Tumin is one of the few sociologists who are willing to *evaluate* social mobility as well as measure it.

14. This has been substantiated by H. Becker and B. Geer, "The Student Culture in Medical School," *Harvard Educational Review*, 28 (1958), 70-81; and J. Coleman, "The Academic Subculture and Academic Achievement," *Am. J. Sociol.*, 65 (1960), 337-347.

15. R. Thomas, "An Empirical Study of High School Drop-Outs," *J. of Educ. Sociol.*, 28 (1955), 11-18.

16. E.g., B. Neugarten, "Social Class and Friendship Among School Children," *Am. J. Sociol.*, 51 (1946), 305-313; A. Hollingshead, *Elmtown's Youth*, (New York, 1949); and W. Warner, et al., *Who Shall Be Educated?*, (New York, 1944).

17. For a delightfully entertaining and insightful account of this process as it occurs in British universities, see Kingsley Amis, *Lucky Jim*, (New York, 1953).

18. This mobility pattern was shown by Howard Becker, "The Career of the Chicago Public School Teacher," *Am. J. Sociol.*, 57 (1952), 470-477.

19. See E. Chinoy, *Automobile Workers and the American Dream*, (New York, 1955); also Chinoy, "The Tradition of Opportunity and the Aspirations of Automobile Workers," *Am. J. Sociol.*, 57 (1952), 453-459. In medicine, see H. Becker and B. Geer, "The Student Culture in Medical School," *Harvard Educational Review*, 28 (1958), 70-81.

20. *The Open Society and Its Enemies*, (New Jersey, 1950).

CHAPTER FOUR

Cultural Lag, Social Change, and Education

The Concept of Cultural Lag

One of the most widely accepted concepts in contemporary social thought is that of cultural lag. The argument in its simplest form is as follows: There are within every society *two* cultures. The first is concerned with the *techniques and devices* used by the members of the society to perform the tasks which are necessary for the continued existence of that society. Thus, in many societies in which fish are a major source of food, techniques and devices useful in building boats, navigating, catching fish, and cooking and storage of the food will constitute a considerable part of the *technical culture* of that society. The second culture consists of the values, goals, and behavioral cues which have to do with morality, religiosity, and purpose. The function of this culture is to make the citizens feel that there is something beyond themselves, that even after death certain values and truths will remain. This culture, which satisfies the need for a feeling of stability and "rightness" can be called the *value culture*. The technical culture can change rapidly, but the essence of the value culture is that it provides a sense of permanence which cannot be achieved if the values are in constant flux.

According to the argument, these two cultures generally exist together in harmony and balance, but in highly industrialized Western societies the technical culture (or the technology) has expanded at such a prodigious rate that the value culture has been left behind. The old values are no longer relevant to the technical culture, and cannot be applied meaningfully to the new technology. Or as Carl Becker put it, ". . . Mankind has entered a new phase of human progress—a time in which the acquisition of new implements of power too swiftly outruns the necessary adjustment of habits and ideas to the novel conditions created by their use." [1]

If we wish, we can conceive of the lag in *spatial* terms by imagining two lines moving away from a horizontal base-line at different angles. The base-line represents time; the line rising steeply represents changes in the technical culture; and the line rising less sharply represents changes in the value culture. At any given time, the gap between the two lines represents the amount of cultural lag:

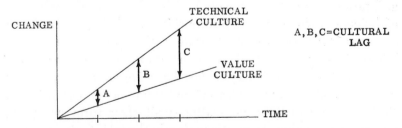

Many writers have defined *progress* as any new development which tends to narrow the gap instead of widening it. [2] The notion has become widespread that if we can just increase the speed of change in our value culture so that it can catch up with the technical culture, then all our problems will be solved. Utopia occurs when the two lines become one.

This concept of cultural lag is an intriguing one, particularly in terms of its implications for education. If we agree that "progress" will occur when the gap is narrowed, there seem to be only two ways to do it—either by *decreasing* the rate of change of the technical culture, or by *increasing* the rate of change of the value culture. The school and other social institutions which may influence the two cultures must accomplish one or both of the above if "progress" is to occur. But both alternatives are untenable as goals for education. It is certainly not possible for the school to arrest the development of technology, which is completely outside the school's influence. It is also difficult to see how the school could increase the rate of change of the value culture. Even if it could, we have indicated that the major function of the value culture is that of providing a firm and stable basis for existence; and increasing the rate of change of social norms would undoubtedly result in greater personal disorganization, not less. What, then, *is* the job of education as seen from the perspective of the cultural lag concept? Perhaps a deeper analysis of the concept is needed before the question can be answered satisfactorily.

The first assumption which should be questioned is that technical culture is not in itself normative, that new devices and processes are not connected with values and the selection of behavior which seems "appropriate," and that there really *are* two different realms. Certainly the automobile carries within it a whole set of value assumptions and prescribed modes and norms of behavior, *just by being an automobile.* Or consider such simple devices as a thermometer and a clock. Both of these devices, no matter what their form or shape, contain many value assumptions simply through their *function.* (The natural world is a thing to be measured; all of the units of measurement are of equal worth; life is governed by a series of known and fixed laws; that which is observable and repeatable is important.) Those who are responsible for programs of technical assistance to "primitive" or "underdeveloped" countries often seem to feel that as long as our personnel do not talk too much about baseball or democracy then no conflict in values has been introduced. In actuality, however, the very processes and products of assembly-line manufacturing scream out the values of the men who devised them.[3] We can alter size and shape and color, but we cannot alter function very well; and it is primarily in the *function* of the object or process that we see reflected cultural values. Thus it is difficult indeed to imagine a technological device or process which would be free of important assumptions concerning values and norms.

If this argument is correct, and it would seem to be, then we will have to revise our cultural lag model. We can no longer speak of the valueless technology zooming ahead of the established values of the culture. We must speak, instead, of the existence of *two value cultures*, one which is produced by the design and function of new devices and processes, and the other which is an accumulation of previous values and standards not necessarily related to the *new* devices and processes, although it probably originated in *previous* devices and processes. If the values and norms which are exhibited in the function and form of the new device or process are compatible with the established values, then the adjustment to the new development will be easy. If they are incompatible, then the adjustment will be difficult and perhaps psychologically damaging to the participants. We have now negated a second assumption implicit in the cultural lag model—that it is the *rate* of change of the new devices and processes that causes the damage. Devices and processes can change with great rapidity and cause no new problems, as long as the values and norms inherent in their form and function are compatible with the existing traditional values.

In order to question a third assumption of the cultural lag concept, we must consider the spatial model again. We said that the horizontal axis represented time, and it is easy to see how time units could be set up which would be compatible to both technical change and value change. But if we are to draw the two lines representing technology and values, we must know what the *vertical* axis stands for. It must be expressed in units which are compatible with both the factors of technology and values. If the horizontal axis represents time, then it seems likely that the vertical axis should represent *rate* of change. But how can we compare rate of change of technology and values in the same units? On the horizontal axis there is no problem—we can call the units months, years, decades, or centuries. But what is the unit for measuring rate of change, especially value change? Values only manifest themselves in human behavior of one sort or another, so that value change could only be measured in terms of changes in human behavior. Even if we could devise a unit for measuring changes in human behavior (*all* kinds of human behavior), it is hard to see how this unit of measurement could also accommodate technological changes without altering the nature of the unit.

The major assumption of the cultural lag theorists is that we must change values as quickly as we change technology. We must *keep up* with technological change. But from what we have just said, what does "keeping up" mean? How would we know it if we had "kept up"? How could we tell how far, and in what specific directions, we would have to move in order to "catch up"?

To its spokesmen, cultural lag is the difference in rate of change in technology and values at a given point in time. What we are suggesting here is that the lag is not a function of rate of change at all, but that it represents the *compatibility* of the values inherent in new technology with the existing values. It must be said that this modification of the cultural lag theory does not provide us with a sound empirical basis for measurement, for we are saying that the spatial model of cultural lag is as dangerous an oversimplification as trying to describe social mobility using only vertical and horizontal dimensions.

In earlier times, people would not have considered technology and values as two separate things, as it was *through* the devices and processes used by the members of the society that these members were able to manifest their traditional cultural values. The patterns of activity performed by the hunter were rich in symbolic value. These patterns enabled the hunter to express religious and ethical values *in the activities of hunting.* Who could say of the worker tightening nuts and bolts on an assembly line that he is also manifesting spiritual and ethical values? For the worker, religion is a Sunday activity; it does not pervade his everyday actions. The significant difference here is in the nature of the environment of yesterday and today. When man saw the environment as trees, rocks, clouds, lakes, seas, and earth, he was able to build deeply meaningful symbolic structures into these things as he worked with them.[4]

In contrast, the environment in today's interdependent technological society is increasingly *other people*, and people make notoriously bad symbols, because the symbol is then merely a mirror image of its maker. This does not mean that we are influenced only by people and not by things, but it does mean that the things with which we surround ourselves are interpreted pragmatically, and these things tend to remind us of the pressures and demands of people. Certainly the objects which we use in everyday life (the toothbrush, the subway token, the instant coffee, the can of beans, the television set) do not fit together to form a meaningful whole, and have little symbolic potential. A rose, a boat, a setting sun, or even a drop of rain has enough connotations which relate to a variety of human experiences to make a richly meaningful symbolic structure. The connotative aspect of a subway token is too limited to be of much symbolic worth, as we see it only in utilitarian terms. Our objects remind us (if we think of them at all) of other selves, virtually identical to our own. As a consequence, we tend increasingly to take our cues from the possessions and behavior of others and not from a tradition providing meaningful symbolic structures which enable us to interpret present experiences *for ourselves.* This means that the contemporary person who does have a deep commitment to certain values will have difficulty in finding significant objects or symbols through which he can express his commitment.

American machines, like other aspects of American life, manifest contradictory values. When one buys a machine such as a car or a major appliance, it is comforting to feel that the product is a superior one. Such a product can be a source of some satisfactions through its brilliant performance, and pride of ownership can be a comforting thing. But because of techniques such as the doctrine of planned obsolescence, the owner must realize that his machine will be eclipsed by next year's model and that it will wear out within a period calculated by the manufacturer, who does not always consider long service a value. Thus the potential value of the machine for its owner is circumvented by the plans of the manufacturer, and its potential value as a symbol is lost. The product is designed to make its owner feel important; but because he does not possess the technical skills necessary to repair the machine, he must feel inferior to the serviceman or mechanic who knows more about it than he does.

As we turn increasingly to other people and new objects for values and direction, we become increasingly influenced by the values which pervade machine technology. One of these is that machines can do physical (and more recently mental) work faster and more efficiently than human beings can, and that therefore all physical work should eventually be done by them.

This idea, commonly referred to as the leisure-pleasure principle, sees work as an evil and the release from work as pleasure. Yet there is considerable evidence that work of some kind is a psychological necessity, both in terms of individual satisfactions and in the feeling of belonging to a corporate activity.[5] Here is one of the conflicts of the values of machine technology with the values of the school. The child is told in school that hard work is beneficial and necessary, while everything outside the school tells him that the goal in life is to do nothing. The ideal car is one in which you have nothing to do; the ideal washing machine is one which requires no effort; toasters are designed so that the toaster itself lowers the bread into the heating elements so that the operator need not exhaust himself by pulling a lever down; and there is on the market a battery-powered cocktail stirrer for those too weak or too incapacitated to stir their drinks with a spoon.

Clearly this is a dangerous point of view. Just as a good diet demands certain proportions of certain elements, so a good psychological "diet" needs variety—work and play, tension and relaxation, happiness and sadness, accomplishment and failure. Yet we find increasingly that we are encapsulated in our wondrous machines which leave nothing for *us* to do, making us the prisoners of that which was intended to set us free. One of the most interesting characteristics of radio and television commercials is that the people involved are seldom if ever *doing* anything. The housewife is gazing at the automatic stove which is cooking her automatic cake mix, while the cigarette smoker reclines in a sylvan woodland with eyes shut, steeped in the pleasure that comes from leisure. The result is that although our lives are more hectic than ever, everything in our environment is screaming at us to relax.

The same sort of process occurs in a factory. The parts to be assembled are interchangeable, and the workers who do the same job on the line are also seen as interchangeable. As a consequence, individuality, either of a part or of a worker, is not rewarded but is often considered a defect. This type of situation is bound to have some effect on the worker in terms of his perceptions outside the plant. This effect might be called the "accept-reject" effect, in that the worker never has to consider the problem of *superiority*. There is one quality standard: Those parts which meet the criterion are passed, those which do not are rejected. Within the accepted group of parts there are still many deviations, but the worker need not concern himself with that. Likewise, in terms of *quantity* of output, he need not concern himself with what a superior performance of his task would be, as a single standard is set up for all workers who do his particular job, which he can surpass only at his peril. This standard must be low enough so that all the workers who do that particular task can accomplish a day's work. The question of what is better than acceptable is a question the worker seldom if ever needs to consider. Thus, outside the factory, our worker may vote for a local man for political office instead of a more highly qualified candidate from out of town, if the local person is "good enough." He will not vote more money for schools if the existing ones are "acceptable." In his own life, the question of what is excellent, what is the very best that can be attained, need never be asked.

This example is simply one of many ways in which attitudes and habits acquired in one situation may transfer to another.[6] It is important to realize that just as the child brings his parents with him (symbolically) when he enters school, so the factory worker may bring the factory to the town meeting. In fact, the attitudes of the factory existence may infiltrate into the schoolroom. If a school has a grading sysem which uses only two grades—pass and fail—then the effect on the student may be very like the effect of the factory on his father. Again, people and things are either good enough or rejects. This type of thinking, whether in education or in industry, leads people to overemphasize commonalities and to neglect differences. But the commonalities are always *minimal* and do not always represent the maximum potential of the people involved. The easy assumption to make when one meets a holder of a doctoral degree is that he is smarter than those who do not hold that degree, but this assumption completely overlooks the fact that there is a great variation *within* the group who hold doctorates. The requirements for the degree only represent the least, but acceptable, accomplishment of which the doctorate holder is capable; in no sense do they measure the *maximum* achievement of the person. No matter how high the standards, the group selected will never be identical in ability or achievement, because there is no such thing as a *completely* homogeneous group.

Now we can see that the problem brought about by social change is not the problem of changing values as rapidly as we change technology, as suggested by the advocates of the cultural lag analysis. Rather, it is the compatibility of the values and attitudes inherent in new technology and new products with previously acquired values and attitudes. We have seen how the factory value of interchangeable parts and people conflicts with our notions of excellence in achievement and the fullest possible exploitation of a person's abilities.

There are similar incompatibilities between our time sense and our marketing patterns. Americans have always been known for their optimism, for their belief that tomorrow will be better than today. This willingness to give up present gratifications in order to reach future goals, to make sacrifices now for a better tomorrow, has been a major article in the American creed. Weber and others considered this attitude to be the essence of the spirit of capitalism. Yet today, in order to expand the economy and provide more goods and services for more people, we have resorted to installment buying, which directly contradicts the capitalistic spirit by saying that there is nothing that you can't have *today*. Why save for something when it can be yours now? There is no basic difference in the purchasing process. In the earlier time the individual saved his money and when he had enough saved, he made his purchase, while now he makes his purchase and then makes the payments which are the equivalent of enforced saving. But certainly the result has been to make the future much less important and to make *present possessions* much more important. (There may be psychological differences as well, as there is nothing particularly exhilarating about making the last payment on a car which has long since been retired to a junkyard.) Thus, contemporary economic, marketing, and manufacturing practices can only survive by the *refutation* of the notion that we should make sacrifices today for a better future, at least in terms of our functions as consumers. In this case, values do not lag behind technology. The values inherent in production and distribution techniques appear to have conquered the opposing values of an earlier age.

Thus, our major problem is that we find ourselves in more and more situations in which the old values and codes are simply inoperable. Such virtues as honesty are not generic; they are situational and need to be re-established for each new situation,[7] in terms of the new action possibilities inherent in the new situation. That which constituted the crime of usury a century ago is today the completely legitimate Friendly Loan Company. The evolving role of the white collar worker has made it abundantly clear that "criminal" behavior occurs when moral codes are not specifically defined for a new and often tempting situation, which may include such practices as lavish expense accounts or cooperative bidding on orders.[8] The difficulty is that we do not recognize the value implications in new devices and procedures *as values*. We often tend to think of them simply as new practices, divorced from all questions of ethics and values. This is exactly the same error we have pointed out in the thinking of the advocates of the cultural lag model. One of the most insidious aspects of highly complex technological processes is that it is so easy for the participants to become lost in their tasks and overlook the value assumptions inherent in what they are doing. This is a problem in all technological societies, for they have all failed to redefine values in light of technological objects, processes, and *behaviors*. This leaves the citizen with no frame of reference for values except that inherent in the technological processes with which he is engaged.

The situational nature of values and the need for redefinition in new situations cannot be overemphasized. Even a concept as straightforward as plagiarism needs redefinition in various situations. The undergraduate who writes a term paper without acknowledging the sources for direct quotations has undoubt-edly used the ideas of others without giving credit. But in a college classroom, an overwhelmingly large proportion of the ideas presented by the instructor did not originate with him. Every book that has been written is based on the ideas of others. The completely original lecture is a myth (one which many teachers enjoy perpetuating), yet we do not call this plagiarism. Many freshmen leave college every year simply because the values of scholarship were not defined in terms of the behavioral situations in which the freshman encounters them. Unless the student has had specific indoctrination con-cerning what is plagiarism and what is not, he is at a loss in the realm of scholarly values, and his previously developed notions of morality will be of little use. Thus, the student, like the worker engulfed in rapidly changing technological proc-esses, needs some redefinition of values in terms of the immedi-ate situation. He must know the *behaviors* which are acceptable and appropriate in an unfamiliar context.

In the case of the student, there is little question of the re-sponsibility for this redefinition. The college or university generally establishes a program for freshman orientation ad-ministered by the Dean or some other agency in order to meet its responsibility for clarifying student responsibilities in new and unfamiliar areas. However, from the broader perspective of technological change in American culture, the obligation is not so easily seen. In a democratic society, who *is* responsible for cultural redefinition?

The Problem of Authority in a Democracy

The relationship between freedom and control in a demo-cratic society is a complex relationship indeed. Superficially, we could say that freedom exists only when there is no control, and conversely, when there is control there is no freedom. This statement may have satisfied idealistic thinkers of an earlier age, but it is no longer applicable today. Through increased technological development and interdependence of peoples, many situations in which we find ourselves are equipped with *built-in controls* which are inherent in the situation.

Freedom and control are not as dichotomous as some people suggest. Certain freedoms are dependent on controls. For example, an artist is not free to express himself unless he has mastered the controls of the discipline in which he will work. A very young child may sit at the piano and bang away with both fists, totally unaware of anything except self-expression, but this form of expression is not satisfactory to the adult, at least not for very long. In order to break rules meaningfully, you must know and respect the rules first.

In order to protect ourselves against harmful impurities in food and drugs, we must set up a federal agency and grant it certain rights to exercise controls. Without these controls the agency would be powerless to protect our freedom from harmful and impure substances. We could make an infinitely long list of examples, but in every case what we call freedom occurs in a context of regulation and control.

It is the interrelationship of freedom and control that may give us a clearer idea of what freedom actually is. If we see a man in prison who is about to be executed, and who has a choice of dying by electrocution, hanging, or the gas chamber, we may say that he has a certain amount of freedom in his situation; the control of those around him is not *complete*. Still, few of us would rejoice at being given the freedom this man possesses. We usually feel that freedom is a function of the number of possible choices available to the person involved, but in this case we could add hundreds of other ways of taking away the life of the prisoner without increasing his freedom. Adding to the number of choices the individual has does not, in this example, reduce our *control* over him. Similarly, we might ask ourselves whether or not our freedom is greater in the selection of television programs than that of Soviet audiences, when we may have many kinds of mediocre programs to select from while they often have only one choice—watching the one excellent state-sponsored program or turning the set off. Choice then has both qualitative and quantitative aspects, and both must be considered in assessing the degree of freedom and control.

Clearly the number and quality of choices alone does not produce a condition of freedom. Some feel that freedom is basically a subjective reaction; *you are free when you feel free.* A situation which produces a feeling of freedom in one individual will not necessarily produce the same feeling in someone else. The very idea of freedom as *spontaneous* action is unacceptable to the determinist who contends that every human activity is caused by previous events and circumstances; that people make the choices they do because they are forced to make them, because they are what they are. The determinist would say that if we knew enough about the background of an individual, we could predict exactly what the individual would do in a given circumstance. From this perspective, we cannot imagine a situation in which a person is *not* controlled.

However, this does not mean that we are necessarily conscious of these controls. One of the most important and frightening contributions of Freudian psychology is the insight that we are often completely unaware of the major determinants of our behavior. Even if we quarrel with the Freudian model of the human psyche, it would be difficult to substantiate the notion that a great deal of human behavior is spontaneous, and somehow "uncaused."

In a society with egalitarian premises like our own, this notion that freedom cannot exist without some forms of antecedent control is difficult to grasp. Yet the processes of socialization are basically authoritarian, a fact which many teachers will not accept. That is, the child cannot choose to become a Chinese or a Malayan. He must accept the values and norms of his culture, at least until he is mature enough to criticize them.[9] If we look at the examples of children who have grown up "free" from the coercive influence of a culture, who have developed without interacting with other people, we find not a glorification of human virtues, not the Noble Savage, but a mockery and a distortion.[10]

Our conception of unrestricted freedom makes us feel guilty about using power and control over others, *even if we have their consent.* These notions of freedom and power must be made compatible if democratic institutions are to compete with totalitarian ones. The most distinctive attribute about the free citizen is his right to select the individuals and institutions which will control him.[11] If he is dissatisfied with the way in which this power and authority is being used, he is allowed some acceptable mechanism for expressing his feelings and ultimately altering the system. In a totalitarian society, alteration of the system by the people can come only through revolution.

Most people would probably agree with this definition of the free system, but they would restrict the areas of choice to the most obvious one, that of the political arena. If one were to suggest that in social and cultural areas the same principle of selecting and submitting to controls might apply, it is doubtful that Americans would agree. This suggestion is distasteful, and smacks of Orwell, Huxley, and Big Brother. Yet at the present time the amount of social control present in our culture is tremendous, and this control rests largely in the hands of those who control the mass media. This type of control is usually seen in terms of the selection of program content for the medium. (And here it would be difficult to argue that the mass media are operating under the consent of those who are influenced by them.)

But there is another kind of social control in the mass media, and that is the control of consumer *desires* through advertising. In presenting an image of the kind of person who buys his product, the advertiser may be directly influencing social norms, for as products become more alike, people increasingly seek personal identity with the products they consume. For many, the purchase of a tube of toothpaste means more than clean teeth; it means that the buyer is a certain kind of person.

Cars, gasolines, soft drinks, soaps, cosmetics, and alcoholic beverages are often seen as devices for the establishment of one's identity, but this identity is selected in advance by the advertiser. The impact of advertising on social norms has not yet been investigated empirically,[12] but certain developments could be anticipated. The tremendous increase in sales of deodorant products could only occur if people became more concerned with the effect of their physical presence on others. Sales of preparations to control skin blemishes could not increase unless certain elements of the population (particularly adolescents) were made increasingly sensitive about their complexions.

One impact of advertising on social norms might therefore be an increasing sensitivity to what would have to be called rather superficial criteria for judging the worth of other persons. As a corollary, we would expect that the concepts of business and social *success* will have to be altered to include these same superficial criteria. Our concepts of masculinity and femininity may also be changing in accord with the models presented to us, both in advertising and in program and text content. Our notions of certain professions, particularly those of the scientist and the doctor, may be changing. (It has often been said that a man in a white coat who *looks like* a doctor can sell anything in a magazine or on television—but what has this done to our image of the doctor?)

Even though we are short on empirical evidence, it seems safe to say that in contemporary America, social norms and values are now being altered by vested interests whose chief concern is in the sale of products, not in the alteration of social perceptions. In fact, spokesmen for the mass media have repeatedly and emphatically denied any responsibility for the social consequences of their activities. The general populace seems remarkably unconcerned about these consequences, in part because the mass media have been given no legally constituted authority for influencing social change. Because they have no *formal control* over people, the mass media have been relatively free to ignore this responsibility. Because people know that television, for example, is not legally designated as a device for the control of social norms, they feel secure in succumbing to its message. The image of Big Brother is terrifying chiefly because the process is government-operated; in the hands of free enterprise the danger is apparently eliminated, even though the control of the audience is still present.

The Problem of Social Control in a Democracy

All of the material presented here indicates the need for some sort of social control, but the problem is a very sticky one. Our criticism of the control exerted by the mass media is that it is not directed toward the best interests of the society. (Even the most avid advocate of a particular toothpaste would find it difficult to explain how American society would be better if everyone used his product.) But what *are* the best interests of American society? Who should have the right and the responsibility to define these interests?

The most obvious answer to the question is that those most familiar with American society, those who have studied the social problems which confront us, should be the most qualified people. However, the social scientist who fits these qualifications generally does everything possible to avoid such a responsibility. To a large degree this avoidance is caused by his commitment to the methods of empiricism, his belief that the social scientist, like the natural scientist, must be objective and remain aloof from the phenomena he is investigating. To get personally *involved* in a social problem or a program of action is to be "unscientific."

The fallacy in this type of thought should be clear. Social scientists are not divorced from their own culture; they are an integral part of it. They select certain problems for study and overlook other problems which may be just as vital because their perceptions are guided by cultural norms. The social scientist is a part of his culture, and so is *social science*.

The results of social science research may have considerable impact on the people who are influenced by them. The very process of interviewing people may have a marked effect on those interviewed, in that the questions asked may open up new areas of thought or may force the person to come to a conclusion on a matter which had not been decided prior to the interview.[13] Therefore, we cannot say that the social scientist is exempt from the responsibility of controlling social change because of his need for objectivity and empiricism. He seems like the most qualified man for the job.

This argument seems very clear and straightforward, yet there is something very disconcerting about it. We have already indicated that social change is now being directed by powerful private groups who are acting in their own best interests. This is clearly unfortunate, but is the alternative to set up a *state-controlled* mechanism for the control of social change?

Cultural Pluralism

The very essence of American culture is that it is pluralistic —it allows people with different values and behaviors to intermingle. This process has a very real advantage over a monistic, totalitarian system which allows but one set of norms. This advantage can best be seen by considering a concept borrowed from research into the nature of group interaction which we call *situational leadership*. According to this concept, different situations require different abilities from the person who leads the group, so that as the group moves from problem to problem, different members of the group will lead when their competencies are needed, then make way for another member or members when the situation the group is facing has changed. In similar fashion, the pluralistic society should be able to adapt to a changing environment more quickly than a totalitarian or monistic one, in that a variety of values and behaviors are available to meet the new situation, instead of just one. However, this advantage is nullified unless the society is constructed to allow these subcultures to express themselves. If these deviant groups have no influence, if they cannot be heard, then their deviance will be of little use to the society as a whole, and the major advantage of pluralism will be lost.

We can extoll the virtues of pluralism to our heart's content, but most recent social analysis indicates that Americans are becoming much more alike in nearly all aspects of life. The era of the geographical frontier is over, and the waves of immigration which brought into America deviant sets of social norms have passed. Most of the ways in which people may differ are now carefully defined in advance. If it is true that American culture is becoming increasingly monistic and less able to deal with deviant social norms, then we cannot rely on the advantages of pluralism in our dealings with other nations and in our internal affairs. If we are becoming a monistic society, we cannot expect to surpass other societies which are *avowedly* totalitarian and can exploit a single system of social norms to the fullest extent possible.

There is every reason to believe that the present trend toward homogenization and standardization in American society and in American culture will continue. If so, we may find that many of our institutions, which were originally conceived in a pluralistic setting, are no longer fulfilling their function. Clearly there are two directions in which we might move. First, we might continue on the road toward a completely homogenized, monistic state, either trying to run it as a democracy or as a totalitarian state. Second, we may return to a more open condition and encourage the development of divergent and vocal groups, resulting in a truly pluralistic society. The first alternative seems totally unacceptable, as it violates most of the assumptions of the American heritage. The second seems desirable, but unrealistic in that it is difficult to see how the trend toward a monistic system could be arrested, how more diversity could be intentionally injected into the culture.

There are those, of course, who feel that the first alternative will be the prevailing one, and that we should therefore plan accordingly,[14] on the grounds that men have always controlled their fellows in one way or another, and that it is morally acceptable for one man to dictate the *entire* life patterns of other men. On the other hand, there are those who say that the essence of the human condition occurs when people of disparate points of view interact, that no one man has the right to engineer the life of another. For them, man may try to live like the termite, but he does not possess the termite's equipment. Human society must be more than the insect society, which is primarily a mechanistic unit that adapts through genetic mutation. Human society must rely for adaptations on *social* mutations, and this means interaction and conflict. We can do no more than outline the positions here. The reader must decide for himself which point of view is more acceptable.

The Role of Education in Promoting Social Change

Before proceeding further, we must indicate the meanings of the term education in the above heading. Education can be defined both as a process and as a social institution. In the broadest sense, the *process* of education occurs whenever any influence produces a change in the physical or mental behavior of any person. In this sense, the television screen, food, electric shock, political speeches, snow storms, and labor unions exert "educative" influences. As a social institution, we can consider education as the sum total of the schools and the people who in some way interact with them.

These two definitions will, of course, overlap, in the sense that the *process* of education does occur in the educational *institution*. But it is very important to see that the process of education, as here defined, also occurs throughout our society. We have seen some of the educative functions which the mass media perform, and it would seem reasonable to suggest that every private interest group wants to "educate" the people around the group, either to become sympathetic toward the purpose of the group or to become members themselves. The major error to be made in thinking of the educative process is to assume that it occurs *only* in schools. American culture is in reality a melange of "educations," all trying to influence each individual along certain lines. Often the educative effect is unintentional. The movie producer and director may never have considered what changes might occur in those who see their product, and the people who go to the movie may not go with the intention of having their patterns of value and behavior altered; but change may occur regardless of this lack of intent.

In a totalitarian state, the educative effects of the various social institutions and groups can be controlled by the central government so that the educative efforts of one group will not contradict those of another group. The over-all effect on the individual citizen will be one of harmony and consistency. Social institutions exist only to serve the state, according to totalitarian doctrine, and the state may regulate them at will. This is why Marxist thought sanctions the rewriting of history, as history is but another institution, designed to serve the state and to be regulated by it. In a democratic society, however, the central government cannot usually alter the social institutions to make them into a completely consistent whole, and the effect on the individual citizen is one of conflicting and confusing messages. The educational efforts of conflicting groups are likely to be contradictory and will not provide the individual with a clear direction for his activities.

The American educational *institution* must be seen as merely one agency among many in our society which utilizes the educative *process*. We have already seen in previous chapters that the values which the school teaches are often opposed to the values which are practiced by the rest of the society. When the school's values become too far removed from the problems of daily existence, these values often become sanctified, and the elders give lip service to them, although the children, who see no use for these values, may refuse to do even that.[15]

Here, then, is the central problem which the school faces in dealing with social change. *The school must both promote it and prevent it.* To help the young in their adaptation to a constantly changing society and culture, the school must keep up to date as much as possible. On the other hand, the school has been entrusted with the transmission of the values of the past, which may not be relevant to contemporary events, and the transmission of these values and norms to the students will undoubtedly slow down the processes of social change. The question now becomes: In what specific aspects of its program should the school promote social change, and in what parts of its program should the school try to slow down the process?

The Curriculum and Social Change

In general, we can say that most schools divide their curricula into two parts—the general curriculum and the special curriculum. Each student's program generally contains elements from both parts. The special curriculum is designed to promote social change by preparing the young for the specific problems they will meet after they leave school, both in terms of their jobs and their use of such things as charge accounts and checkbooks. Here the school must be as up-to-date as possible, in that there is no point in training a boy to be a machinist if the machines he uses and the techniques he learns in school are outmoded by the time the boy enters the working world. On the other hand, the general curriculum is designed to take the students' eyes away from the problems of the immediate present and to make the students aware of the heritage of Western thought and culture, sometimes including even the non-Western world view. Supporters of the general curriculum and the general education movement say that the real aim of these studies is to have the student *reinterpret* the present in light of his newly expanded view of man.

Because the techniques and devices we use change so rapidly, it would seem logical to place the special curriculum in the last years of the school experience. However, because the general curriculum requires the student to possess a considerable amount of emotional and intellectual maturity in order to grasp the content, it too should be placed in the last years of the school experience. As a consequence, the last years of senior high school have become a battleground between the two factions. One result of the junior college movement has been to take some of this pressure off the high school curriculum, but college attendance is still not required by law, and the high school program must be built on the assumption that for a large number of students formal education terminates with the end of secondary education. Thus, a great deal of time, energy, and thought should go into the planning of the last years of high school, especially for those who are not going on to some form of higher education. It seems safe to say that with the increase in college enrollments, many school systems have neglected the needs of the terminal student, particularly in terms of preparing him to live in a society characterized by rapidly increasing social change. It is much easier to ponder the education of the college-bound student, at least in terms of his curriculum, as he is not a "finished product" when he completes his high school courses. The secondary school can see the college preparatory student as being in a transitional phase, and can assume that the college has the final responsibility for the student. With the terminal student, however, no such assumptions can be made. The educative function of the school is a final one here, and the difficulty involves one major question: What does *every* American need to know? In educating the terminal student the school must take a direct position on the control of social change.

Clearly, the functions of the general and the special curriculum in dealing with social change should be complementary, not antagonistic. Special education should give the student the techniques which are needed in contemporary society. General education should give the student a pervasive framework which will allow him to place in perspective present and future changes in his society. Here he should learn to evaluate critically new ideas and new devices and processes in terms of a hierarchy of values. He should learn what things are most important to him and why, and in this process he will inevitably learn a great deal about himself. By developing in the individual a hierarchy of values and an insight into how these values are implemented in objects and behavior, we are trying to make the individual *selective* about which social changes he can accept without dangerously altering his basic commitments.

Because this is still a society dedicated to the idea of pluralism, we cannot in the general education program dictate to the individual what the order of his hierarchy of values should be. All we can say is that he should have one. On the other hand, the school can direct the student by selecting certain problems for consideration in the general education cirriculum and rejecting others, thereby retaining some measure of control over the process.

Before proceeding, it might be instructive to investigate the way in which general education courses are organized to promote the consideration of value questions by the student. Typically, a book is selected by the teacher for its discussion of a problem which he wants to include in the course. The students may disagree about the interpretation of the book, but they have all read it. We might say that the reading of that particular book is one of the experiences that all members of the class have in common. In fact, one of the aims of the general education program is to provide a set of common experiences which can be discussed in class. But knowing what we do about individual differences in motivations, interests, and perceptions, we might question this aim by asking: What *specifically* is the nature of the common experience which all students will have from reading the same book, or being exposed to the same content in any form? Students will obviously select from the content those ideas which interest them, and we could expect a considerable amount of deviation in the selections which different students might make. What we are suggesting here is that if the teacher wishes the students to have the common experience of coming to grips with a given theme or problem, a *wide variety* of materials which present the problem should be used instead of a single source.

Even if the teacher is able to bring the class to a personal confrontation of a social problem by each and every student, what reason do we have for assuming that the process will bring results—that the student's values will actually change, enabling him to be selective in the face of pressures for social change?

One of the favorite comments on the nature of the school's function in America is that the students learn democratic *values,* not just facts. Yet we know very little about how people acquire and change their values. The acculturation studies suggest that in certain cases where the value system of the individual is incompatible with the value system he is supposed to acquire, no change can occur without great personal conflict and disorganization. Even though we have little basis for saying so, we continue to assume that the liberal arts make people liberal, and that the humanities make people more humane. Most of the available evidence (which is not conclusive) indicates that at the college level very little change in the values of students can be noted.[16] Studies at the elementary and secondary levels also are not optimistic.[17]

The social analysts have for the most part agreed with Riesman's assertion that in America people are becoming increasingly other-directed; they take their cues from the behavior of others around them, not from a strong, fixed set of values which provides the individual with a sense of tradition and direction. In such a culture it becomes increasingly difficult for the liberal arts and general education programs to *alter* value commitments, as the students have few commitments on which the teacher can work. In an other-directed culture the tendency for social change to rush ahead unimpeded is great, because people have no fixed set of values which can be used as a basis for selection of desirable social changes, and for the rejection of those which are incompatible with the individual's value system.

There is little reason for believing that the school program can arrest the tendency toward other-directed behavior and harmfully rapid social change *by itself*. It is also unlikely that the other institutions in American culture which exercise educative influences, such as the mass media, will in the near future be willing to correlate their educative efforts with those of the school. We have already indicated that the educative influence of other institutions may *contradict* that which the school attempts to do; and there is no reason to assume that this contradiction will cease, as long as we continue to be at least a nominally pluralistic society.

Given this situation, there are few easy answers or recipes which will indicate clearly what the school should do about it. However, it seems reasonable to assume that a society which is to survive must have clear-cut goals which are a direct manifestation of values. An educational system also must have a set of goals which reflects important values. Many writers have suggested that a society like ours which is in constant flux can find a source of stability in the very process of change itself. There is a parallel argument for education which asserts that the growing, evolving child be made the center of the educational enterprise, not the wishes of the teachers or of the society. Both of these arguments contain an assertion which is at present unwarranted—that the process of adaptation, of constant change with no long-range goals toward which the individual can strive, can result in increased stability and security for the individual. Boyd Bode has pointed out brilliantly the dangers of making the child the center of the educational universe, instead of the society.[18] We have already said that in the socialization process, the child is in what must be a basically authoritarian situation if the society is to remain an integral unit.

There is therefore some justification in seeing the school as a potential source of goals and values, even though we have indicated that the school has not yet developed efficient techniques for producing value hierarchies in its students. Certainly there are few other institutions in our society which can help a young person acquire a system of priorities which will provide him with a sense of direction and stability. Naturally, this system will grow and change as the individual develops. It need not (and should not) remain unchanged throughout the life of the person. It should, however, provide him with some personally valid criteria for the acceptance of some social changes and the rejection of others.

There is one technique which might be of some help in providing young people with a set of values, and that concerns the *analysis of a broad range of contemporary behavior.* The other-directed person is one who accepts the behavior around him without questioning the assumptions or consequences of what he observes, and he is particularly dangerous in a democratic society. We cannot provide students with the direction and values which tradition has provided previous generations, but we can provide students with the tools of social analysis which will enable them to see into the values that pervade every aspect of their social environment.

We are suggesting here that the normal organization of the general education curriculum be reversed; that instead of beginning in the past and leading (ideally) to the present, we begin with an analysis of the present which will lead us to the examination of the same questions as general human problems. As an example, the contemporary automobile might well be a subject for intensive study in the general education sequence. It is generally divided up into thirds: one for the engine (power), one for the passengers (comfort), and one for the trunk (things). Its wheels are continually getting smaller, its gasoline mileage remains about the same from year to year. The most important performance factors are comfort and acceleration. Certainly there is a wealth of material here for investigating the value priorities of the people who make, sell, and buy these automobiles. Similar analyses could be performed on any other object of importance, and patterns of behavior could easily be investigated in the same fashion. A chart of the Gross National Product and its distribution could be just as revealing. Patterns of speech contain many of the unspoken assumptions of every culture, and in them we have an extremely fruitful source of insights into our cultural priorities.

As Becker has said:

> If we would discover the little backstairs door that for any age serves as the secret entranceway to knowledge, we will do well to look for certain unobtrusive words with uncertain meanings which are permitted to slip off the tongue or the pen without fear and without research; words which, having from constant repetition lost their metaphorical significance, are unconsciously mistaken for objective realities.[19]

In the interest of making the process of social change more selective, the general education curriculum should have as one of its primary goals the development in the student of sophisticated techniques of analysis of contemporary objects and behavior. This blurs our former distinction between the general and special curricula, in that both can and should use the contemporary culture as a major source of information. The difference is in the approach. In the special education program a future accountant might learn how to figure interest rates on installment plan purchases, while in the general education program the students might consider some of the assumptions behind the installment plan, and some of its effects upon the consumer.

This program will not provide the student with a set of value priorities directly, but it does give him a chance to determine at least the priorities which exist in his culture. By working at this level of *behavior* and *things,* the student is in a much better position for evolving a realistic set of value priorities. He is also capable of evaluating *future* behaviors and things through his knowledge of techniques of social analysis. We cannot assume, of course, that this process of critical analysis of contemporary cultures will develop a hierarchy of values in every student; but the odds are as good as, if not better than, the odds on the presently constituted general education program, that this hierarchy will develop. Evidence for this assertion comes from the recent studies of the use of television instruction in Hagerstown, Maryland. In school, the students are given constant practice in watching television carefully, critically, and analytically. One unexpected consequence of the experiment has been the increased selectivity of the students in their out-of-school television viewing.[20] Apparently many of them have acquired the ability to evaluate commercial television critically, enabling them to reject, as unimportant, programs which they previously watched. Here the school has *unintentionally* built into many students a hierarchy of values which allows them to be selective instead of being inundated by the steady flow of one program after another. If it can be done unintentionally, why could not the school intentionally develop a program to promote sophistication in analysis of a wide range of social behaviors?

There are, of course, many difficulties in implementing this proposal. Teachers of general education courses are not always proficient in the techniques of social analysis. Many of them possess a reverence for the past which makes analysis of the present seem unworthy and not fit for the truly academic mind. The material which they now teach possesses a certain sanctity, even though this material has seldom, if ever, been shown to be superior to other types of material in producing students who are aware of the sensitivities and complexities of the world around them.

An even more important problem in promoting this sort of critical social analysis is that one outcome would be a dissatisfaction on the part of many students with American culture as it now exists. School boards tend to be composed of conservative members of upper social and economic groups who are quite happy with things as they are, and these boards have legally constituted authority for the control of the schools. For many private interest groups, particularly military and fraternal organizations, critical analysis of American culture is unpatriotic, and the function of the schools is to teach patriotism. Local businesses might well be disturbed if students investigated the assumptions of installment buying.

Because the success of such a program might alter such things as patterns of consumption, we can say that the school is here serving as an instrument of social reform. However, one provision must be added. The school is, through an intensive program to develop the powers of social analysis and criticism in its students, making social reform *possible*. However, the school is not dictating the *direction* of social change; it is simply making students more aware of the changes which are being forced upon them, and more selective about which new patterns of behavior they will accept without objecting. Thus the program could promote social change or retard it, depending upon the actions of the students after they leave the school.

This does not mean that the study of the past is no longer of any use. What we are suggesting here could be accomplished by adding a new course to the present curriculum, or by changing the emphasis in some of the existing courses. The importance of the past will actually be greater for those who see it in relation to the present.

Such a program could conceivably perform a real service, especially for those who are not going on to higher education. Most observers of present non-college "problems of democracy" classes will feel a vague uneasiness about the fact that the votes of these young people will count as much as their own. The kind of program we have been outlining may lead to an increased faith in the social competence of these young people, and a new faith in the potential of the pluralistic society for controlling and directing the increasing forces of social change.

NOTES

1. C. Becker, *Progress and Power*, (Stanford, 1936) 91. For other treatments of the theory of cultural lag, see G. Mead and W. Ogburn, *Social Change*, (New York, 1922), 200-212; J. Mueller, "Present Status of the Cultural Lag Hypothesis," *Am. Soc. Rev.*, 3 (1938), 320-327; J. Schneider, "Culture Lag: What Is It?" *ASR*, 10 (1945), 786-791; D. Marquis, "Psychology of Social Change," *The Annals*, 249 (1947), 75-80; and W. Ogburn, "How Technology Changes Society," *The Annals*, 249 (1947), 81-88. For an excellent summary of theories of social change, see D. Miller, "Theories of Social Change," in F. Allen, et al., *Technology and Social Change*, (New York, 1957); and for a recent discussion of cultural lag in contemporary society with special emphasis on the problem of measuring cultural lag, see H. Hart, "The Hypothesis of Cultural Lag: A Present-Day View," in F. Allen, et al., *Technology and Social Change*. C. P. Snow's, *The Two Cultures and the Scientific Revolution*, (Cambridge, 1960), uses basically the same conception to discuss the scientific and humanistic cultures in contemporary society.

2. E.g., R. Lynd, *Knowledge for What?*, (Princeton, 1939), 109-110.

3. For an excellent discussion of this problem, see Chapter 4, "Specific Mental-Health Implications of Technical Change," in M. Mead (ed.), *Cultural Patterns and Technical Change*, (UNESCO, 1955).

4. The lack of valuable symbolic structure in contemporary culture has been described by Suzanne Langer in *Philosophy in a New Key*, especially in Chapters 6 and 10, (Mentor Books, New York, 1958). For a remarkably lucid and compelling discussion of the importance of symbols in non-technical cultures and relevant implications for cultures like our own, see Dorothy Lee, *Freedom and Culture*, (New Jersey, 1959).

5. See T. Caplow, *The Sociology of Work*, (Minneapolis, 1954); and A. Roe, *The Psychology of Occupations*, (New York, 1956).

6. For an expanded treatment of this phenomenon, see R. Merton, "Bureaucratic Structure and Personality," *Social Forces*, 17 (1940), 560-568.

7. The classic study in this area is H. Hartshorne and R. May, *Studies in Deceit*, (New York, 1928).

8. See E. Sutherland, "White Collar Criminality," *ASR*, 5 (1940), 1-12. Also see E. Sutherland, *White Collar Crime*, (New York, 1949).

9. To see why this is so, see K. Davis, "The Child and the Social Structure," *J. of Educational Sociol.*, 14 (1940), 217-229.

10. K. Davis, "Extreme Social Isolation of a Child," *American Journal of Sociology*, 45 (1940), 554-565; and K. Davis, "Final Note on a Case of Extreme Isolation," *Am. J. Sociol.*, 52 (1947), 432-437.

11. For two of many significant approaches to the problem, see K. Mannheim, *Freedom, Power, and Democratic Planning*, (New York, 1950); and B. Skinner, *Walden Two*, (New York, 1948).

12. For a popular treatment, see V. Packard, *The Hidden Persuaders*, (New York, 1957). There have been investigations of advertising, of course, but not of its long-term characteristics. The research settles around the question of whether or not the advertisement increases the sale of the product and ignores the impact on the buyer's values.

13. For an interesting discussion of the "educative" effects of social science research, see P. Hatt and A. Reiss, *Identity and Interpersonal Competence*, (Glencoe, 1958).

14. See B. Skinner, *op. cit.*

15. For two extremely funny accounts of the divergence of "life" and "lore," see W. Sayres, "The Singular Society of Loscho," *Harvard Ed. Rev.*, 27 (1957), 301-309; and O. Peddiwell (pseud.), *The Saber-Tooth Curriculum*, (New York, 1939).

16. See P. Jacobs, *Changing Values in College*, (New York, 1957).

17. E.g., A. Foshay and K. Wann, *Children's Social Values*, (New York, 1954); and T. Banks and E. Farley, "We Tested Some Beliefs about the Bibliographic Method," *School Review*, 59 (1951), 157-163.

18. *Progressive Education at the Crossroads*, (New York, 1938).

19. *The Heavenly City of the Eighteenth Century Philosophers*, (New York, 1932), 47.

20. Reported by the Director of Public Relations for the Washington County Experiment in Television, Mr. Robert F. Lesher.

CHAPTER FIVE

Motivation

Introduction

Perhaps the most significant question which can be asked in the behavioral sciences is "What makes people do the things they do?" When stated in such large and vague terms, the question could be answered in an infinite number of ways. Notice, however, the word *makes* in the above question. This term suggests that however we wish to define it, all behavior is caused. There is no such thing as spontaneous behavior produced without a factor or series of factors behind it which dictate the direction and strength of the behavior. Just as the theory of the spontaneous generation of life was overthrown by the doctrine of causality, so the idea of spontaneous behavior has been overthrown by the deterministically-oriented behavioral scientist, who uses the tools and methodologies of his somewhat more successful counterpart in the natural sciences. When we speak of motivation, then, we are speaking of the assumed antecedent factor or factors which *cause* behavior.

It is important at the outset to make clear this assumption about motivation. The word assumption is used here advisedly, as the statement that *all* behavior is caused by a finite set of factors has yet to be, and perhaps never can be, fully substantiated. In fact, there are certain examples of investigations of human behavior which are not tied to a closed, rational, deterministic system of analysis. Sociologists are now concerned with functional *and* dysfunctional (or non-functional) behavior; some psychologists are studying extra-sensory perception or parapsychology; while others are studying both rational and irrational behavior.[1]

It may well be that the two views of behavior represented by the Gestalt (spontaneous behavior is possible) and Behaviorist (spontaneous behavior is impossible) schools of thought can be resolved.[2] It is perfectly possible that a given behavior is *simultaneously* part of a closed chain of cues and responses, and also is produced by a selection of that one chain from many others in the repertoire of the individual.

Before discussing some of the various theoretical systems of motivation, we should point out that most human behavior occurs in relation to other humans, that there is a social correlate to the behavior we observe in ourselves and in others. For example, the intake of food is supposed to satisfy one of the basic needs of existence, yet only certain foods are *socially* acceptable in a given culture at a given time. The revulsion with which people regard strange foods (even though they may have excellent nutritional value) is often astonishing. There are even cases of people isolated in strange environments who simply could not digest nutritional elements readily available but socially unacceptable—the final result being starvation. Any action which the individual chooses will have to be mediated through, or translated into, culturally acceptable patterns of behavior. This is as true for the thief (who has his own definition of "socially acceptable" in the context of other thieves) as it is for the bank president.

It is a great temptation to include, in the following discussion of motivational theories, many ideas which have not been used in empirical research. Certainly Marx, Sumner, Spencer, Ward, Simmel, Veblen, Turner, Beard, Weber, Cooley, and George Herbert Mead, to name only a few, had fairly well-developed ideas about the structure of motivation. However, to do this would be to invite an excursion into the realm of literature, then to philosophy, then to other fields. Because of the all-encompassing nature of the term, a *complete* chapter (or book, or series of books) dealing with motivation is an absurdity. We will confine our discussion to theories on which empirical research is based.

THEORIES OF MOTIVATION

We have pointed out that human behavior does not exist in a vacuum, that all behavior has some sort of social context. Theories of motivation, then, could emphasize either the factors in the external environment which "make" the individual behave, or could emphasize the internal urges, sets, and capacities which the individual must translate into the terms dictated by the environment. We might say, then, that certain theories stress aspects "outside" the individual, while others stress those aspects which are "inside" the individual. This debate between inside and outside emphasis resembles the swing of a pendulum, with research studies being formulated to correspond with the swing of the pendulum, although the studies may be somewhat behind the swing. Like the heredity-environment controversy, which still finds some ardent advocates on both sides, the most sensible position here is that of interaction, with the "inside" sometimes controlling the "outside," and at other times vice versa. The relative strengths of the two forces will vary as the individual moves through time and space. We shall begin with the theories which tend to stress the individual, then move to the theories which stress the environment.

Murray's Theory of Emergent Needs

Murray's classification and interpretation of the concept of need has served as the basis of much empirical research, as we shall see.[3] For Murray, needs (forces which direct and define behavior) exist in a hierarchy of potency, beginning with the primary (viscerogenic) needs which are concerned with the maintenance and continuance of biological existence, and leading to secondary (or psychogenic) needs which are concerned with the maintenance and continuance of the person in his social context.

Our interest here is not in performing an intensive analysis of Murray's specific categories, but in pointing out the *developmental* aspect of his theory; that is, certain needs must be satisfied before the individual can progress to other (and perhaps "higher") needs. The most obvious example of Murray's theory in action would be the futile task, attempted by some, of trying to convert a semi-starved people to a political ideology without first satisfying their need for food, which takes primacy over all other needs. In similar fashion, a worker whose need for security has not been met might find it difficult to enjoy a job with built-in risks, challenges, and ambiguities, even though another worker, who had somehow satisfied the need for security might find such a job very appealing because of its opportunities for stimulation.[4]

Murray's picture of the evolving individual, whose needs differ as the evolutionary process continues, is certainly a useful and justifiable one. However, we must ask certain questions of his position. For example, what are the *functional* relationships 'between the various needs and need levels? What criteria should be used in the analysis of behavior to determine which need or needs are involved in the behavior? Can we tell, for example, whether a mother's behavior is related to the need for succorance or need for nurturance? In a classroom, can we spot behavior which reflects a need for exposition, and distinguish it from the need for cognizance? Murray has, along with others, developed a method of testing which is intended to answer some of these questions. This method will be discussed in the section on measurement.

Freudian Theory

Basic to all the writing of Freud is the concept of conflict *within* the individual. Before the individual can be effective, he must reconcile the conflicting demands presented by id, ego, and superego.[5] The location of these designations in the anatomy of the human brain has not been accomplished, and therefore we cannot say that Freud's theory has been substantiated biologically. Freud did not want his position interpreted in this way. However, we can say with certainty that blind impulses (id) must be reconciled to high standards of morality and conscience (superego) through the mediating influence of the conception of self (ego) which selects satisfactory ways of releasing the pent-up energy of the blind, biologically-linked impulses. Even if we disagree with Freudian terminology, we must at least accept the Freudian analysis of the most difficult of all social and cultural problems—that of the necessary conflict and compromise between biological impulses and moral codes, and through this process the establishment of a sense of personal identity.

As a general statement of the human condition, then, it would be difficult to argue against the Freudian position.[6] However, as an all-encompassing explanation of the sources of motivation, it may leave something to be desired. The primary

Freudian conflict for the young boy concerns his perception of his father as a threat, both as a barrier to the attentions of his mother, and as a person who can render the boy impotent sexually. It is from these perceptions in the young boy that the basic patterns of conscience are laid down. But if we are to accept this theory, how then do we explain the development of the superego in the female? Oedipal rivalries and the castration complex are inadequate for this task, as are the more specialized concepts for the examination of feminine characteristics.[7]

It may be, then, that Freudian theory is not equally applicable to all persons. The theory of conflict it suggests seems much more applicable to advanced, Western cultures than it is to primitive or to Eastern cultures. In certain societies it may not be applicable at all,[8] even though Freud has suggested that his theory of *individual* conflict can be extended to include human *societies,* without clearly stating any exceptions to this general rule.[9]

The utility of Freudian concepts in psychotherapy is easily substantiated; however, this only indicates that it is a useful tool in diagnosing mental *illnesses.* Whether or not the theory is broad enough to explain the motivational patterns of a range of people who might be described as "normal" has yet to be shown.

The Homeostatic, or Drive Reduction Theory

This theory is one of the simplest of the models for motivation, particularly of those which stress the "inside," and depends on the supposition that there are internal states or conditions which must be satisfied. Certain individuals do not recognize the existence of such internal drives. Skinner, for example, does not find the concept compatible with his use of independent and dependent variables only. Instead of postulating "Hunger" as an intervening variable, he simply measures as extensively as possible the *external* conditions which occur when the animal is not fed.[10] However, there is widespread feeling that much behavior is a product of some inner force, or drive, even though this same behavior has been acquired or modified through social learning.

These drives, then, put the individual in a state of tension and discomfort. His goal is to reduce, through appropriate behavior, the tension produced by internal drives, with the goal of a condition in which all drives have been satisfied and all tensions have been released. This condition is known as homeostasis. The major source of motivation is the reduction of drives leading toward homeostasis.

Clearly, the theory, as stated, leaves something to be desired. The discipline of self-denial, the enjoyment of stress, the taking of a calculated risk, are all incompatible with homeostasis. All of Browning's poetry suggests strongly that our reach must exceed our grasp, that the major motivation of a social being is the *denial* of homeostasis. It may be, however, that the approach will make better sense if we admit certain factors: (1) Some people have a need for tension of certain types. (2) Those things for which a person has suffered or worked hard will be of great value and satisfaction to him. It may be, then, that the "overworked" executive who seems to be punishing himself continually is in what is *for him*, a condition of homeostasis. The skilled surgeon in the operating room, the pilot in the air, may find in their complete and utter concentration on the task at hand a kind of homeostasis which makes their nonworking hours seem less satisfying. If we see homeostasis in this light, and not as a Roman orgy ending in unconsciousness, the concept has considerable utility as a theory of motivation. There is a large amount of evidence to support Festinger's contention that ". . . rats and people come to love things for which they have suffered." [11] A sense of well-being can therefore be established in a state of tension. Without some tensions, no creative activity could occur.

Theories of Discrepancy

This research is based on a rather simple central principle. People enter situations with certain expectations—they have generally defined the most probable events and they have a "set" concerning that situation. Once in the situation, they may find that their *perceptions* of what is actually going on do not square with their previously established *expectations*. If there is no discrepancy, the most likely result will be boredom. Certain small discrepancies can be positively motivating in certain circumstances. For example, consider the fact that women continually vary dress and hair styles, even though they receive compliments for previous styles. Also, most humor is simply a small discrepancy between what we expect and what actually happens. This is as true for the "shaggy dog" story as for the custard pie which seemed to appear from nowhere when the audience was least expecting it. The pun is also a slight discrepancy between the words we expect in a given context and the words we hear.

On the other hand, too great a discrepancy can produce fear, and we will do our best to avoid the situation, as is the case in seeing a severe physical deformity unexpectedly, or in being suddenly confronted by a stranger on a road which appeared to be deserted. Everyone has probably been in the position of being suddenly surrounded by strange, unexpected events with the inevitable result of wanting urgently to be somewhere else.

There are many excellent aspects to this theory. It presents the entire range of personal expectations, from physical objects to values and attitudes, and contrasts this with the entire range of perceptions. In a sense, then, it combines inside and outside aspects of motivation, and as a theory it describes nicely the squaring of predispositions with reality.

Yet, from the theory, we would predict that when a person about to receive a severe electric shock knows that he will get a shock and knows what sensations he will undergo—that person should feel boredom, as his expectations and perceptions are perfectly matched. It seems unlikely that this will be the case. Also, large discrepancies tend to become smaller through repeated contact, so that the person who "enjoys" the horror and monster movies has somehow minimized the discrepancy. He *expects* monsters on the screen while others expect people. Some people seem to be able to minimize these discrepancies by revising their expectations.

Cognitive Dissonance

As a specialized aspect of the discrepancy model, we can consider the work of Festinger, who has dealt with discrepancy from another point than that of expectations and perceptions. There are many bits of knowledge possessed by an individual which are incompatible, contradictory—dissonant. They lead the person in opposite directions. Consider, for example, the person who knows that he is very smart and very wary, but who also knows that someone has just picked his pocket. Or, in similar fashion, consider the person who is very good at advanced mathematics but who cannot, at a given moment, subtract three from eight.

This dissonance creates a source for motivation, as the person must resolve the incompatibility, or must reduce the dissonance. In several experiments, subjects were able to alter their perceptions in a drastic way in order to avoid dissonance. Their behavior became, in one sense, "irrational." If an individual has to work very hard to reach what is actually a rather dull objective, he will have a strong tendency to persuade himself to overvalue the objective, and think it very stimulating. In this sense, then, he has reduced the dissonance by changing his perceptions of the goal.

It may be that the concept of cognitive dissonance can help us in understanding some difficult problems in motivation. For example, why did the German middle classes and intelligentsia support Hitler long after it became clear what was about to happen? As in our previous example, it may be that they overvalued their perceptions of the Hitler regime in order to reduce the dissonance with their own personal commitments. Or, why do certain groups cling to prejudices which have long ago been shown to have no basis in fact? It seems that the more they are bombarded with logic and clear argumentation, the more secure and dedicated they are in their position. Instead of calling this irrational behavior, it is far more helpful to see it as an attempt to reduce cognitive dissonance.

The implications for teaching are obvious here. Every teacher has had the experience of dealing with a student who is clearly in error on a given point, but refuses to admit it. The more logical, kind, understanding, and tactful the teacher is, the more aggressive, illogical, and determined the student becomes, even though the error is obvious. In one such instance, the teacher proceeded with a long and complete analysis of the child's error, after which the child looked her straight in the eye and stated with great sincerity, "You have an ugly face." This behavior is not socially acceptable, but it is *not irrational* either. The student had to resolve a normally favorable impression of herself with her performance in the situation. Some other alternatives might have been to raise the importance of past achievements (The child who is wrong in history who retorts, "I got an A in English") or to lower the importance of the present performance ("Who cares about history anyway?").

The student here simply decided to reduce dissonance by derogating the person who seemed to her responsible for the dissonance—the teacher. This does not mean that teachers should cease pointing out errors in student work. It does mean, however, that teachers should revise their strategies in this connection so that whenever possible they provide a *positive* alternative for the reduction of dissonance, instead of forcing the child to choose between several negative alternatives. We know very little about what happens to a child when we tell him that he is wrong, and some very creative research could be done on the question.

Lewin's Field Theory

We now come to the theoretical models which tend to emphasize the "outside" rather than the "inside." [12] One of the most widely known models is that of Kurt Lewin, which is based on principles of geometry, topology, and force analysis as used in physics. Lewin sees the individual in spatial terms; that is, he exists in a certain social space at a certain time. This social space, which is comprised of all the factors which may influence his behavior, is known as his *life space*. Remember that we are now plotting a range of *social* determinants as if they had *physical* location. Within this space, or field, there are various forces which push the individual in different directions. These forces vary in strength, and the relative strength of each is shown by vectors, which indicate both the direction and intensity of the force. Any of these vectors within the life space of the individual can be considered as potential sources of motivation. [13] Some vectors may be positive, leading toward some aspect of the field, while others may be negative, pushing the individual away from certain other aspects of the field.

Lewin's basic analogy between physical and social forces is a very useful one which has produced some important research, both in motivation and in group dynamics. Its adaptability to a variety of situations and its susceptibility to empirical treatment make it a good research tool. Nevertheless, like any theoretical model, it has some limitations. The first of these is a major one, and concerns the basic analogy used in Lewinian theory. To what extent *can* we interpret and/or predict social actions on the basis of a vector model? Every vector has at least two characteristics—intensity and direction. Can we ever plot the exact direction or intensity of a *social* force? Also, according to this theory, if a series of forces is working on an individual with equal intensity, and acting equidistantly with the individual at the center:

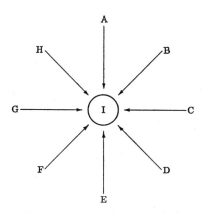

then by definition the individual will be powerless to act, as each force will cancel the effect of its opposite. As in the case of the mythical beast who starved by being placed exactly between two equally appealing bales of hay, it is hard to postulate a real situation which would be in accordance with the theory. Even Hamlet did *something*, although we may disagree about his motives.

This gets us to the heart of the matter, if we consider attempting to diagram the vectors at work on Hamlet. The model leaves out, as the Hamlet example should indicate, that the situation may change *instantaneously*. An accurate view of an individual's motivational patterns would have to include a continual realignment of forces, more in the fashion of a motion picture than a slide from a "still" camera. The simulation of motivational processes in an individual is as difficult (if not more so) as the simulation of physical reality with a movie projector. Lewin's theory does not allow for rapid change and development through time.

Miller and Dollard's Social Learning Theory

Central to the position of Miller and Dollard is the notion of imitation.[14] The individual (particularly the child) is under some pressure, often quite intense, to imitate those around him. Certain imitations will be positively reinforced and will tend to be repeated, while others which are negatively reinforced will be discarded. These reinforcements exist outside the person and are to some extent imposed on him. Through this process of imitation, the person comes to *identify* himself with those whom he imitates. That is, he acquires not only the behavior of others, but their attitudes, values, and goals as well.

This position explains clearly the concern that most psychologists have for the child's early years, in that the child's immediate family form the major goals for imitation and identification which will determine to a large extent the motivational patterns used in adult life. The child is, in a very real sense, father to the man. As the child grows, he is subjected to the influence of many other people, but none has the potential for identification which the family possesses. We usually think of the teacher as the child's first imitation and identification model outside of the family, but the amount and quality of identification with the teacher as a role model has not been clearly substantiated in research. Long before he reaches the school doors, his playmates will have provided him with many behavior patterns *and* models for identification. As an identification figure, the leader of Johnny's group of playmates has a tremendous advantage over Johnny's teacher, in the amount of behavior which can be imitated, in closeness of personal contact, and in the amount of time spent together.

It is difficult, however, to explain all imitation and identification processes strictly in terms of positive and negative reinforcement. Certain behaviors are often imitated by children even though severe punishment is bound to follow, as in the case of the child who imitates his father's profanity even though he knows that dire consequences result. In some cases, children have somehow acquired patterns of behavior which were not practiced by those around them, and have maintained these patterns even under strong pressure to stop. Pascal, for example, was told by his father that he had to stop playing with numbers or face severe consequences, yet in his own room at night he worked out amazingly advanced mathematical formulations.

In short, there seems to be an autonomy, a single-mindedness about the behavior of some people, which transcends simple imitation and conditioning. The process is not completely external; there are occasions when an inside fire seems to be lit which requires no further assistance from outside the person. In fact, all efforts to put the fire out may well be in vain.

The exact nature of the process whereby some people develop areas of activity in which their behavior is self-initiated and autonomous, while others simply do what they are told, has not been determined, either theoretically or experimentally. The implications for education are obvious here, since we would like to create the same motivation for autonomous and self-initiated behavior concerning academic activity that can be found on and off the football field. Nevertheless, intellectual (in the sense of academic) activity is largely teacher-directed and occurs within the classroom, while athletic activity is considerably self-directed and occurs not only on the field but also in every free movement. We do not really know why this difference exists, nor do we know how to encourage autonomous intellectual behavior.

RESEARCH ON MOTIVATION

Research on motivation is a vast area of endeavor, reaching from neurological and chemical research to sensory deprivation studies, from psychiatric reports to the well-known "rumor clinic." Although we can only skim the surface here, there are several recent books which have summarized what has been done.[15] The only research presented here is that which has obvious implications for education.

The Controversy Over Direct and Projective Methods

In general, there are two approaches to the measurement of motivational states. First, we can attempt direct measurement of the person's motivational condition, either by measuring his physiological condition (a person deprived of food will show certain biological characteristics which allow us to say that he *needs* food) or simply by asking him how he feels about the condition in which we are interested. In the above situation we simply ask him if he is hungry. It should be pointed out here that these two external measurements are not identical. Immediately after eating we may report that we are no longer hungry, even though the nourishment is still in the stomach and has not yet satisfied bodily needs.

Second, if we make the assumption that people are not always conscious of their motivations, we can ascertain motivational patterns through indirect means. For example, we give our hungry man a series of ambiguous pictures and ask him to make up stories about what is going on. The person must structure the situation himself; that is, he must *project* something of himself into his interpretation of the picture. The argument here is that even though a person can consciously control and sublimate his "real" motivational states, he will often reveal them unwittingly through his structuring of relatively unstructured situations. For example, our hungry man would tend to use a great deal of food imagery and themes in his stories, particularly if he is unable to express these motivations consciously. Also, at a dinner party, it might not be appropriate for a person to talk about how hungry he is before food was served. On a camping trip, however, expressions of being hungry after a vigorous day in the open air might be perfectly acceptable.

A central question, which has not been adequately answered by research evidence, can now be asked. Are projective measures valid *only* when overt, conscious channels are *not* available for the expression of motivational states, or are they valid constantly, regardless of the chances for open expression of motivational states? In other words, would we expect our friend to respond to ambiguous pictures with a great deal of stories and imagery dealing with food if he were in the dinner party situation where his outward expression of hunger is repressed? Would his projections have less to do with food if he were in the camping situation, in which his open expression of hunger is acceptable and encouraged? Or would his projections remain about the same, regardless of the possibilities for expressing his feelings openly? At the present time, these questions cannot be answered satisfactorily, but they indicate the boundaries of one of the most exciting controversies in contemporary social science.

There are, of course, staunch defenders of both projective and direct measurements of motivation. Stagner has stated, "Projective tests are more useful than reality situations for diagnostic purposes." [16] On the other hand, Allport says, "You may therefore take their motivational statements at their face value, for even if you probe you will not find anything substantially different." [17]

During the past forty years, there has been a steady expansion in the use of projective devices for the measurement of motivation. The methods of Jung, Rorschach, and Murray were seized eagerly by those in the field, often without proper consideration of the limitations of these methods. The basis for this eagerness lies in a whole stream of irrationalist thought, beginning with Schopenhauer, Darwin, McDougall, Bergson, and culminating in the work of Freud. All of these writers have pictured man as being relatively helpless in the grip of blind forces which dominate his existence. His behavior, then, is often misleading, and the investigator must search beneath the surface to find the "real" sources for motivation. This line of thought has led to a contempt for what Allport has called the psychic surface of life—the person's outward expression of his needs and desires is only a cover for what is going on inside, of which he is not usually aware.[18]

So goes the argument. On inspection, however, it seems to leave out a great deal which may be of importance. A projective may reveal that a person has certain anxieties, but what is just as important is to find out whether or not the person is *aware* of them. Has he, through his awareness, been able to work out these anxieties in a productive way? It is, therefore, the relation *between* direct and projective assessments that may be of the greatest significance in our knowledge of how people are motivated. For example, one study of conscientious objectors has indicated that projective tests of people in a semi-starved condition do not show any unusual amount of interest in food, although this was the major preoccupation in the subjects' lives. However, they were continually talking about food during their waking hours. In this case, the projective did not reveal the major source of concern, while simply listening to the subjects' conversations was more than adequate.[19] The subjects did not need to repress their concern with food, and their direct expressions of concern with food were completely valid. Even if their projective responses *had* indicated a concern with food, this concern would not have altered information obtained at the direct level.

It is the person whose projections reveal deep anxieties not shown in any direct responses who may be understood more completely by the testing. The psychoneurotic, for example, may exhibit great differences in his direct and projective performances, while in the so-called "normal" range there is a great deal more consistency between direct and projective data. In order to determine this consistency, a comparison of the two performances would seem to be of more worth than either one alone. Certainly such direct questions as "What would you *like* to be doing ten years from now?"; "What do you *expect* to be doing ten years from now?"; and "What is the one thing in your life that you would most like to eliminate?" are of great importance. Other direct methods are also of importance, such as having the person write an autobiography, or asking him if he prefers one activity to another. The vocational preference tests and interest and value inventories are basically examples of the kind of useful information which direct questioning can provide. The combination of direct and projective information would seem to be of greatest use, if we are interested in both internal tensions and the individual's knowledge of, and responses to, these tensions. Certainly a complete analysis of motivation should take into account both of these aspects.

The Achievement Motive

For those involved in education, research on the achievement motive should be directly relevant to their concerns. Every human being has some sort of goal, whether this be wealth, security, fame, happiness, or a collection of these or other factors. These goals are as important for the juvenile delinquent as they are for the student in medical school, although the specific means of achieving the goal would differ. By the achievement of goals, we establish our social status and find out in part who we are. The need for achievement is in some measure the need to find our identity, and thus is a part of all people in all cultures, although not consistent in form. The strength of the need for achievement will, of course, vary widely between individuals and within a given person as he moves from situation to situation.

A vast amount of research has been stimulated by the work of McClelland, who has argued that the achievement motive can best be studied in a projective situation by allowing the subject to invent or make any associations which come to him.[20] This belief that basic motivations are revealed in fantasy is also at the heart of Freudian thought. McClelland accomplished this by flashing a picture on a screen for twenty seconds. The subject was to write a story, not just to describe the picture, but to tell what was going on. Emphasis was placed on making the stories creative and dramatic, and four questions (adapted from Murray's earlier research [21]) were used:

1. What is happening? Who are the persons?
2. What has led up to the situation? That is, what has happened in the past?
3. What is being thought? What is wanted? By whom?
4. What will happen? What will be done?

The stories were then scored, with particular emphasis on reference to competition with a standard of excellence, unique accomplishment, and long-term involvement with a task. This scoring system has been very carefully explained and has been used with a very high degree of reliability, determined by comparing the ratings of two experienced judgers.[22]

However, it should be pointed out that there is a strong "middle class" bias in the criteria for scoring stories for the achievement motive, in that the situations shown point toward achievement patterns characterstic of a limited range of our population, and the scoring criteria bring the bias out more clearly. According to the criteria, we could safely predict that individuals like John Dillinger, Baby-Face Nelson, Adolph Hitler, and any leader of a juvenile gang of delinquents, would score *low* in need Achievement, even though their lives may testify to their tremendous drive for leadership and power. The test fails to spell out the *specific dimensions* of achievement which the *individual* sees as being of the greatest importance. (The best way of acquiring this information might be to *ask* him.)

Armed with a reliable (although not necessarily valid) index of achievement motivation, McClelland and his colleagues set out to answer many questions, all relating to the central source of concern: What differentiates those who score high in achievement motivation from those who score low? Do high scorers on the projective test also score "high" in achievement *behavior?* Here, of course, agreement is necessary on what behavior (in the real world, not on a projective test) represents a high need for achievement.

The conclusions are, in general, of significance. Those who score high on the projective also tend to do more problems in a timed test, improve faster in doing anagrams, get better grades, recall more incompleted tasks, use future grammatical constructions in talking about themselves, and recognize achievement-related words faster. Also, those who score moderately high seemed motivated by a fear of failure, while those who scored very high seemed to be actuated by a hope for success.[23]

These studies also suggest that achievement motives develop in situations which emphasize the *independent* development of the person, both in terms of families and of cultures. However, this finding should not be seen in the light of oversimplified statements about democratic versus authoritarian homes. If the child must subordinate his own interests to those of the family, then low achievement motivation tends to follow. This subordination may occur just as often in "democratic" homes in which all must submit to decisions made by the group. This development of independence training may come with careful planning on the part of the parents, or it may occur through parental neglect. It produces, however, the sense of personal autonomy and responsibility that was discussed earlier in this chapter.[24]

Another finding which is of interest is that women have achievement drives which have to do with getting along successfully with other people, while men see achievement in terms of social mobility—getting a promotion, being seen by peers as a *superior* person, etc.

One of McClelland's most fascinating studies involved a comparison of the kind of person described in Weber's classic interpretation of the Protestant Reformation with the kind of person who has a high achievement motivation. The parallel is a striking one, particularly in terms of the development of individual independence from authority, and greater reliance upon the individual's abilities and performances. Weber related the development of the protestant ethic to the development of capitalism and advanced technology in protestant societies, and McClelland has pointed out that in these societies, independence training in the home and the inculcation of a high need for achievement in the children have *produced* the development in technology and economy which concerned Weber.[25]

However, there is some recent evidence that the pattern of child rearing McClelland described may not be the dominant one in contemporary America, that parents are emphasizing the child's group performance more than his independence. Also, the Soviet Union, which does not share the heritage of the Protestant Reformation, has nevertheless managed to develop a sophisticated technology, and may promote individual incentive as effectively as does American culture. There is also some evidence that the protestant ethic, if interpreted in the light of high need for achievement, may be more a characteristic of behavior of members of the Jewish religion than of the protestant. Even with these objections, McClelland's analysis is stimulating and provocative.

Motivation and Education

There is some additional evidence that tends to support some of the conclusions drawn by those interested in the achievement motivation. Much of this research has already been discussed in the chapters on stratification and mobility, for some kind of motivation is basic to any person's desire to increase his status in any way. We have indicated that academic performance can be predicted more effectively through an analysis of the family background and the values of the parents than by a rating of economic criteria so commonly used in stratification research. Coleman's study supports McClelland's contention that males see achievement in terms of establishing superiority, while females see achievement largely in terms of being well liked.[26] It should be mentioned that there is no evidence that these differences are biological and genetic, that school children simply make responses which seem to them to be socially acceptable, either to the school, to their peers, or to both. In this connection, there is no reason to suppose that parents are consistent in the way they train boys and girls. Most parents undoubtedly expect and encourage boys to develop independence, while girls are encouraged to develop social skills and dependence on the reactions of others to their social behavior.

In another area of research, there is little evidence that a permissive classroom climate produces a higher motivation for academic achievement than a rigid, completely structured one. In the same vein, the research on cooperation and competition as incentives indicates generally that competition, which is intended to increase individual differences in performance, may actually decrease differences. Although some slower students may tend to speed up under competition, the faster and more able students may tend to be retarded, resulting in a leveling of performance. Cooperative activities, on the other hand, may often increase differences instead of creating uniform performances which are often intended to be the result of group process and "consensus."

In general, then, we can say that the school operates in ways which support those with high need for achievement, as those students get better marks and more school rewards. However, there are notable exceptions.

First of all, high achievement motivation is supposed to be correlated with the development of independent and autonomous attitudes. Yet, the student who gets good marks is often the student who *conforms* to the wishes of the teacher, the one who subordinates his own interests to those he is supposed to have. There would seem to be a notable difference between the behaviors which produce good grades in school and the behaviors which produce high achievement motivation.

Another important exception comes from the Coleman study. Although girls get better grades than boys, the girl is in a dilemma which the boy does not share:

> She is pushed toward doing well in school by her allegiance to parents and teachers; but if she wants dates and popularity,

she is constrained from going all out scholastically. . . . Modern
middle class adolescents are no longer children, and the girl
who is admired and sought after by boys is the *active* girl, not
the one who is still conforming to adult standards by her concern with studies and good grades.[27]

In this way, the motivational patterns which produce high
intellectual status for the adolescent girl actually serve to lower
her *social* status with boys and diminish her popularity. In a
culture which emphasizes social acceptance, we put the bright
adolescent girl in the middle of a severe role conflict, particularly difficult because it occurs at precisely the time when she
is supposed to be developing her own standards. With these
factors in operation, it is easy to see why many bright girls get
only reasonably good grades, without extending themselves to
the point of losing popularity. Also, certain subjects have become sex-linked by the student culture, so that the boy who is
highly motivated toward poetry, art, or classical music often
faces the risk of losing popularity. The same holds for some
girls who are highly motivated toward the mechanical aspects
of science.

We also know more about the motivational patterns of those
who are preparing for college than we know about those students in other curricula, especially those in the "general" programs who often give no visible evidence that there is any
motivation present at all. As more and more students prepare
for college, we may expect that even less concern will be exhibited for motivating the non-college group, many of whom
are now graduating from high school with reading skills equivalent to those of normal fourth- and fifth-grade students. The
figures on cost of education per pupil are somewhat misleading
in this connection, as they are usually compiled by dividing the
total education budget by the total number of students, assuming that each student gets an equal amount of the total. It
would be interesting to see a breakdown of educational costs
for students of various curricula, although the compilation
would be different. The investment of time, money, and talent

in motivating the college preparatory students may be far greater than that invested in the student with no clearly defined goals.

There is little knowledge of how motivational patterns develop and change through time. We know something of how students see occupations at various stages of development, but this represents only one small aspect of the motivational patterns which educators need to know about. There is an urgent need for longitudinal studies which analyze the development of *specific* motivational patterns, not just those of occupational aspirations.

Conclusions

The research on motivation answers many questions, although it raises as many as it answers. The research characteristically attempts to isolate rather general factors instead of focusing on the specific ways in which the person implements the motivation. For example, knowing that a person has a high motivation for college would be much more meaningful and helpful if we knew also whether he was primarily interested in getting *into* college, getting *out of* college with a degree to get a lucrative job, or perhaps in learning something during his college years. A high need for academic achievement is not as important as knowing the specific subject areas in which the student feels this motivation. We do not yet know how to motivate students effectively in terms of producing initiative and self-direction in a subject area. Many students appear to be interested in a class, yet they never think of it again after its conclusion, indicating that no important motivation in the subject had ever existed.

We have already indicated that the motivational patterns required by the school conflict with those of the student subculture. It could be pointed out that the school's attempts at motivating students may also conflict with many of the demands of adult society as well. The fact that communities are willing to support so much expensive social pageantry in school programs (even though the educational benefits of these activities have never been more than nebulously defined) might indicate that many communities feel that the major function of the school program is to provide the young with satisfying social experiences, and not to develop analytical powers of thought. The teachers may want the children to think, while the community wants them to be happy.

It should also be mentioned here that there are many other institutions in American society which attempt to create motivational systems in the young. These enterprises (particularly when working through the mass media) have developed techniques of producing the kinds of motivation they desire which are far superior to those available to the classroom teacher, even with all the recent developments in educational technology which are at the teacher's disposal. Youth possess both present and future purchasing power, and therefore are being wooed by virtually everyone with something to sell. By creating and intensifying "needs" for clothes, cars, and clear complexions, these enterprises often give the child a vision of the good life, plus immediate ways of achieving it, which makes the motivational patterns of the school seem very unreasonable and inadequate.

Some recent research has returned to a rather old idea—that people come to overvalue the things for which they have worked hard. It may be that the expenditure of student effort is one of the best motivational techniques available to the teacher who wants students to develop deep and long-lasting interests in a subject. One of the reasons that boys who play football tend to value the activity highly is the amount of time, effort, and ego-involvement they have invested in their skills. This phenomenon has occurred without any social planning at all. With some intelligent social preparation, could not the same kind of intrinsic, autonomous motivation occur in the academic area as well?

NOTES

1. An interesting research question concerns the formation of methods for handling what appear to be non-systematic behaviors. How can "irrational" behavior be studied in a rational way?

2. An illuminating discussion of the resolution of this conflict can be found in D. O. Hebb's presidential address to the American Psychological Association, "The American Revolution," *American Psychologist*, 15 (1960), 735-743. For recent work in experimental psychology that suggests a merger of the major factions, see the "Plan-Metaplan" approach of G. A. Miller, E. Galanter, and K. H. Pribram, *Plans and the Structure of Behavior*, (New York, 1960); also L. Festinger, *A Theory of Cognitive Dissonance*, (Evanston, Ill., 1957). These approaches suggest that behavior can be analyzed at different levels simultaneously, some of the levels being more susceptible to Behavioristic analysis, some to ideational, or Gestalt, analysis. Miller's approach mentioned above suggests two levels of behavioral analysis; the first being Plan, which controls moment-to-moment behavior, the second being Metaplan, which controls which one of a number of possible Plans will be switched into operation at a given moment. The alliance of Plan and Metaplan in the analysis of behavior suggests the merger of Behaviorist (Plan) and Gestalt (Metaplan) factions in social science. See also D. O. Hebb, *A Textbook of Psychology*, (Philadelphia, 1958). The most complete account of social science investigations of motivation is P. T. Young, *Motivation and Emotion*, (New York, 1961). Another summary is by R. H. Dalton, *Personality and Social Interaction*, (Boston, 1961).

3. Murray's most influential book is *Explorations in Personality*, (New York, 1938). Another approach to the theory of motivation based on the concept of need is A. H. Maslow, *Motivation and Personality*, (New York, 1954).

4. Some possible support for Murray's analysis can be found in E. Chinoy, *Automobile Workers and the American Dream*, (New York, 1955).

5. Probably the most readable and illuminating accounts of Freud's position are *The Basic Writings of Sigmund Freud*, A. A. Brill, trans., (New York, 1933); *The Interpretation of Dreams*, (New York, 1933); *The New Introductory Lectures in Psycho-Analysis*, (New York, 1933); *An Outline of Psychoanalysis*, (New York, 1949); *and The Psychopathology of Everyday Life*, (New York, 1914). The extent of his analysis can be seen in his *Totem and Taboo*, (New York, 1918), and in literature by E. Jones, *Hamlet and Oedipus*, (New York, 1949).

6. Difficult but by no means impossible. The conflicts in Freud's own life and in his analytical system are those which are magnified in Western cultures, not in Eastern or "primitive" ones. For example, many of the

cultures described by Dorothy Lee have no conception of self which is compatible with Freud. *Freedom and Culture,* (Englewood Cliffs, 1959). See also Erving Goffman's perceptive book, *The Presentation of Self in Everyday Life,* (New York, 1959).

7. For an account of how the concept of ego-involvement can be used outside the bounds of psychoanalysis, see M. Sherif and H. Cantril, *The Psychology of Ego-Involvements,* (New York, 1947), particularly with regard to identification as a social force.

8. See some of the account in D. Lee, *op. cit.,* esp. her discussion of the Dakota (pp. 59-69) and the Trobriander (pp. 89-104). Another work which could be used to undercut some Freudian assumptions is G. Ryle, *The Concept of Mind,* (New York, 1949).

9. *Civilization and its Discontents,* (London, 1930).

10. B. F. Skinner, *Science and Human Behavior,* (New York, 1953).

11. L. Festinger, "The Psychological Effects of Insufficient Rewards," *Am. Psychologist,* 16 (1961), 1-11. See also his *A Theory of Cognitive Dissonance.* Another study which supports Festinger's contention is E. Aronson and J. Mills, "The Effect of Severity of Initiation on Liking for a Group," *Journal of Abnormal and Social Psychology,* 59 (1959), 117-181.

12. The deletion of McClelland's nAchievement concept from the theoretical section is based on his personal emphasis on constructing a sound basis in research before attempting an elaborate theory. For his defense of this position, see his introduction to *Motives in Fantasy, Action, and Society,* J. Atkinson, ed., (New York, 1958). See also his *The Achievement Motive,* (New York, 1953). It should be pointed out here that the "inside-outside" distinction is a matter of relative emphasis. No "inside" theoretician would deny the existence of "outside" forces, and vice versa.

13. See K. Lewin, *A Dynamic Theory of Personality,* (New York, 1935). Also his contribution to the *Manual of Child Psychology,* (New York, 1954, second ed.); and his *Principles of Topological Psychology,* (New York, 1935). For his classic experiment, which has set off a whole chain of research, see K. Lewin, R. Lippett, and R. K. White, "Patterns of Aggressive Behavior in Experimentally Controlled Social Climates," *Journal of Social Psychology,* 10 (1939), 271-299.

14. N. Miller and J. Dollard, *Social Learning and Imitation,* (New Haven, 1941). On the phenomenon of imitation, see F. Elkin, *The Child and Society: The Process of Socialization,* (New York, 1960).

15. See P. T. Young, *op cit.;* also R. H. Dalton, *op. cit.* The nAchievement studies have been carefully reviewed in Atkinson, *op. cit.* One of the best and most readable of recent overviews of problems in motivation, both theoretical and empirical, is G. Lindzey, ed., *The Assessment of Human Motives,* (New York, 1958). See especially the article by G. A. Kelly, "Man's Construction of his Alternatives," 32-64.

16. R. Stagner, "Homeostasis as a Unifying Concept in Personality Theory," *Psychological Review,* 58 (1951), 5-17.

17. G. Allport, "The Trend in Motivational Theory," *American Journal of Orthopsychiatry,* 23 (1953), 107-119.

18. For a good summary of this intellectual development, see Allport, *op. cit.*

19. J. Brozek, H. Guetzkow, M. Baldwin, R. Cranston, "A Quantitative Study of Perception and Association in Experimental Semi-Starvation," *Journal of Personality,* 19 (1951), 245-264. An excellent summary of the studies and techniques used in direct and projective assessment has been done by D. T. Campbell, "The Indirect Assessment of Social Attitudes," *Psychological Bulletin,* 47 (1950), 15-38. He reports a good correlation, in general, between direct and indirect measurements, but asks the crucial question as to whether or not this correlation extends to "real life" situations (p. 33). He also claims, after a thorough review of the evidence, that there is no reason to believe that indirect measurements of attitudes have a higher validity than direct measures (p. 30).

20. D. McClelland, *The Achievement Motive.* See also his *Studies in Motivation,* (New York, 1955).

21. H. A. Murray, *Explorations in Personality.* The pictures used by McClelland are mainly from Murray's pictures used in his Thematic Apperception Test, or more commonly, TAT.

22. See McClelland, *The Achievement Motive.*

23. *Ibid.,* p. 327.

24. The intricacies of this problem can be seen in F. L. Strodtbeck's perceptive analysis, "Family Interaction, Values, and Achievement," in D. McClelland, *et al., Talent and Society,* (Princeton, N. J., 1958), 135-194.

25. D. McClelland, "Some Social Consequences of Achievement Motivation," (Lincoln, Nebraska, 1955). This whole series (*The Nebraska Symposia on Motivation*) is highly recommended.

26. J. Coleman, "Social Climates in High Schools," *Cooperative Research Monograph,* OE33016 (Washington, 1961).

27. *Ibid.,* 49-50, 53.

CHAPTER SIX

Learning

The Problem of Perspective

The problem of learning, like motivation, represents a vast and divergent array of human energy and skill. The immediate tendency in assessing this literature is to reduce it all to a series of "warring factions" within the social sciences. Actually, this is a consummation devoutly to be wished, at least in certain respects. Not that social scientists should go to war, but in the sense that various points of view should be argued openly and the merits of each should be determined from situations *which are fair to all concerned*. There is a tendency toward insularity within many circles in the social sciences, for in truth, as Kenneth Burke has stated, "Men build their cultures by huddling together, nervously loquacious, on the edge of an abyss." This statement is as true for subcultures as it is for cultures, and the social scientist needs group support as much as anyone else, even though he may spend his time analyzing the group relations of others.[1]

College departments in the social sciences tend to attract like-minded people who share the views of the department, so that often there is insularity *within* the college department. At conferences, people tend to go to hear papers "in their area of interest," so that the insularity continues. It is in this sense that it might be profitable if proponents of the various points of view within the social sciences could face each other more often. One result of such a confrontation might be the development of an eclecticism which would enable us to say that *given such a situation*, theory A is the most useful, or method B seems to produce the most reliable and valid results. Hebb's recent call for a merging of "schools" within psychology indicates the need for an eclectic point of view. No one theory, no one method can now claim to be *the* answer, as was too often the case in the past.[2]

The problem for the educator is in the development of this eclectic perspective, so that ultimately the teacher can say, "In this situation I should use theory A," or "Research X is relevant to the problem here." However, this knowledge may be a long time in coming, as the social scientist (like everyone else) is not too eager to put his ideas into a situation in which their virtues *and deficiencies* will be assessed in relation to other theories and research designs, in a framework which is fair to all. Also, this eclectic use of theory and research implies a sophistication with the social sciences which the teacher of today generally does not possess. In an earlier chapter, it was suggested that the tools and findings of the social sciences become an integral part of the general education segment of the public school curriculum, but certainly this cannot be done effectively until teachers are well versed in, *and committed to,* materials in social science.

Theories of Learning

In the interest of developing the perspective mentioned above, we should point out that learning theory is not a new development. Because of the relationship between learning and knowledge, every theory of learning is to some extent also a theory of knowledge, or know*ing*. Thus all of epistemology, which is devoted to the nature of knowledge, is relevant here, and might provide a useful background, even if sketchily presented.

Probably the earliest approach to the nature of learning and knowing is the Faculty approach, which developed out of deductive Aristotelian thought. The mind is seen as a series of compartments, or faculties, each responsible for a certain kind of mental activity. The study of phrenology is simply one of many adaptations of the Faculty approach, based on the assumption that one could spot the faculties, and their relative importance, by the configuration of the skull. We might think of these faculty centers as compartments or baskets with very specific labels on each one—memory, emotions, abstract thinking, will, etc. The individual was born with these baskets, and at birth they were thought to contain *innate ideas*. These ideas did not develop out of individual experience; they were thought to *precede* experience. However, through experience, *associations* could be built up between the faculties and the outside world. One of the best-known examples of this position is that of Plato, who by clever questioning of an ignorant peasant boy, was able to "bring forth" the boy's innate or inherent knowledge of the Pythagorean Theorem. Through practice or exercise, the associations between the innate ideas and experience could be increased, thus strengthening that particular faculty.

As a consequence of this view, the exercise or "mental calisthenics" view of learning arose, and it still dominates much of current educational practice. Proponents of this view feel that the role of the learner is basically passive. The learner has his innate ideas; he has experiences; and the associations between the two are formed *without effort* on his part. The role of the learner is much like that of Aristotle's sculptor, as every block of marble contained *within it* an ideal form, and all the sculptor had to do was to chip away the excess. He, like the learner, *creates* nothing which is not already there. The way to develop the memory faculty of the learner was simply to memorize as much and as often as possible. Understanding was seen as something innate, so that learning was simply a matter of drill and practice.

Like the Trivium and Quadrivium of old, "liberal arts" subjects of today's school and college curricula are revered in part because they "discipline the mind," and because they are thought to contain the eternal verities (innate ideas) which are applicable in all times and in all cultures. These subjects are often seen to be good in and of themselves, *by definition*, making a utilitarian defense of them not only irrelevant, but also something to be feared as a sign of "giving in to the enemy." In many schools and colleges, an impartial observer might still see classes which appear to be operating in accord with the faculty theory. Students are passive, and the assumption seems to be made that simply by the process of being in the same room with the ideas of the instructor, those ideas will be transferred *without alteration* into the appropriate faculties, or compartments, in the student's mind.

An important impetus to the faculty theory of learning was given later by Descartes, who established at least to his own satisfaction that personal existence can only be substantiated in terms of *mental process*—Cogito Ergo Sum. As a consequence of this split between mind and body, the role of the senses in learning was definitely restricted, and data which came from the senses was not to be trusted. Therefore, the mind had a separate existence from the body, and was seen as a clear white beacon, shining through the fog and haze of sense impressions. Learning was considered a mystical affair, occurring through the contact of one mind with another.[3] (One crucial question for the Cartesian here is, how do minds communicate with each other—how do teachers teach—*without* using the same sense impressions that are supposed to "contaminate" the mental processes?) The French educational system is still very much Cartesian in nature. For the French, feeling, smelling, listening, and making models with one's hands have little to do with learning. As we suggested above, many American schools also exhibit practices which are compatible with the faculty or Cartesian theories of learning.

There is, however, another development in learning which might be called the activist point of view. One of the initial breaks with traditional theories of learning probably occurred with Locke's refutation of the doctrine of innate ideas. For Locke, the newborn infant is like a blank slate or tablet, a passive recipient of sense impressions written there by the environment. The person is still basically passive as he learns, but at least he is not controlled by innate ideas which are immutable and often unknowable, but by the environment, over which he may have some control. Thus, the possibility for direction and modification of the learning process now exists.

Hume also emphasized that experience was the basis of all learning, adding to the importance of the individual learner. Berkeley added his famous dictum that the existence of things occurs only in the *perceptions* of people—Esse Est Percipi, or "to be is to be perceived." Thus, the perceptions of the *learner* will dictate the learning, not necessarily those perceptions of the teacher. William James' concept of the stream of consciousness also emphasized the personal, subjective nature of the processes of learning and thinking. He saw, as clearly and poetically as anyone, that mental processes have continuity through time, that we do not shut off our minds when the arithmetic lesson is over.

The teacher should, therefore, be concerned with all of the mental activity of each individual student, but he should also be aware that these intensely personal states may not be communicated to him in reliable form. Life is a process of organizing experiences, beginning with the baby who sees only "a great blooming, buzzing confusion," to the adult who has a well-developed set of categories and responses for dealing with the environment. The Darwinistic notion of adaptation is useful here, in that instead of adapting through the changes in genetic structure, human beings adapt through changes in *mental* or cognitive structure—that is, through learning. Through communication processes, this learning or adaptive behavior can be passed on to future generations [4] so that they need not start from scratch. The individual, according to the activist view, *must* be active if he is to learn (adapt) and therefore survive in a changing world.

Finally, Herbert Spencer pointed out that learning is a *social* phenomenon as well as an intensely personal one. Because the social context is important, learning can be justified only in terms of the ends which it is designed to further, and in terms of whether or not the individual is more successful in his social context *with* this learning than he would be without it. Thus, curricula must now be justified in terms of the life experiences *of the learner*. This need for the pragmatic justification of certain kinds of learning is still not acceptable to some, but Spencer's central question—what knowledge is of most worth— *must* be considered by every educator, regardless of his answer.

Thus, epistemology has moved from a passive and static notion of learning toward an active, changing, continuous, and intensely personal view. Attention has shifted from the world of innate ideas to all aspects of the environment which "write" experiences on the individual, and then to the individual himself, who is responsible in some respects for *his own* success in dealing with his environment through adaptation.

There is at the present time no universally agreed-upon definition of learning. However, the definitions are interesting in that they indicate the predispositions of the writer, and one can forecast quite successfully what sort of research will be done by those holding the definition. Here are a few major examples:

In the most general sense, learning is any change in the behavior of an organism.

It is that reconstruction or reorganization of experience which adds to the meaning of experience, and which increases the ability to direct the course of subsequent experience.

Learning is any response made by an organism to any stimulus.

Learning is any change in the cognitive set or field, not necessarily a change in behavior.

Learning will occur under conditions of positive reinforcement.

Learning is a relatively permanent change in behavior potential which occurs as a result of reinforced practice.

Learning is the acquisition of insight into the nature of the problem.

It should be clear from these definitions that there are many ways in which theories of learning can be categorized. Probably the simplest is the division between those who see learning as a *molecular* phenomenon and those who see it as a *molar* phenomenon. The first group will see learning atomistically, and will concentrate on an analysis of the specific components or parts which can be identified. The second group will see learning as a single whole, a process or function which is greater than the sum of its parts.

The "Parts" or Atomistic Theories

These theories are all characterized by one thing—a desire to find the one *indivisible* unit of human learning. Since the time of Lucretius, there has been the same urge in the physical sciences to find the one indivisible particle, or atom, of which everything else is composed. (The social scientist is often discouraged by the success of the "atomists" in the physical sciences, but he should remember that the "indivisible" atom has turned out to be electron, proton, neutron, and now neutrino, positron, and other sub-particles whose identity can only be guessed at.)

Thorndike's Connectionism

One of the most important of the atomistic theories was that of Thorndike, who saw the human being as a sort of neural switchboard, capable of making and breaking connections. His position has therefore come to be known as Connectionism, or the making of associations between certain stimuli and certain responses made by the individual.[5] Not all connections are of equal strength, but the strength is determined by the "association" of stimulus and response. These S-R bonds can, however, be modified, and the ways in which these modifications can take place form two of Thorndike's most famous Laws. The *Law of Effect* states that reward strengthens the S-R bonds, while pain decreases the bond strength. The *Law of Exercise* states that the increased use of a connection or bond will strengthen it. Therefore, practice in itself will increase the S-R bond strength, leading teachers to believe that practice in itself will lead to greater learning. Thorndike, a thoroughgoing empiricist, modified the Law of Exercise in 1929, when experimentation convinced him that practice, *in and of itself*, did not necessarily result in increased learning.

Thorndike's theory is grounded in a biological approach to learning, which is simply a "stamping-in" of certain connections or S-R bonds performed in a mechanistic way by the nervous system. As a consequence, Thorndike saw transfer (the use of learning acquired in one situation in a *different* situation) as a rather simple problem. Transfer might occur whenever there were *identical elements* in the original and the new situation, thus avoiding all references to learning as insight, concept formation, and reorganization.

As a consequence of this theory of transfer, many teachers tried to create classroom situations which were *identical* with those the child would meet in the outside world. If he needs to know how to make change as an adult, we teach him in school to make change, even trying to duplicate the outside setting of a grocery or department store, so that the S-R bonds which are produced in the classroom will have identical elements with the situations he will meet later. In this sense, many of the practices of what has come to be known as progressive education can be attributed as much to Thorndike as they have been to John Dewey.

Learning is, then, the connection *in the nervous system* of a given stimulus with a given response. Intelligence becomes, for Thorndike, the sum total of S-R bonds which the individual has acquired. Learning can be used in new situations only when there are identical elements in the new and in the original situation in which the S-R bond was first formed.

Thorndike had considerable influence on educational practice, particularly because of his simple, mechanistic definitions of learning and of teaching. If you present the appropriate stimulus and a positive reward, learning *will* occur. If the curriculum is introduced gradually, with identical elements as a bridge across each step or increase in difficulty, learning *will* occur. In the minds of many, Thorndike had isolated the "atom" of behavior—the S-R bond.

However, others were not so sure, particularly Judd and Lashley. Although Thorndike's "atom" was supposed to be in the nervous system, it was never isolated empirically. If this stamping-in of S-R bonds occurs as a *physical* change in the connections between neurones and their synapses, the change should be measurable. No such measurements have been made which validate the S-R bond theory. Learning cannot successfully be measured as a change in energy potential within the nervous system; thus Thorndike's Laws remain as hypotheses, since the "atom" on which they were based (the neurological S-R bond) cannot be empirically shown to exist. As Lashley has pointed out, the same objection can be used to Thorndike's concept of transfer, which implies a "switching" of identical elements within the nervous system. After systematic experimentation, Lashley concluded that transfer had nothing to do with specific neurones at all.[6]

Another objection, which can be made in relation to all of

the relatively hedonistic theories of learning, concerns the over-confidence surrounding the use of the term "reward." The Law of Effect, which is still generally supported by teachers, states that learning will take place more readily in a situation in which reward follows, or is associated with, the learning. But what is "reward"? Is it the same for all people? Can we compare rewarding a rat with a piece of cheese with the reward a person may feel from playing a Beethoven Sonata? Will a reward which works on Monday also work on Wednesday? In the same sense, what is "punishment"? It is clear that there are different *kinds* and *intensities* of reward and punishment, that qualitative as well as quantitative aspects should be taken into account. Fortunately, recent studies in reward have become much more sophisticated in their use of the term.

As an example of these differences, consider a classroom in which one boy, Johnny, is a continual discipline problem. The teacher may administer what *she* calls punishment, only to have the boy continue in his previous behavior, perhaps even intensifying it. From *his* perspective, her "punishment" is actually a reward in that it may increase his status with his peers. The work of Festinger and others suggests that we tend to overvalue the things for which we have worked hard and seems more useful than the often unclarified use of reward and punishment as single, independent entities.[7]

As a theory of learning to be used by teachers, Thorndike's S-R Bond approach leaves much to be desired, although the impact of the Law of Effect may have forced some teachers to give up harsh and cruel educational practices. The insistence on identical elements when these elements could not be isolated successfully, the emphasis on the neurological, mechanistic side of learning was often difficult to translate into *effective* classroom practice. The teacher simply cannot depend only upon a molecular learning theory in class,[8] as varying situations will call for varying techniques of analysis.

Although these objections to Thorndike's learning theory have been raised, it should be noted that he was the first man to bring empirical rigor to the study of learning. Although his connectionist approach did not yield a great many answers to questions which plague teachers, he performed a great service in putting many assumptions and presuppositions about learning into a framework in which their validity and reliability could be tested.

Conditioning Theories

The most famous exponent of the concept of conditioning is undoubtedly Pavlov, who discovered that under certain conditions, two stimuli could become associated to the point of producing the same response. Note that there is a view of association here, but not that of Aristotle or Locke. Association was for Pavlov a physiological, organic process which had nothing to do with ideation. When the association was completed, and the animal was responding to the second stimulus as he did to the original one, we can say that conditioning had taken place. Learning is therefore the change in behavior which occurs as a result of the association (or "transfer") of a response with a different stimulus. As was the case with Thorndike, learning is *behavior,* but here behavior is not considered at the atomic level, but in terms of quantifiable laboratory measurements.

Pavlovian methods and concepts have had immense impact on Russian education, as one might expect, both from Pavlov's nationality and because of the philosophical compatibility of Pavlov's behaviorism with the basic goals and concepts of the Russian state. Because the production of the desired behavior *is* learning, and because attitudes and values stem from behavior, the conditioning process begins while the infant is still in the nursery. Every day, parts of his body are exercised in a systematic way, so that the child becomes accustomed to being manipulated in an orderly fashion by others and accepts it without question.[9] It is clearly the hope of the authorities that this response pattern will become associated with other situations which will require physical *and mental* subservience, so that a conditioned response of submitting to authority will be produced in a variety of stimulus situations.

Pavlovian concepts were brought into this country by Watson, who also used physiological conditioning in child rearing. As learning *is* behavior, and vice versa, all we have to do is to produce the desired *behavior* in children; and we can then assume that the necessary learning has taken place. No mention is made of attitude, consciousness, cognition, or other mental states, as these cannot be observed *directly*, and have no relation to the learning (behaving) process.

The epitome of this type of behaviorist conditioning was the so-called "Watson Baby," a product of pre-Depression years. The child's will, desires, and attitudes had *no part* in the child training process whatsoever. Feeding occurred on a rigid schedule, whether the child was hungry or not. At a specified time, the child was "ready" for toilet training. The child was then strapped onto a training chair and left alone for half an hour. Regardless of the child's reaction to the schedule (which incidentally was also "behavior") deviations were not permitted. Naturally, no attempt was made to encourage the child to *want* to learn the required behavior, as the child's will was irrelevant to the acquisition of habit, which occurred more or less automatically when the response patterns desired occurred in proximity with the stimulus patterns which produced them.

It would be interesting indeed if good longitudinal studies were available on the lives of those who were "Watson Babies." There is no doubt that the learning of habits did occur, but the learning of attitudes and values which may have occurred simultaneously (denied by Watson because learning *is* behavior, and that alone) meant that parents often paid a terrible price for the "well-regulated" child. This price was particularly visible later when parents attempted independence training; that is, removing the child from the role of subservience to which he had become accustomed, and attempting to allow him to become functionally autonomous in certain areas of his life. In fairness, we should point out that present ideas of conditioning are much more sophisticated than Watson's, but his impact on child training cannot be questioned as an historical fact.

Unfortunately for parents, the training of children involves much more than the simple solution of *forcing* him to produce the desired behavior. Differences in growth rates, maturation levels, and readiness in children have produced a different approach, perhaps exemplified by the great popularity of Spock. He believed that each child should be considered as an individual, having within certain broad outlines his own readiness and maturity levels which are *for him* the optimum time for the development of certain responses. Even in rats, we now know that the process of learning to run a maze is more than a simple neural chain of conditioned movements.[10]

For the advocate of conditioning, therefore, learning *is* response. If no behavior occurs, no learning has occurred. Let us let Watson speak for himself:

> Behavior is thus the central problem. Thought can be safely left to itself when safe methods of regulating behavior can be obtained. *What a man thinks is only a reflection of what he does.*[11]

The behaviorist position can be pushed no further than this. It is possible to contend, however, that doing and thinking are not this far apart, that learning involves a *functional* relation between doing and thinking. Others feel that learning is mainly non-behavioral in nature.

The situation is somewhat akin to that of the famous "black box" problem in physics:

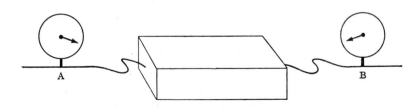

Wire A leads into the box and wire B comes out the other side. Nothing is known about the contents of the box. However, it is found that by varying the electric current which is sent into A, certain variations occur in B, although not *identical* with those in A. After a wide range of variations have been induced at A, it may be possible to set up general laws governing the relationship between variations in A and the consequent variations in B, ignoring all the while the presence of the black box itself. Others, however, on the basis of the relations between A and B might begin postulating *what must be in the box.*

So it is with learning. Some are content to stay outside the individual (who now becomes the "black box") measuring the relationships between inputs of stimuli and outputs of responses and thus setting up certain systems based on all the previous trials. Others, however, are much more interested in deducing from these patterns of stimulus and response the *processes which must be going on within the individual.* Still others, who are not interested in patterns of input and output, might reflect on the ultimate nature, or social significance, of black boxes, or of people.

Guthrie and Hull

Both of these men are characterized by their emphasis on learning as *adaptation.* For them, all behavior is not learning, only that which leads to an improvement in the situation of the individual in relation to his environment. They represent a break with other behaviorists in that they partially refute the building up of response strength through trial and error. (The greater the number of trials, the greater the strength of the response pattern.) Guthrie contended that one trial is often enough for full associative strength, and no further improvement could necessarily be gained with increasing trials.

Because of their conception of learning as adaptation, they saw that learning occurs not only in the development of appropriate responses but also in the discarding of *in*appropriate or unsuccessful ones. In other words, the individual (or animal) who can say, "I'll certainly never try *that* again in this situation," even though he has not yet found a successful adaptive response, can be considered as having learned. This type of learning, the elimination of unsuccessful alternatives, can be most enlightening, particularly if the person can discover *why* the response was a failure. Many new teaching devices, which are so well programmed that the student can *not* make a mistake, may be overlooking a vital part of the learning process, at least as seen by those who stress learning as adaptation.

Hull, who formed one of the first really systematic theories of learning,[12] broke with Thorndike and Pavlov in that he saw the organism as being able to *discriminate* among responses. Because of this discrimination, habits were more than blind collections of S-R bonds. Although he admits the existence of these intervening variables between stimulus and response, his system does not include them. Hull saw, however, that the external world was in a state of constant flux, and *variation* in behavior patterns, instead of fixed patterns of conditioned responses, might aid the individual in his struggle to survive. Hull is therefore a step away from the pure mechanists in his emphasis on the *interaction* of the individual and the environment. Hull's adaptive conception of learning can be seen in the work of Dollard and Miller, who explain the existence of neurosis and psychosis as a failure to build up adaptations (learning) which are compatible with the environment.[13]

Skinner's Descriptive Behaviorism

Skinner, on the other hand, sees no need for a complex theory like that developed by Hull. For him, there is no entity such as a mind which operates at abstract, non-behavioral levels. On the other hand, his version of the stimulus-response pattern is much more complex than that of Thorndike and Pavlov. He admits that there are certain responses which can occur without being immediately preceded by a stimulus:

nevertheless, the relationship must be there. Skinner is much more interested in *describing* behavior in a systematic way than he is in *explaining* it. In this sense, referring back to the Black Box analogy, he is interested in the relationships of A and B, not in what goes on inside the box. Such concepts as need or states of feeling, as they exist *inside* the organism, are of use only in terms of the responses they produce. He therefore uses drive strength only in terms of the intensity of response,[14] stating that drive is ". . . a hypothetical state interpolated between operation and behavior." [15] Young points out that "The majority of psychologists, however, think of drive not as behavior *per se,* but as an organic state which motivates behavior. Behavior is *driven* and the impetus comes from some bodily or hypothetical factor that is assumed to exist outside of the *driven* behavior." [16]

Skinner also conceives of learning as a hypothetical state occurring between stimulus and response. Like other conditioning theorists, he states that learning is the production of appropriate behavior. (The kind of learning that comes from accidents, from pursuing a wrong answer, from striving when no striving is indicated by the situation, from high achievement when mediocrity would suffice—these things have no place in Skinner's analysis of learning.) Because verbal behavior is no different from other behavior, and is therefore subject to the same laws,[17] the teacher should produce conditioned associations between words and *specific* things. Ambiguity, which is the lack of specific associations, stemming from inability to discriminate appropriate stimulus-response patterns should be eliminated. The teacher should therefore avoid universal terms, words which cannot be identified with specific things or examples. Generalities should be avoided unless they have direct behavioral implications.

Unlike many of his colleagues, Skinner seems to be willing to talk about the specific techniques of teaching. He has asserted in at least one educational journal that teachers in America make two serious mistakes. First, there is too great a time lag between the presentation of the stimulus by the teacher and the rewarding of the appropriate response made by the student. (Teacher assigns a theme due Monday; the corrected papers come back to the student two weeks later.) Second, there is not *enough* positive reinforcement given by the teacher, either in terms of frequency or intensity. (Teacher asks a question for which twenty students know the answer; only the one called on gets the reinforcement.) [18] He also asserts, "The simple fact is that, as a mere reinforcing mechanism, the teacher is out of date . . . If the teacher is to take advantage of recent advances in the study of learning, she must have the help of mechanical devices." [19]

These machines are now available to all teachers, and they meet Skinner's major objections to present practice already mentioned. He has, naturally, been a major figure in the development of these devices. Although there is some variation, the basic pattern of the device is as follows: The programmed material is inserted into the machine, which is then operated by a single student. Through a window arrangement, or a simple locking device, the individual student knows immediately whether or not his answer is "correct." If it is, he is then allowed to proceed to the next item. It is felt that the positive reinforcement of getting the correct answer, and being informed immediately that his answer is correct, will provide more than enough positive reinforcement and will provide it rapidly.

This system then supposedly frees the teacher from those tasks in which he has previously functioned as an inferior machine: "Of course the teacher has a more important function than to say right or wrong . . . the teacher may begin to function, not in lieu of a cheap machine, but through intellectual, cultural, and emotional contacts of the distinctive sort which testify to her status as a human being." [20] It is interesting that a thorough empiricist could make a statement like this without defining these contacts operationally, and without stating why they should be considered distinctive. If the teacher is to be freed by the machine to do those things which only a human being can do, it would seem to be appropriate to have a list of those things, spelled out in typically Skinnerian detail.

Skinner has translated his theory into productive practice, and for this he deserves much credit. Also, powerful conditioning principles do exist and can be used very effectively. It should be noted, however, that other reputable psychologists have a different view of the learning process and that perhaps a single series of correct answers with minute gaps in "level of difficulty" between them may not be the ultimate goal of education. Bruner has put the problem this way:

> I have yet to see a teacher present one way of doing division and then put it squarely to the class to suggest six other ways of doing it—for there are at least six other ways of doing it than any one that might be taught in school.[21]

The "Whole," Field, or Gestalt Theories

We come now to the second major division of learning theories. In terms of the Black Box analogy, these theories emphasize an understanding of what is going on *in* the box, not a descriptive interpretation of changes in input and output. The quest of Thorndike and others was the discovery of the indivisible unit of human behavior; the atom around which all behavior was structured. The goal was to reach a state of certainty and predictability parallel to that of physics and chemistry, in that they had discovered and isolated the indivisible *physical* particle. However, such is not the case in contemporary physical science:

> The fact, however, that the day of the self-sufficient, self-contained atom has passed, or is passing, is fairly clear. Every atom is located in a "field," and is continuous with that field, and every field is, in turn, overlapping with other fields, world without end. The field, and not the atom, is now being regarded as the unit of action. A change anywhere is a change in the whole field; it is a manifestation of a process that is as wide as the field itself. Thus saith our oracle, modern physics.[22]

In similar fashion, the study of learning involves not only particles, but also the fields in which they move. Basic to Gestalt psychology is a new theory of perception, introduced by Max Wertheimer in the early years of this century.[23] This theory was developed around the so-called phi phenomenon, seen at its simplest in the fact that although a motion picture is only a collection of still pictures, we perceive in the still pictures definite movements. The perceptions of the motion picture, therefore, cannot be explained effectively by an analysis of the individual still pictures which compose it. If we cannot deduce the whole from an analysis of the parts, then we can say that the whole is *greater than* the sum of its parts, or at least different from this sum.

The assumption is therefore made that phenomena are *wholes,* not merely the sums of their atomistic parts. In a reversal of the customary mode of analysis, we can say that the behavior of these wholes is *not* determined by the nature and activities of the component parts, but that the intrinsic *nature of the whole determines* the meanings we attribute to the components. This may be a difficult notion to grasp, but the example of the motion picture should be helpful.[24]

For the Gestaltist, then, learning is not the conditioned formation of S-R bonds under the influence of positive reinforcement, measurable only through consequent behavior. It is instead the development of *insight,* the ability to see wholes, the reorganization of a jumble of meaningless perceptions into an *organized entity.* William James, among others, claimed that perception was not completely mechanistic or automatic, that perception was a *selective* phenomenon, based on previous experience. The individual thus organizes *his own* perceptual field in a highly subjective and selective way. This un-Lockian notion of the development of perception has become one of the major tenets of Gestalt psychology. It is a declaration of what goes on inside the Black Box.

The Gestalt position, unfortunately, does not lend itself to rigid experimentation as readily as do certain of the conditioning theories. However, optical illusions and other reorientations of the perceptual field with no change in the conditions of the field, offer some evidence that field theories can be applied to actual behavior. For example, there is little experimental doubt that the addition of understanding (organization) to learning will lead to greater recall, and will also make new learning easier.[25] Also, certain of the experiments with animals have indicated that insight can occur *without* trial and error.[26] It is possible, however, that in insightful learning, a number of approaches to the problem have been tried out mentally, along with their hypothesized consequences. Thus, in a process very like Dewey's "dramatic rehearsal," the person or animal can give the *appearance* of a sudden burst of insight when he has actually been engaged in *mental* trial-and-error.

Insight, which has an "all-or-nothing" connotation for Kohler and Koffka, may be considered in varying *degrees* as well. For example, if a man read *Hamlet* as a high school junior, a college sophomore, a young businessman, and again as a retired chairman of the board, his insight into the play will change in accordance with the experiences he brings to it at various stages in his life. We can therefore look on the acquisition of insight as a *developmental* activity, one which can be improved with practice, one which can be learned.

Gestalt theory has many implications for education. The basis for learning has become the *entire perceptual field* of the learner, and the teacher must be aware of all the facets of the field which may influence the learner, even though some of these facets may not be directly measurable. For example, Tolman, who tried to bridge the gap between conditioning and Gestalt theories, admits the importance of insight, or as he puts it, the development of "cognitive maps." [27] He also states that just because two people *behave* alike in a given situation, there is no reason to assume that their *mental* processes are identical. He uses *purpose* as one of the major factors in an individual's formation of a perceptual field, even though most S-R psychologists find the concept untenable.[28] However, the fact that purposes, wishes, emotions, and felt needs cannot be measured *directly* does not mean that they are of no importance to learning and behavior. The vital importance of felt needs to behavior and learning is easily documented.[29] Also, Gestalt theory allows us to consider the learner's *ego-involvement* in the tasks we place before him, an aspect of learning which is of obvious importance.

From the Gestalt argument, we are in a position to consider one of the major (although seldom admitted) dilemmas in the process of teaching—the often vast deviation between the *teacher's field and that of the student.* Consider a college fresh-man class, studying literature. The teacher, far more advanced in years and experience than the students, proceeds to develop interpretations which are compatible with *his own* field, but not with those of the students'. The students may rattle off interpretations which *sound* insightful to the instructor, as they are compatible with his own field, but a student's response, like that of the parrot, is simply a response and does not indicate any increase in insight. *This is as true for correct answers as it is for incorrect ones.* Many teachers feel that education ends when the student answers, but it is what the teacher *does* with the response that makes the experience educative or not, from the perspective of the *student's* field.[30] A statement like "Shakespeare is the world's greatest dramatist," is just as full of insight coming from the mouth of a high school junior as it is from the mouth of a parrot.

Many teachers try to surmount this problem by a technique which forces the student to modify his field, or at least gets the instructor into the student's field, to some extent. For example, in a chemistry class, the instructor might ask at the conclusion of an experiment, "Now, what would have hap-pened if we had used *half* as much silver nitrate?" The English teacher might say, "Substitute the word infirm for elderly in that passage and see if that changes your analysis."

Arguing from the Gestalt position, we can say that the "creative" field trip to the zoo can be just as mis-educative as the drill session on material which the children already know. America is a production-conscious culture, and our educational system is naturally geared toward the production, *in quantity,* of correct answers. However, thinking and producing remain somewhat independent entities.

The Functionalists

A final theoretical word should be given to those who have tried to see learning in an even larger perspective. Dewey's definition of learning seems concerned with field development, with the addition of a Darwinistic criterion of utility. He says of education:

> It is that reconstruction or reorganization of experience which adds to the meaning of experience, and which increases the ability to direct the course of subsequent experience.[31]

The matter was put even more simply by Bode when he said that learning involves not only the discovery of new meanings but also the *validation* of them.[32] It follows that as a consequence of learning, the individual should be more effective in dealing with his environment (field) than he was previously. Because of this Darwinistic conception of the function of education, learning was seen by Dewey to be the solution of problems. This is, of course, just as one-sided a definition as that which states that *all* learning is the acquisition of neural chains of S-R bonds. For example, an individual may have a task to be done which is not *in his opinion,* a problem to be solved, and yet from doing the task he may reorganize this experience so that his ability to direct the course of subsequent experience is improved. If a problem to be solved is *identical* with the problem we solved the week before, it would be hard to claim that *all* problem solving is learning, and *vice versa.*

The functionalists, like Tolman, insist that learning is purposive, but the relevant purpose is that of the *learner,* not that of the teacher. How often do we work our way out of a situation without *any* particular purpose at all? Purpose, like the definition of a problem, can occur at many levels. The high school student in a college preparatory curriculum may see as his major purpose gaining admittance to a good college; *that* is the major problem which he must solve. Or, as one student said to the author, "There are two problems to college—getting in and getting out." How many teachers see the educational experience from the purposive and problem-solving perspective, or field, of the student? It may be that some of the problems with which we confront our students are simply not compatible with their field of long-range problems which must be solved. We should therefore not be astonished when they become bored with our carefully structured set of exercises.

There is nothing *inherently* motivating about a problem; people will differ greatly in terms of the problems which they think are *worth* solving. For the budding mechanic, a malfunctioning car may be a problem in which he can become completely ego-involved, while another student, trained from infancy that getting his hands dirty was evil, might reject the notion that there was a problem there *for him*. We know virtually nothing about how, and why, students become ego-involved in some situations and *create* problems out of them, while other situations are simply passed through. Much remains to be learned, by social science and by teachers, about the problem-solving field of students, and about its relationship with the field of the teacher.

SOME EXPERIMENTS ON LEARNING

The range of experiments on learning is so vast that we must select only a handful of studies for analysis. They will indicate conclusively, however, that the assertion made in the first page of this chapter was essentially correct: that most studies, being carefully "controlled," will allow for *only* the kind of learning in which the investigator is interested. Lord Russell has put the matter in a typically amusing and devastating way:

> One may say broadly that all animals that have been carefully observed have behaved so as to confirm the philosophy in which the observer believed before his observations began. Nay, more, they have all displayed the national characteristics of the observer. Animals studied by Americans rush about frantically, with an incredible display of bustle and pep, and at last achieve the desired result by chance. Animals observed by Germans sit still and think and at last evolve the solution out of their inner consciousness.[33]

Hilgard has stated that we need to know more about different *kinds* of learning, each of which may operate within its own set of laws.[34] Also, as teachers, we need to know when a situation requires one sort of learning, and when another would be more productive. Although educational theory has generally failed in this matter thus far, Hullfish and Smith are unquestionably right when they say:

> It is the business of a theory of education to indicate whether it is uniformly organized patterns of meaning or relatively unique constructions which are most likely, in a given case, to increase control over the course of subsequent experience.[35]

Since this research is not designed for comparative purposes, experimental research on learning will be of little avail to the theorist who seriously wishes to attack this most difficult of educational questions.

Kohler's Apes

Kohler's experiments, performed at the Yerkes Observatory, are of great importance in establishing the fact that insightful learning exists as a different *kind* of learning from trial-and-error learning. The experimental situation was generally as follows: An ape is in a cage, while some bananas are beyond his reach, either outside the cage or hung from the ceiling.

There are implements inside the cage which must be extended or altered before they can be used to reach the fruit. For example, two short sticks, neither of which is long enough in itself, can be put together to form a single longer stick which will then reach the fruit. This could be done, often *in one trial*. Often, the fruit would be hung from the ceiling of the cage, and the ape would have to drag two boxes under the reward and pile them up. This too often occurred in one trial. These animals had obviously grasped the principle of *extension*—through mechanical means they could extend their arms and their control over things.

The animals' obvious understanding of the principle of extension is clear in this description by Kohler:

> The ape climbs on to the man's shoulder after he has dragged him underneath the object, and the keeper quickly bends down. The animal gets off complaining, takes hold of the keeper by his seat with both hands, and tries with all his might to push him up. A surprising way of trying to improve the human implement.[36]

It should be noted here that although the experiment substantiates to a large degree the idea of insightful learning, it is a biased experiment. Trial and error would be a ridiculous approach to the situation, as there are no buttons to press, no bars to push, no choices of going left or right at a turn in a maze—in short, *there is nothing to try.* Take the same ape and put him in a T-maze, and he might well begin to learn by trial and error.

There is, however, one discovery from this experimentation which should be mentioned. In situations in which insight is required for the solution of the problem, the presence in the cage of tools which had been used successfully in previous situations tended to inhibit the discovery of new tools, even though the old tools were totally inapplicable to the new problem. There are obvious implications for education here, as one major strategy of students is to try to use previously acquired techniques (even though totally inappropriate) instead of developing the techniques the situation calls for. This "interference" aspect of previous learning is at least a frame of reference in which we can place *some* student errors. At the moment, we know little about student mistakes. We are so interested in getting the correct answer out of him that we cannot take the time to investigate the source of the error.

We have no coherent theory of error, but we can certainly say that all mistakes, like all learning, will not be of the same *kind*. For example, Kohler's apes often made a *clever* error, one which showed a grasp of the problem to be solved, but which left out some necessary detail. On the other hand, one of Thorndike's cats, who had been trained to pull a string in order to get reward, and who, after the string had been moved to another point in the cage, went to the initial location of the string and made string-pulling motions, could be said to have made a *stupid* mistake. It may be that here we have an example of the interference effect of previous learning, as the cat's conditioning had produced a rigid "set" toward the cage and string. (It is also possible that cats are rather stupid animals when it comes to insight.)

Pavlov's Dogs

In this classic experiment, already described, we can see the same factor. The dog was faced with no problem to solve, no cage to get out of, no situation in which insight into the situation would do him the least bit of good. He had no choice but to obey the demands of the experimental situation.

However, from the studies of animal learning performed by Pavlov on dogs, Guthrie on cats,[37] and Skinner on pigeons, it should be possible to develop considerable appreciation for the *frequency, exactness,* and *intensity* of behavior which can be produced without any apparent insight on the part of the animal. Teachers often tend to derogate trial-and-error and rote learning of fixed patterns of behavior as being inferior to insightful learning. This may be true, but only in terms of the *uses to which the learning will be put.* If we wish to inculcate a fixed pattern which can be reproduced on command, then systems of conditioning can do the job superbly. For example, most children learn the principles of language in a very haphazard way before they ever get to school. The same is true of the basic concepts of number and spelling. It may be that some of these rules are arbitrary and do not require *immediate* understanding (saying "It is I" instead of "It's me").

One immediate task for teachers would be, therefore, to attempt to gain agreement, at least within a given school, on *which* material should be treated insightfully, and which should be treated using the principles of conditioning. Certainly when the eighth-grade teacher deals with grammar as a series of prescribed behaviors while the ninth-grade teacher stresses a functional, insightful approach to language, a great deal of the "interference" and confusion already mentioned will result. It may also be that *within* each of these two broad categories (insightful and conditioned learning) there may be many autonomous *sub*-categories, each operating under its own rules, and it may also be true that both major categories can occur *simultaneously.*

Also, one wonders occasionally why it is so important to know so much about learning patterns in rats, mice, pigeons, apes, and all the way down to the lowly planarian: "The planarian (flatworm) which has bilateral symmetry and a cerebral ganglion, seems to be the simplest organism which is certainly capable of forming *classical* conditioned responses, although its performance is not impressive." [58] (One student is known to have remarked at this statement, "What on earth did they *expect* from a planarian?") If the argument is that from studying simple forms of life we can discover the *basic* processes which exist in man at a more complex level, then the researchers are obliged to demonstrate these specific processes, and also their utility in analyzing *human* behavior. The number of conditioning experiments on animals far exceeds the number using human samples. In fact, we probably know far more about the learning strategies of lower forms of life than we do about humans.

The Measurement of Human Learning

Leaving the flatworm aside for the moment, we might observe that in terms of the measurement of human learning, the behaviorists have the upper hand over the Gestaltists. If the important thing is the production of the correct *behavior,* the problem of testing is a relatively simple one. The development of the standardized aptitude and achievement tests will obviously be involved with behavior, and these tests are becoming a major success criterion in our culture. As a consequence, for every major test one can find on the open market a book which will (or claims to) enable the buyer to get a high score on that particular test. (One wonders what would happen if *everyone* who was to take the test read the book beforehand.) The Regents Examinations in New York State form a good example of how a test can dominate the educational scene, as they not only select and reject students, but also *teachers,* who are in part evaluated on the basis of how well their students do on the Regents Examinations. The Scholastic Aptitude Test is of increasing importance in gaining admittance to college. Also the test bestows status on any institution which requires it for admission. For machine scoring purposes, these tests generally require the student to select one answer from a number of alternatives.

It is very difficult, if not impossible, to write a test item which will measure the students' *insight* into the nature of the problem. Speaking in Gestalt terms, it is a great advantage if the student's perceptual field is somewhat like that of the tester—the closer the field, the better. The biases of the tests as a measure of intelligence (and intelligence can be viewed as the totality of what has been learned) has been cogently pointed out by Combs:

Is the delinquent, with rich and varied perception on how to elude the police, less intelligent, or has he simply not perceived things society wishes he had? Since perceptions are always closely affected by need, by whose need shall we sample perceptions—yours, mine, society's, the subject's own? For the most part our tests are based on the assumption that academic, upper middle-class, intellectual perceptions are important. But are they? Can we assume that the expert machinist, who can perceive things "out of this world" for most of the rest of us about a piece of stock on his lathe, is less intelligent than a diplomat who perceives many things about foreign affairs? Can we blame the machinist for his lack of perception about foreign affairs without asking the diplomat to be equally skilled in the machinist's field of perceptions? [39]

Problems arise in such test items as this one mentioned by Sorokin. The student is shown a harp, drum, violin, and piano, and is asked to identify the one which is *different*.[40] The "correct" answer is the drum, but some student may realize that the violin is the only one capable of generating a continuously sustained tone, that the harp is the only one which can be tuned instantaneously (unless the drum happens to be a kettle drum), and so on. If intelligence is taken to be the sum of a person's learning, we might question whether this item, or others like it are indicative of learning at all. Even if the student gets the "right" answer, what does it indicate about that person or his future behavior? The skeptical reader is here invited to construct a multiple-choice test item which will test insight or reasoning ability and not simply rote memory, and which is completely free from ambiguity.

We will probably never be able to develop large-scale, standardized tests which will measure insight, as learning which occurs by reflection and reorganization will be *relatively unpredictable, and the patterns produced will not be uniform.*[41] Thus we should be very much aware of the fact that a standardized test, *either of aptitude or of achievement,* is an instrument which is very partial to the behaviorist position.

The more important standardized tests become in the selection of people for higher educational and occupational roles, the more teachers will teach for *the kind of learning the test requires*, as their success as teachers will be linked with their students' test scores. The test makers are thus entering the area of curriculum selection, value priorities, and criteria for teacher competence, even though they have no intention of doing so. Another possible consequence of testing is that the *range* of human thought may have been noticeably diminished by the impact of standardized testing on our educational system. Along with various radio and television quiz shows, they may be creating the impression that the principal characteristic of the scholar is instantaneous recall.

Conclusions

It should be clear that many aspects of current educational practice favor the behavioristic conception of the nature of learning. Certainly the development of educational *technology*, which is one of the most influential and far-reaching innovations in our time, is slanted toward behaviorism. Technology is inherently mechanistic, and can only provide a mechanistic approach to the educational process. As teachers we should always be aware of what technology *leaves out*, as well as the many fine things it can do.

One of the central assertions of this chapter is that the teacher should become eclectic and autonomous in making learning *decisions*. The teacher must decide, for each given case, whether uniformly organized patterns of learning or unique insightful constructions of individuals will be more appropriate and of greater value to the students. Unfortunately, the teacher's subject matter preparation will not serve as adequate preparation for this task; neither will the typical teacher education curriculum. The psychologist, who does not claim to be a subject matter specialist, cannot and should not do the whole job. Courses in special aspects of the curriculum may someday be organized to consider the *learning* implications of the particular content area; unfortunately, until that time, and until social scientists are more willing to work in areas of content, the teacher will be more or less on his own.

There are, of course, things the teacher can do by himself, or with other interested educators. First, a reassessment of the existing curriculum on the basis of the *learning* assumptions implicit within it might be helpful. Second, the construction of a unit, or specific day plans, organized around the most appropriate learning theory could be very helpful. Third, a teacher could investigate the cues he gives to students which tell them what type of learning strategy they should employ. He may not even be aware of these cues, and the students may not consciously realize the adaptations they are making. As a consequence, many confusions may occur between the teacher's tacit signals as to the learning strategy to be used by the students and the strategy they actually adopt. Discussions of the tactics and strategies of learning, which are now seldom held openly between teacher and students, might be a profitable venture.

Some readers may get the impression that they are being forced to *choose* the "correct" point of view, which will then be held for all time. Such is not the intent. The hope here is that the teacher can come to use all forms of learning, but that a *justification* for the selection should be available in each specific case. The behaviorist and Gestalt approaches to learning are *not* mutually exclusive. The task before us now is the isolation of specific educational situations, attempting to discover what practices and theories regarding learning are of greatest value to the students.

Stereotypes of Learning

Perhaps we might conclude this chapter with a listing of several commonplace ideas about the nature of learning which are not substantiated by the evidence available:

1. *The smaller the size of the class, the more learning will occur.* There are, of course, *upper* limits beyond which certain

kinds of learning are restricted by class size. However, no single figure has been found which can be considered as THE ideal number for all kinds of teaching and learning.

2. *The greater the students' motivation, the greater the learning.* This depends in large part whether the motivation is intrinsic or extrinsic in relation to the required learning. There can be too much motivation, or motivation unrelated to the problem, which may cause the student to overlook obvious factors in his desire to get the correct answer. The *Umweg* experiments may help to point this out:

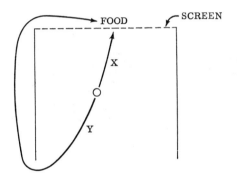

The experiment is basically an open-backed cage with a wire screen across the front. Food is placed in front of the cage, observable to the subjects inside through the screen. Very hungry chickens would continually try a *direct* approach (X) through the screen, which was clearly not warranted. Chickens who were not so hungry would engage in exploratory behavior (Y) which led them to a successful solution (indirect approach) much more frequently. If the reward is *too* great, the human being may spend so much time thinking about the reward that he is blind to the nature of the problem. Thus, reward can be so high that it sets up *interference*. Also, the *relevance* of the reward to the situation at hand should be considered, particularly in terms of whether or not the students and teacher agree that the consequence in question *is* a reward.

3. *Active participation is better than passive reception.* This may be true, but the statement does *not* mean that discussions promote more learning than do lectures, which is the common interpretation. Gifted lecturers can often produce a great deal of *active, vicarious* participation as the student follows an exciting argument, or tries to find clues to the solution of a difficult problem. On the other hand, many discussions, revolving around such crucial issues as whether students prefer malted milks to milkshakes, do not achieve much active intellectual interest. It should be clear to everyone that the production of sounds from the mouth does *not* necessarily indicate a working mind. Active *mental* participation can occur without any talking by the students at all.

Most of us look for cues from the students as to their relative activity, in terms of their eye movements, the amount of restlessness and whispering, watching the clock, playing with pencils, etc. Many of these cues may be highly misleading, as the bored boy in the back of the room may have been following the flow of ideas very carefully and actively. In the same vein, students know that certain activity cues are positively reinforcing to the teacher, and the smiling girl who nods her head in indication of complete understanding and admiration, and also gives many indications of sudden flashes of insight, may simply be attempting to raise her grade. We know little about the "matching" of cues and responses of teachers and students, but we can be sure that there is a considerable margin of error in interpretation on both sides.

4. *Democratic teachers produce more learning than authoritarian teachers.* We have already indicated that, first, the variables are not clearly defined, and second, the evidence suggests that even with the above terms, no consistent relationships exist.

5. *The more money spent per child in a school, the greater the learning.* This statement indicates a belief which is almost universally accepted in America. (The more you pay for anything the better it is). Yet, from the statement, we would have

to say that in schools in which a high amount is spent per student, *measured achievement would be closer to measured aptitude* than would be the case in schools which spend a small amount per student. This generalization has not been substantiated. In fact, there are many schools in which a very small amount of money is invested per student, yet the achievement of the students is at very high levels. Such factors as parental influence, school climate, and student attitudes can easily override the single-minded economic view of school achievement.

6. *It is dangerous for children to learn more than our aptitude measures indicate is appropriate for them.* One of the most ridiculous concepts in American education is that of the "over-achiever"—the child who learns more than he is *supposed* to. As well as being a logical impossibility, it suggests a finite ceiling to learning and a validity and reliability which our best measures of aptitude do not have. If a child achieves more than aptitude tests indicate is normal, it is the *test* that is wrong, not the child. If, on the other hand, the phrase "over-achiever" is taken to mean a student who *strives* to do things which are completely beyond him and fails consistently to show any improvement, then there may be a real issue. However, the problem is not over-*achievement* but over*striving* for achievement—the child tries but consistently fails to learn. There is no reason to believe that a child will be damaged in his social adjustment because he *actually achieves* more than his aptitude level.

NOTES

1. It would be extremely interesting to study the in-group, out-group relations *within* social sciences, particularly in reference to criteria for in-group membership ("talent," publications, sociability, degrees, professorial rank, etc.). Also, what sorts of intellectual differences create in-groups and what sorts do not?

2. D. O. Hebb, "The American Revolution," *American Psychologist*, 15 (1960), 735-745.

3. One of the best refutations of the Cartesian position is G. Ryle, *The Concept of Mind*, (New York, 1949), Ch. 1. For an excellent critique of Ryle's distinction between knowing *how* and knowing *that*, see Marcus Brown, "Knowing and Learning," *Harvard Educational Review*, 31 (1961), 1-20. Also relevant is I. Sheffler, *The Language of Education*, (Springfield, Ill., 1960).

4. A central problem for man and other forms of life is that adaptation of necessity takes some time. Thus the mutant fly that survives will pass his genetic structure on to others who may have to deal with new conditions. In similar fashion, the learning which is passed from one human generation to the next may be non-adaptive in the new situation. (For example, "Schools should be closed in the summer months so that the children can help out on the farm," is no longer an adaptive mode of behavior, although it once was. This is a restatement of the problem analyzed in chapter three.)

5. E. L. Thorndike, *Educational Psychology* (2 vols.), (New York, 1913-14). Volume 2, *The Psychology of Learning*, is the more relevant here. See also his *Human Learning*, (New York, 1931), and *Selected Writings from a Connectionist Psychologist*, (New York, 1949). There are available for the interested reader a number of good summaries of the central issues in learnings: W. Estes, *et al.*, *Modern Learning Theory*, New York, 1954); E. R. Hilgard, *Theories of Learning*, (New York, 1948); J. Deese, *The Psychology of Learning*, (New York, 1958, 2nd ed.). One of the most readable summaries of theory is L. Thorpe and A. Schmuller, *Contemporary Theories of Learning*, (New York, 1954). The best summary of research is *Hilgard and Marquis' Conditioning and Learning*, (rev. by G. A. Kimble), (New York, 1961). Teachers will find much information relevant to their problems in H. L. Kingsley and R. Garry, *The Nature and Conditions of Learning*, (Englewood Cliffs, N. J., 1957, 2nd ed.). A very exciting book, seldom discussed in the field of education, is O. H. Mowrer, *Learning Theory and the Symbolic Process*, (New York, 1960).

6. K. S. Lashley, *Brain Mechanisms and Intelligence*, (Chicago, 1929), 173.

7. For an excellent account of "reward" confusion in a public school setting, see J. Henry, "Working Paper on Creativity," *Harvard Ed. Rev.*, 27 (1957), 148-155; also in the same journal see E. T. Ladd, "The Perplexities of the Problem of Keeping Order," 28 (1958), 19-28. It is interesting that so little has been done on the problem of discipline, either in terms of theory or research, particularly as teachers almost always list it as one of their most pressing problems. There are many theories of behavior, but almost no work has been done on *mis*behavior in the school setting.

8. One of the best single chapters on this vital issue is Chapter 11, "A Theory of Learning for Teachers," in H. G. Hullfish and P. S. Smith, *Reflective Thinking: The Method of Education*, (New York, 1961). The

entire book is highly recommended. See also B. Wellington and J. Wellington, *Teaching for Critical Thinking*, (New York, 1960).

9. From a conversation with Mrs. Eleanor Roosevelt in 1960, after her return from an extensive tour of Russia.

10. A typical methodology for such studies is as follows: Train rats to *swim* through a maze filled with water; then build in a false floor just under the water level so that the rats could *walk* the maze instead of swimming it. There is no increase in errors when this is done, evidence that refutes the notion of kinesthetic chaining as the basis for maze learning.

11. J. B. Watson, "Practical and Theoretical Problems in Instinct and Habits," *Suggestions of Modern Science Concerning Education*, (New York, 1918), 51-100. (Italics added.) Of particular interest is his discussion of standardized intelligence tests and his plea for "real behavior" testing,

12. Clark L. Hull, "Conditioning: Outline of a Systematic Theory of Learning," in 41st yearbook of the National Society for the Study of Education, Part II, *The Psychology of Learning*, 61-95, (Chicago, 1942). This whole volume is still very pertinent, and is highly recommended.

13. J. Dollard and N. Miller, *Personality and Psychotherapy*, (New York, 1950). Dollard and Miller's four principles of learning—drive-cue-response-reinforcement—fit nicely into Hull's theoretical framework. However, Dewey's theory of learning, based on a problem-solving assumption, is not compatible with them. *His* five steps of learning (as one might suspect) are recognition of the problem, search for clarity, hypothesis, application, and verification.

14. This lack of willingness to admit variation in drive strength is not in accord with many carefully controlled experiments which have established quite clearly the existence of *internal* states which cause changes in behavior even with no change in the external stimulus conditions.

15. B. F. Skinner, *The Behavior of Organisms*, (New York, 1938), 368.

16. P. T. Young, *Motivation and Emotion*, (New York, 1961), 101.

17. B. F. Skinner, *Verbal Behavior*, (New York, 1957).

18. ———, "The Science of Learning and the Art of Teaching," *Harvard Ed. Rev.*, 24 (1954), 86-97.

19. *Ibid.*, 94-95.

20. *Ibid.*, 96-97. See also his Utopia, *Walden Two*, (New York, 1948).

21. J. Bruner, "Learning and Thinking," *Harvard Ed. Rev.*, 29 (1959), 184-192. See also his *The Process of Education*, (Cambridge, 1961).

22. B. Bode, *How We Learn*, (Boston, 1940), 216. This book, a revision of his earlier *Conflicting Theories of Learning*, is an excellent treatment of the various views of learning. Those who find Dewey's *How We Think* (Boston, 1933) too difficult should find Bode's discussion of many of the same problems much more readable.

23. Probably the most exciting example of Wertheimer's kind of analysis is the new edition of his *Productive Thinking*, edited by his son Michael Wertheimer, (New York, 1959).

24. The best and most readable volume is W. Kohler's *Gestalt Psychology*, (rev. ed.), (New York, 1947). A good description of the empirical uses of field theory can be found in K. Lewin, *Field Theory in Social Science*, (D. Cartwright, ed.), (New York, 1951).

25. G. Katona, *Organizing and Memorizing*, (New York, 1940).

26. W. Kohler, *The Mentality of Apes*, (New York, 1925). See also a fascinating account of a family that raised an ape along with a child. At one stage, Gua, the ape, solved a problem in one try which took Donald, the child, four or five tries. Even though there is a lack of empirical control in such a situation, the results are of great interest. W. N. and L. A. Kellogg, *The Ape and the Child*, (New York, 1933) esp. pp. 200-219.

27. E. C. Tolman, "Cognitive Maps in Rats and Men," *Psychological Revue*, 55 (1948), 189-208.

28. ———, *Purposive Behavior in Animals and Men*, (New York, 1932).

29. For example, see W. Sargent, *Battle for the Mind*, (New York, 1957).

30. On this point, see Hullfish and Smith, *op. cit.* An excellent discussion of the use of Gestalt theory in specific educational situations can be found in E. Bayles, "The Idea of Learning as Development of Insight," *Educational Theory*, 2 (1952), 65-71.

31. J. Dewey, *Democracy and Education*, (New York, 1916), 89.

32. See B. Bode, *op. cit.*

33. Quoted in Martin Mayer, *The Schools*, (New York, 1961), 71. This book is probably the best report available today of what is *actually happening* in American schools.

34. E. Hilgard, *op. cit.*, 326.

35. *Ibid.*, 185.

36. W. Kohler, *The Mentality of Apes*, 146.

37. E. R. Guthrie and G. P. Horton, *Cats in a Puzzle Box*, (New York, 1946).

38. Hilgard and Marquis, *op. cit.*, 49.

39. A. W. Combs, "Intelligence from a Perceptual Point of View," *Journal of Abnormal and Social Psychology*, 47 (1952), 662-673. This article asks a series of extremely provocative questions which should be asked more often.

40. P. Sorokin, "Testomania," *Harvard Ed. Rev.*, 25 (1955), 199-213.

41. Hullfish and Smith, *op. cit.*, 185.

CHAPTER SEVEN

Education in Social
and Cultural Perspectives

Although no specific attempt will be made here to summarize all of the preceding material, there are several concepts which have occurred throughout the analysis which can now be looked at more closely before we consider some concluding statements.

Multidimensionality

It should be obvious by now that human behavior is *not* single-minded or single-sided. The observer (the teacher as well as the social scientist) *selects* aspects from the totality which we call action and fits these into a meaningful pattern. There is a tendency, already noted among teachers and researchers, to argue from one or two factors to the totality. Thus we find people making pronouncements about social class, mobility, motivation, values, and learning, on the basis of a very small number of

208

factors. In identical fashion, teachers will say, "Jane just doesn't want to do the work in my class; that's why she is failing," "Bill is just inherently lazy; no one will ever teach him anything," or "John tries hard, but he just can't work with numbers."

All of these statements indicate a faith in the idea that behavior of a wide range of sorts can be initiated by a *single factor*. This faith is not merited, even though single factors often give what seems to be good predictability in terms of consequent behavior. There seems to be, in the course of general human interaction, a certain optimism concerning our ability to "see inside" other people. This optimism is seen in the teachers' statements mentioned above, and in the social research we have discussed. It implies a deterministic world, but in terms of our conversational pronouncements about our fellow men, it is a *determinism based upon intuition*. We generally feel confident about the judgments we make of ourselves and others, but how often do we pause to reflect on the criteria and the methods we use?

Some of the social tendencies we have discussed would indicate that with increased technology comes a decrease in our knowledge of aspects other than our own of the occupational world, and therefore a decrease in our knowledge of those around us. Increased geographical and social mobility, plus new products creating new values and motivational patterns are operating to make us "all one big happy family" when we ride the subway or go to a football game. But in less superficial situations where genuine and meaningful interpersonal contact might be made, we often prefer the glib, pat responses we put forth as part of the mass pattern, to those unique reactions which make us individuals, but which are so difficult (and often dangerous) to communicate. Thus, in the same breath, we are becoming more alike in terms of the things we buy, the places we go, the recreation we enjoy, the things we want; yet we probably know less and less about each other, as the chances for intense and personal interactions are minimized.

thanks largely to the vastly increased amount of structured group activity in contemporary America.

It may be possible that because people are behaving in very similar fashion we make the deterministic leap to the assumption that they *are* similar. The current pattern of childhood and early adolescence is one in which group activity is largely established through adults. There are few times when a child is free to construct his own games, either alone or with his peers, without an adult to supervise. The advantages to adult-supervised activities are many. For example, a large number of children can be kept occupied at a single location and level of skill may improve from adult instruction. However, there are also very important advantages to spontaneous activity which is not dominated by adults. Except for very crowded areas in some big cities, where children still chalk *their* games on streets and sidewalks, there is little opportunity for a child to engage in spontaneous, unplanned activity. For example, one Little League team used to meet for practice on Saturday mornings, and, although the boys arrived at 8:30, not a baseball was batted or thrown until 9:00 when the *adults* arrived to organize the day's activities. For one who grew up with sandlot baseball, in which *the players* made up the rules, and in which the players felt perfectly free to go swimming or play football if they were tired of baseball, this is a curious and unwelcome development.

The recent developments in the production of children's toys also indicates the trend toward adult-imposed similarity. In middle range suburbs, virtually every house has the same outdoor gymnasium (which actually provides the child with very little exercise, compared with climbing a tree) and the same plastic swimming pool. In fact, in a well-known toy catalogue can be found a terribly elaborate toy which duplicates the operation of an airplane in realistic fashion. According to the description, this is the ultimate toy because "It leaves absolutely nothing to the child's imagination." Imagination, whch is unique, personal, spontaneous, and unpredictable has apparently become something for the adult and child to guard against.

It would seem that we can make just as good a case for the lack of opportunities for spontaneous, creative activity in the lives of children as we can for adults. Thus, people are *behaving* in increasingly similar patterns. As Ralph Linton put it, "People are trying to live like termites without half the termite equipment." As a result of this commonality of behavior patterns, it becomes even easier to use our intuitive determinisms and conclude that people who are doing the same things *are* similar. Thus, the Japanese child twirling a hula-hoop is no different from the American child twirling an identical hula-hoop.

If only international relations could be so easy! Arguing the criterion of similarities in behavior, we could say that when everyone in the world drinks Coca-Cola (which is possible) there will be universal understanding and friendship. When everyone owns a car, brushes his teeth twice a day, wears a white shirt and tie, and watches television, world brotherhood will be a living reality.

What is missing in this sort of easy, intuitive, single-minded determinism is our multidimensional model of the human being. *Two people behaving alike are not necessarily alike inside.* Overt activity is only one dimension of humanity, just as occupation is only one measure of social class. We tend to overload the dimension of behavior, just as the sociologist often overloads the dimension of occupation. As people behave in increasingly similar fashion, the multidimensional view becomes more difficult to maintain, because differences have become submerged below the surface level of activity and cannot always be readily observed. Also, there is something so overwhelming in the sight of a large number of people doing exactly the same thing (a large number of soldiers doing close-order drill, for example) that we forget to look for differences.

The multidimensional view, which allows and even forces

us to see the complexities behind obvious similarities in be-havior, is of tremendous importance for our time, as increas-ingly we shall have to be aware of differences in other social and cultural systems, even though their peoples *seem* to be-have as we do. This is as true in religion and economics as it is in politics and science. Our foreign aid programs often give the appearance of providing enough aid so that the citizens who receive it can behave like Americans, on the assumption that this is all that is needed for happiness.

The teacher who has a measure of sophistication in the social sciences can perform a great service by encouraging students to look for differences as well as similarities, both in their own behavior and attitudes and in the behavior and attitudes of others. This teacher, if a member of a social studies depart-ment, could do a great deal to point out *differences* in other cultures in a way which may cause students to respect these cultures for what they are, instead of admiring only those which look like miniature Americas. This teacher could em-phasize the fact that all cultures must adapt to many of the same conditions and must provide people with many of the same things.

For example, the problem of war has often been handled rather effectively by certain "primitive" tribes. In one, when a dispute occurs with another tribe, the two tribes gather together and the *two leaders* fight, after which everyone goes home. In another, the two tribes face each other in two long single rows. Then heads are counted and the tribe with the largest number of people in attendence is declared the victor, after which everyone goes home, unhurt. The problem of death also has to be resolved in a meaningful way. In one culture when an adult dies and a child asks about it, he is told that the lost adult has gone into the sky to count the stars, and that when he is finished, he will return. Even if the solutions of other cultures and other times are not realistic solutions for us, we can nevertheless develop an appreciation for another culture *as an integrated whole,* and not just in terms of the amount of behavior produced which is identical with ours.

This teacher, if a member of the English department, would realize that a particular poem may produce several different effects in one student, several other reactions in another, and no reactions at all in a third. He thus would be conscious of a wide range of aspects of the lives of his students, and would not tie his teaching down to a single-factored approach. He would attempt to interpret student responses from a number of aspects, instead of interpreting them only in terms of whether or not the student's answer was identical with his own. He could develop, in his students and in himself, an appreciation for the literature of other cultures, as well as their use of language, not in terms of how it compares with ours, but as an independent entity to be approached on its own terms, not on ours.

Teachers who see individuals and cultures in a multidimensional light will be less prone to commit the crime of *ethnocentrism*—judging other cultures only by the standards of our own. Likewise, they will judge their students by more than just one standard, especially those which may not be too closely related to the students' learning. Such a teacher would realize that many "middle class" values and desired behaviors, such as being scrupulously clean and neat, wearing certain types of clothes, always agreeing with the teacher on everything, always being punctual, never expressing aggression physically, never using such expressions as "I ain't" and "He don't," may have little connection with the ability to learn.

Such a teacher would try to break down single-dimensioned thought wherever it was found, on the conviction that it represents the best way to misunderstanding. There are many people who would claim that there is *only* one important way of evaluating others and that the dimension is dichotomous (Negro *or* white, Protestant, Catholic, *or* Jewish, rich *or* poor, Democrat *or* Republican, northerner *or* southerner, labor *or* management, Communist *or* American).

Our teacher would also see that the status system of the school age group is basically single-factored, operating around a dimension of "athlete *or* not," both for boys *and* girls, since the girls share the conviction about athletics, as seen in their dating preferences. (It would be interesting to know whether students' perceptions of parents and teachers are as single-factored as their status perceptions of each other, but authoritative research has not been done on the question.) This teacher would also be conscious of the single-factored generalizations made by his colleagues ("These students all flunked and they are therefore alike." "Our school board is only interested in economy." "My principal is a good one because he is young." "If I got a $500 raise next year I could really enjoy teaching.").

The life of such a teacher (or principal, or superintendent, or parent) is not an easy one. The analytical judgments he makes, and those he helps his students to make, are rigorous and demand a good deal of hard work. Also, they are subject to evaluation and revision. In certain schools, there are maxims (such as those listed in the conclusion of chapter five) which are not to be questioned, and the teacher who tries to use an analytical approach in the "wrong" areas may not be too popular. His conclusions and those of his students will emphasize a *number* of dimensions for the analysis of human behavior, an appreciation for a *variety* of cultures and their values and activities, an awareness of differences which are just as important as similarities, a feeling for different ways of doing the same thing.

Many people in the community will be critical of him, regardless of the subject he teaches. The superpatriots will be concerned over his respect for the virtues of other cultures and his assertion that nationalism is not good by definition but should be carefully evaluated and perhaps ultimately be replaced by world government. The Rotarians and Chamber of Commerce will be concerned with his probing into the economic and psychological effects of installment buying, and his fellow teachers may be concerned with the fact that he wants a *defense* for the statement that the *Mill on the Floss* is a classic. The D.A.R. may object to the conclusion his students reach that the goals of American foreign policy have not in every case been completely altruistic. His assertion that being liked by everyone in the group is not necessarily of paramount importance may arouse the guidance office or the school psychologist. His feeling that success in life may mean more than getting into a high status job will probably incur the wrath of many parents with occupational aspirations for their child. His resistance to televised instruction, team teaching, and extensive use of audio-visual aids, on the grounds of their failure to perform in a *superior* way over his present techniques, may be looked upon by educational administrators as backsliding.

The methods and conclusion of such a teacher would violate the intuitive determinisms which most of us find so easy and compelling. However, if America is really a pluralistic society in which every individual and group can influence others, such a teacher is not a rabble rouser, but a model of what a good citizen should be. It is through people like him that the confrontation necessary for a truly public philosophy, to use Walter Lippmann's famous phrase, could actually occur. In actuality, however, it may be that we have a *pluralistic culture* but a *monistic society,* in that although we give lip service to the value of conflicting ideas and their interplay, our social institutions—the church, the military, the mass media. large-scale government, and bureaucratic business organizations— are not equipped with any *functional* devices for allowing and even encouraging a variety of points of view. Thus our pluralistic *ends* clash with bureaucracies which often depend upon monistic, inflexible *means.* This conflict is often eliminated by the bureaucratic technique, described so aptly by Max Weber, of allowing means to *become* ends.

The Reconstructionists to the contrary,[1] the teacher we have described here will not alter the bureaucratic tendency which

seems to be associated with increasingly complex and technological societies. "Big" organization is here to stay. However,
if we had enough teachers who fit our description, it might
be that in a new generation we could impart the techniques of
analysis which could produce, perhaps for the first time on a
mass level, a meaningful *discussion of the translation of ends
into appropriate means.* It is therefore not enough to reaffirm
our faith piously in the Bill of Rights and the Constitution as
ends, without analyzing the means we have available to promote these ends. It is here that our idealized teacher type
could make a singular contribution by his insistence upon the
importance of the means-ends relationship.

Recent developments in educational technology (accompanied, as Weber might predict, by an increase in educational
bureaucracy) may make the job of our teacher even more difficult, as technology promotes the discussion of means more
than it does ends. (This is logical, as ends, being based upon
values, are not compatible with technological language or
methodology.) Educational technology, like any other sort,
can be very productive, but this productivity needs assessment
and direction. As a consequence, the main question—*What
knowledge is of most worth, and why?*—should be of greater
importance today than ever before, as we will have an astonishing array of educational devices in a short time.[2] These
devices have often been produced without a sound theoretical
base or a realization of the aspects of the curriculum which
will be favored by their use. Our teacher, who is willing to
discuss ends as well as means, can perform a vital service here
for the educational profession. Ultimately, through his students,
he can serve the society by creating citizens who see man on
a *number* of dimensions, who have the analytical techniques
necessary to evaluate innovations as well as established practices, and who can exercise some autonomy and selectivity
in *all* the choices they make. Their dedication to the multidimensional approach will enable them to function in opposition to a wide range of intuitive determinisms, getting us

nearer to the creation of a *pluralistic society* as well as a *pluralistic culture.*

Determinism and Spontaneity

In most of the literature of the social sciences we have discussed, there can be seen one major assumption: Man can be viewed as either a completely predictable machine, operating under definite cause-and-effect relationships, *or* as a free agent, capable of reversing these relationships and acting in creative, spontaneous, uncaused ways, *but never as both.* It goes without saying that the social sciences, like the natural sciences, have dealt mainly with the deterministic side.

We have already suggested that this attempt to emulate the physical sciences distorts reality. We may now consider the possibility that the image of the physical sciences as dealing *only* with determinisms is questionable. In recent years, particularly in physics, there has been an increasing awareness of the field as well as the particle; and the notion that measuring a particle's speed will distort its size, while measuring size will distort speed, leaves one in a difficult position. The point has been well stated:

> A kind of general expectation of over-all determinacy is not the essence of science. It is what keeps the enterprise going, however . . . modern science, when it encounters some special indeterminacy, develops special techniques, usually statistical ones, for dealing with it and marches on, much as the modern mobile army flows around little pockets of resistance with its strategic eye on the larger objectives.[3]

For example, consider the problem which begins, *"Neglecting friction,* calculate the acceleration of a ten-pound ball rolling down an inclined plane. . . ."* The truly deterministic position cannot neglect friction or any other variable, such as temperature, humidity, or barometric pressure, which might influence the results. As suggested above, statistical techniques can be devised to produce a calculation that is extremely close, but there will always be some deviation from the predicted rate of speed, even though our instruments may not be sensitive enough to record it.

Another example, perhaps closer to the central issue here, is that light is seen by the physicist as *both* a wave and a particle. In certain circumstances it behaves as a wave form, and in others as a collocation of moving particles, capable of exerting physical force. The determinist is bound to say, "But it must consistently be one *or* the other! It cannot be both." The physicist, however, sticks to his dual model of light, as it explains reality better than any other.

Thus, the Heisenberg principle and the dual theory of light, both of which are relatively indeterministic positions, *explain reality better* than any completely deterministic model available. With this sort of position in the physical sciences, is it not possible, reasonable, and perhaps admirable, that we view man as being both a machine *and* a free agent simultaneously? Like the elusive beam of light, whose "real" nature seems to be two things, we can view the human being as composed of deterministic *and* indeterministic elements.

It is thus perfectly consistent and reasonable to bridge the major gap in educational theory and practice by saying that some aspects of human behavior are indeterminate, while at the same time striving for a scientific theory of education. Such a theory will contain both determinist and indeterminist elements. The task which remains is that of classifying, as carefully as possible, the conditions which fit into each category. Of particular importance to education is the classification of situations in terms of *creative and imitative* behavior. That is, when do we want the student to imitate the agreed-upon skills or facts as such, and when do we want him to engage in spontaneous, non-uniform behavior which is relatively unpredictable? When this sort of question can be answered, educational theory and practice will have come of age. However, in order to answer the questions, we must have a set of educational priorities which will indicate the patterns of meaning which are worthy of being learned. Such a set of priorities is certainly not on the immediate horizon.

The need for the concept of indeterminacy is easily seen in many situations which affect teachers. Once a prediction is made known, *the prediction itself* becomes part of the perceptual field of the person about whom the prediction was made. Thus, in a situation somewhat parallel to the uncertainty principle, attempts at predicting a human phenomenon may alter the nature of the phenomenon itself. A simple illustration of this would be that of a man holding an object in his hand, whereupon someone else makes a prediction as to whether he will continue holding the object or will drop it. No matter how much data are gathered in making the prediction, in terms of the individual's background, interests, needs, etc., it is theoretically impossible to *know in advance* what the effect of the prediction will be on the decision. In a chemical reaction, it makes no difference if the prediction is made public in advance. In human situations, however, the prediction itself introduces a new factor.

This does not mean that we have no idea of the impact of predictions. Every teacher knows that the self-fulfilling prophecy is a useful aid in the classroom. These are predictions which *cause themselves* to come true; such as "I think that everyone will do very well on the test today," or "You're such a smart class that I am sure you will do better than the class across the hall," or "John, I think you can get that problem if you work on it," after which, the desired behavior *does* occur, partially because of the prediction. However, predictions of this sort (which are in one sense simply rewards) will probably have a different effect every time they are used (usually diminishing in potency) and thus are not a stable, reliable item on the teacher's list. They do indicate that the impact of a prediction itself can influence the behavior of students as well as teachers.

This sort of indeterminacy is only one type, which we could call the uncertainty of prediction impact. The various indeterminacies which impinge on human activity have never been categorized adequately, but we could certainly mention indeterministic aspects of the creation of new ideas, of certain decision-making situations, of accidental and spontaneous behavior, and of the impact of such concepts as honesty, loyalty, and love on human behavior. A taxonomy of these and other indeterministic aspects of man would be an ambitious effort, but well worth it if educational theory is ever to contribute much to educational practice, and vice versa. With such a taxonomy, it might be possible to begin to produce a system of educational priorities which would contain both deterministic and indeterministic elements, producing a more complete composite picture of the end product of education than we have had before.

It should be made clear that indeterministic end products are just as capable of *being achieved* as are deterministic ones. Also, in many cases both kinds of analysis are represented in a single end product. For example, freedom of thought is in part the result of conditioning or training in the uses of various kinds of logical analysis, a set of acquired skills. However, the *specific conclusions* produced by a given individual using these skills or processes are unpredictable. It is much easier to measure the deterministic component of the acquisition of the skills and techniques of thinking than it is the indeterministic component. Yet it is conceivable that these indeterministic components are also susceptible to statistical analysis, although the question has not been investigated carefullly.

The presentation of reality fostered by the school is often slanted toward the deterministic pole. Historical events have a finite cause or a finite number of causes, as do poems, verbs, symphonies, lab experiments, results of elections, etc. The idea of an event without a specific cause or finite number of causes is inconceivable to the typical student, or teacher for that matter, yet it is, in relation to the uncertainty principle, a good possibility. The school program does little to develop appreciation for the spontaneous, the creative, the unplanned responses and perceptions which are an important aspect of life, particularly in a bureaucratic, technological era. If our educational goals contained both deterministic *and* indeterministic components, the balance might be shifted away from a complete domination of skills and attitudes which are *imposed upon* the student. For example, when we say that we want our students to develop an understanding of the American heritage, we really mean that we want the student to acquire *our* understanding of it. It ought to be possible to structure a goal such as this one to include techniques which will allow the students to develop independent, spontaneous evaluations of certain aspects of the American past, and to understand how the past influences the present.

To teach children that life is simply a collection of pre-defined responses to pre-defined situations is misleading. The S-R model is misleading, in that it neglects the important fact that human beings can select and *seek out* stimuli in the real world, even though most laboratory experiments do not allow for this fact. We can decide *between* deterministic chains, and in certain situations *we can reject them altogether.* Such a statement is not incompatible with a scientific theory of education, as we have indicated.

The major difficulty in the indeterministic aspect of teaching is the teacher, not the student. Expressions of awe, wonderment, and mystery are not the least bit difficult for most children. Their almost intuitive response to certain situations in nature—the birth of a kitten, the power of a thunderstorm, the majesty of a mountain range, the mystery of the stars—indicate that children can appreciate situations without establishing cause-and-effect relationships. However, in school and out, it seems that as puberty nears, the creative, spontaneous use of words, music, and the visual arts gets driven out of them. Why and how this happens is not known, but it *does* happen.

Thus the adult comes to feel that indeterministic elements such as spontaneity and creativity belong only in the realm of children, and the elimination of these elements becomes a mark of maturity. The teacher, as representative of adult society, generally subscribes to this view, and as a consequence presents mainly a connection of deterministic chains. It is largely for this reason that our educational system does such a poor job at producing in students a sense of wonder, awe, and amazement at the feast we spread before them. Anyone who grasps the concept of infinity, the feeling of human history, the mysteries of language, or the miracle of life has a great deal to wonder about, even in our sophisticated age.

Many teachers have a vested interest in a static, relatively permanent and deterministic notion of truth, as this is what they know. Any attempt to introduce concepts of spontaneity, wonder, indeterminacy, and creativity will be seen as a threat to the teacher who knows "The Truth" and simply wants students to say the same things. Creative behavior, being essentially indeterministic, can never be *completely controlled* by the teacher, and thus teachers who are uncertain of their ability to dominate the class have additional reasons for sticking with a completely deterministic approach to education.

A central problem in teacher education, unsolved at the moment, concerns the development of teachers who have the stability, courage, and insight to deal with indeterministic elements, in the physics class as well as in the English or history class. In order for this to happen, we will need *college* teachers who can produce the indeterministic reactions of awe, amazement, and a sense of wonderment in connection with a certain subject area. It is questionable whether or not such teachers exist in quantity at the college level. However, there is little doubt that the teacher who can convey the sense of the wonderful, the miraculous, has at his disposal one of the most powerful motivating devices yet known, probably far superior to the reinforcement which comes from simply getting the correct answer to someone else's problem. As soon as we relinquish our control over students, either at the end of the day or of the year, they seem very uninterested in carrying their education along with them. Thus, we have failed to develop in the students an *autonomous* interest in the subject, largely because they see the subject only as a collection of skills and facts, not as something wonderful, beautiful, or amazing. The indeterminist aspects of every discipline could well provide this incentive.

Education Versus Society

Another theme which has run through many of these pages is that of the conflict of the values and desired behaviors promoted by the school and those promoted by the outside world. As we have indicated, many areas of American life contain inherently contradictory values. For example, free enterprise capitalism has always emphasized the importance of the *individual's* acquiring capital for himself, while the altruistic ethic has always held that giving to *others* is always better than seeking personal gain. The school is thus fundamentally caught between capitalism and altruism, as is the rest of the society. Thus, by subscribing to *both* horns of the dilemma, we tell students to be ambitious and acquire the good things of life, while at the same time we tell them that charity is necessary to care for the human waste which accompanies a competitive system.

In many other areas, the conflict is not so easily sidestepped. The teachings of the school generally support the values surrounding a *future* time dimension. Thrift, regular savings, putting profits back into the enterprise instead of spending them, acting in relation to future consequences more than present ones—these are values sanctioned by the school.

The culture, on the other hand, has been moving toward a present-oriented, hedonistic ethic. Through the installment pattern of buying, immediate enjoyment of things has become possible and very desirable. People often figure purchases not in terms of total cash outlay, but in terms of the size of monthly payments, seldom going to the effort of multiplying the monthly payments by the number of months they will be paying. Because the retailer can charge very high interest rates in this situation, he often prefers the installment buyer to the cash customer. The person without a charge account or a record of installment purchasing may find it difficult to get credit, simply because he has never had to borrow money before. Signs proclaim the joys of immediate ownership of anything desired. The school's future orientation is clearly in conflict with business patterns, producing some conflicts in students, who have now become a very important consumer market. They are able to own products, such as cars, which establish their rights to claim maturity, because people who drive cars are generally not considered to be children. Because they can buy things as immediately as their elders, the adolescents have little reason to show deference to their parents. Thus, the buying pattern, which we accept, produces in the young a greater feeling of independence, which we dislike.

Another area of conflict concerns the relative values of work and pleasure. The school's position seems to be "Work hard, both because you'll get ahead and because hard work is enjoyable." American society, on the other hand, seems to be moving toward a leisure-pleasure principle, at least judging from mass media advertising, which seldom emphasizes the *productive* use of leisure. In the same vein, the schools often exude a rather rigid, Puritanical approach to morality and value commitments, while outside we have moved toward a relativistic conception of morality in which the right thing is that which is being done by most of those around you. This is exemplified in Riesman's concept of the "other-directed" man.

One difficulty with American schools, and one reason why there is a great deal of argument among those responsible for them, is that various groups having to do with schools are spread out between the so-called "traditional" and the more recent "emergent" values. Spindler, in a provocative paper, diagrammed the situation as follows: [4]

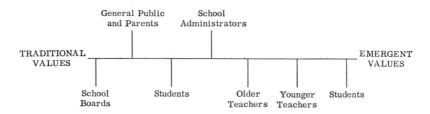

The school boards, having gotten where they are through succeeding in the system *as it is,* feel a heavy commitment to the *status quo* (traditional values), while the younger teachers, who have no roots in the traditional and were influenced by the modifications in values as they grew up (and *also* may possess the multidimensional point of view, and may admit and enjoy indeterminacy), may be closer to the relativistic, less individualistic, Emergent pole.

There are other individuals and groups interested in public education besides those in the above diagram. One of the new major roles which our society is forcing on us is that of consumer. This new role is often proclaimed as one of our principal ways of asserting our individuality, even though the products from which we choose are often virtually identical. (The Chevrolet, the Pontiac, and the Cadillac seem to be more alike each year.) Because of the consumer power of the young, and because there is some evidence that early consumer habits are retained through time, there is a great interest in selling the adolescent his first pack of cigarettes, the younger child his first bottle of pop, first package of gum, first candy bar, etc.

Thus, private interest groups are often very interested in the school program. In the schools one has a captive audience of large size which will be buying products longer than any adult audience. In this connection, consider the rapid spread of driver education courses in American schools. A decade or two ago, they were a rarity, while today they are considered virtually an essential. How has this curriculum change come about? Who decided that, although independent driver training schools are available, the *schools* should be responsible for teaching young people to drive? One can make a very reasonable case for the assertion that the *manufacturers* of a product have an obligation to instruct buyers in the use of that product, but such programs have not been developed.

One possible hypothesis is that driver education programs entered the high school curriculum because the cars, complete with prominent signs giving the name of the auto firm, were *donated* to school committees. When one considers the amount of free advertising, from the signs and from word-of-mouth, it was a splendid investment for the local dealer. As support for this hypothesis, how many cars donated for driver education programs are donated *anonymously* and contain no advertising? [5]

This is only one tenuous example of something which must be watched carefully. Many people in many fields would like to get into the schools or the school program *in order to sell things to students*. Many organizations send out teaching units, complete with pictures, text material, and tests, which somehow manage to project the organization's name and/or point of view to the students. In similar fashion, publishers of textbooks, who determine a considerable portion of the public school curriculum, are not always immune to private interest groups. Also, they must produce a version which will sell both in the Northern states and in the 50 per cent of our states, mainly in the South and Southwest, which have a central adoption or purchasing committee. Thus, many texts, particularly in the area of history and social studies, represent a rather ineffectual compromise. This compromise is easily seen in treatments of the Civil War and the United Nations.

It should be clear that various enterprises are interested in selling *ideas* as well as things, both to students and teachers. Labor and management groups want to make sure that their points of view are treated sympathetically in the schools, while patriotic groups wish to protect students from influences which they term un-American. As an example, during the so-called "Robin Hood Riots," all books which mentioned Robin Hood were banned from libraries because of his socialistic tendencies in taking from the rich and giving to the poor. In similar fashion, *The Nation* magazine was banned from libraries in the city of New York, presumably because of material by Paul Blanshard which was not favorable to certain positions taken by the Catholic Church. Teachers have been fired for teaching *Catcher in the Rye, Brave New World,* and *1984.*

One of the best ways to sell things is to eliminate competition. Thus, if you have a point of view to "sell," it is often a very successful move to simply remove from public access other points of view which conflict with yours. This happens often in the public schools. In some states, a reading from the Bible is required each day, schools with Jewish majorities (a rapidly increasing occurrence in many suburbs) celebrate the Christmas holidays, and released time for religious instruction is often given—except for children of atheists.

The schools of a truly pluralistic society should be either open to *all* ideas, or else closed to all, with the former preferred over the latter. At the present time, certain ideas have greater dissemination through the schools than others. These ideas are not necessarily superior in terms of their logical structure, but they are often held to be self-evident truths, and not areas of *debate.* In Spindler's terminology, they represent the Traditional pole far more than the Emergent.

The greatest service the American school can perform in our society, with its increasingly bureaucratic and single-minded tendencies, is to exist as a model of pluralism. The way to fight certain ideas or tendencies is not dogmatically to denounce them, but to provide, through the curriculum, a confrontation of *all* ideas, not just those which are passively accepted as the truth at the local, community, or state level. In earlier times, local educational programs could be geared to local values, as most of the students would spend their lives in the town, and a case could be made for helping the young to "fit in." Today, however, when one of every four or five Americans changes residence *every year,* the local value perspective may not be adequate for those who will complete their education a thousand miles or more away.

It will be difficult for the school to function as a pluralistic model as long as we retain the notion of *complete* economic and intellectual control of public education through locally elected school boards. These groups, often highly dedicated but occasionally using the school board as a steppingstone to higher political office, have been elected because of their interest in the town or city, and therefore attack educational problems and practices from a local point of view. As long as the schools remain localistic in outlook, they cannot operate as a pluralistic model. Education is no longer merely a matter for local concern. The student who begins in Cleveland may graduate from high school in Denver, and Denver should therefore be informed about, and concerned with, the Cleveland public schools.

There is often poor articulation between elementary and secondary programs within many school systems, but there is even less *between communities*. Those who oppose increasing articulation between communities do so on the grounds that anything other than complete local control is totalitarian. However, totalitarianism is not necessarily a function of size, and the small town of 1,200 people, as we have indicated, may be the *most* totalitarian educational unit of all. As a consequence of this lack of articulation, we have in this country over 40,000 autonomous local educational systems with little, if any, communication between them. Increasing the *communication* would certainly not increase non-local control, but it would improve the ability of the local school to operate in a pluralistic fashion by widening the local perspective to include state, national, and ultimately world problems and points of view. The French educational system is not necessarily *undemocratic* simply because it is a national system. It is to some extent not pluralistic, but we have argued that *within* each local school system, our system is also not very pluralistic.

The ideal school, in terms of the pluralistic model, has a

Darwinistic ring to it—not in terms of people, but of ideas. It should exist as an arena in which conflicting ideas can meet and struggle for survival. The job of the school is to train students in the techniques of analyzing these ideas, so that in the present *and in the future*, they will be able to evaluate new ideas in non-school settings. Unless the techniques learned in the school program can be used in a variety of situations, the analytical approach developed will be of little use. Many students seem to feel that they know how to analyze Plato and English literature, but analytical techniques have no place in questions of whom to vote for, whom to marry, or what to buy. It is this lack of transfer of analytical skills to life situations which suggests that the techniques and goals of school programs need reassessment.

From the preceding chapters we can select several notions which could be made the focus of the teacher's actions, and by an analysis of *all* the alternatives, the problem could be diminished. The problem of status is one such problem. A unit on status in a social studies course might produce a high degree of motivation in the students, because status is a *life problem* for everyone, the teacher included. Investigations of the status systems of other countries, of the change in American status systems from the colonial era to the present, and statements of the status goals of each student, as well as those of the teacher, might produce an awareness of the importance of other dimensions of status than those belonging to a high status occupation. We cannot all have prestige, as we cannot all be at the top of the occupational status hierarchy; but students could realize that in many respects, the status which comes from esteem (doing a task better than anyone else) may be of a richer and more personally meaningful sort than occupational prestige. This is not to say that occupational status is unimportant, but that *it is only one dimension* of human existence.

In the same vein, occupational mobility (which functions through prestige and not esteem) could be shown to be only one aspect of life, and one not closely related to personal hap-

piness and fulfillment. Students might consider whether more
happiness comes from being a lawyer or from being the
best plumber in town.

The school has, it would seem, some obligation to provide
avenues for *esteem* for those who cannot, or do not wish to,
compete for the *prestige* positions in our occupational structure. People should be able to develop feelings of personal
worth without changing jobs. The extra-curricular program of
the school should, if effectively utilized, provide areas in which
those not going on to college (those not competing for high
prestige occupational positions) could acquire esteem. However, as presently constituted, these activities are undertaken
by exactly the students who have little to gain from them—
the college preparatory students. Through a carefully executed
program to develop activities which would interest students
not preparing for college, the schools might be able to alter
the notion so prevalent in our culture that *position is more
important than competence.*

Perhaps one of the reasons that football is such a status-full
activity is that it combines prestige and esteem elements. Just
being a football player carries some prestige, but the most
important reward is the esteem which is given to those whose
actual performance is outstanding. The school should recognize
a much wider range of excellent performances in its extra-curricular activities than it now does, so that a wide range of its
students can taste the rewards of high competence.

We should also consider the specific motivational mechanisms
in American society which are organized to enable individuals
to raise their position on any dimension. These also should be
subject to critical analysis in the school program, perhaps
through an analysis of the kinds of motivational patterns which
bombard the consumer. What sort of appeals are made to him?
What view of "the good life" is presented? How does this view
square with what we know to be the *realities* of American
life? What sort of criteria should be used by the consumer in
coming to a decision? How can one be an individual when

he is considered by others as simply a statistical aggregate? How can one influence the range of products from which he can choose?

One possible conclusion from our analysis is that as patterns of ownership become more and more alike, people may search for other avenues of status which will allow for *meaningful differentiations* between people. One often neglected consequence of the revolution caused by the development of automation (particularly the concept of feedback, which allows machines to check the performance of other machines) is that wealth, which had been produced only through the intense efforts of individual men, can now be produced *automatically*. As a result, economic status will also become an area of differentiation which has lost most of its meaning. The graduated income tax, and other devices which reduce great disparities in individual wealth, also operate to reduce the effectiveness and meaningfulness of economic status differentiations. Most of the studies of college graduates indicate that the status motivations of earlier times are no longer so important. The drive for economic status and power is now seen as not being worth the accompanying strains and tensions. Comfort and security are beginning to replace economic and occupational status as major life goals. One reason for the steady decline in applicants for medical schools can be seen here. The effort and risk involved, the deferral of "the good life" until future years instead of present enjoyment, have caused many young men to desire middle-management positions which will provide them a "comfortable" income without strain. Consider the following remarks of a college senior as being somewhat typical: [6]

> I'm not money-mad by any means, but I'd like enough to buy a house, and have transportation, and of course good clothes for the family. Plus entertainments: I'd like to be able to see the good plays and movies. And I suppose I'd want a trip every year: visit around in the big urban areas, you know, Berlin, Paris, Rome. I can't set any exact amount I'd like to make, so long as it's enough for the *necessities* of life.

One very likely hypothesis about this attitude is that the major status dimensions of income and occupation are losing their ability to motivate people. Even the area of status through "consumership" is seen as superficial by many college students. (Whether or not young people who have *not* gone to college agree on the superficialities of the status dimensions of occupation, income, and purchasing things is open to speculation, as most studies of values have been done on college populations.) [7] Recent fiction would also indicate a dissatisfaction with these dimensions of status in the adult sector of our population as well. The "do-it-yourself" movement is also evidence of a search for *meaningful* sources of *personal* evaluation.

It is here that the school, particularly through its extracurricular program but also through the formal curriculum, can perform a vital function. The job is not that of *eliminating* status systems, but of *creating* dimensions of status differentiation and mobility that are personally meaningful and that can provide a sense of identity and worth in each individual. For example, the school could influence the passive nature of spectator sports by providing instruction in sports that can be played for life, for every student without serious physical defect. High school athletics, which are definitely "ability-grouped" in that only the best play, should be designed for *all*. Games like tennis, volleyball, badminton, and golf, which can be played throughout life, ought to be given equal consideration with the "major" sports of football and basketball, which are not suited to informal recreation. Any male who has ever tried to retrieve a hard badminton smash will realize that this is not a female sissy sport; yet most of the above games are considered girls' sports and are often not available in the boys' athletic programs. The feeling of physical competence in *some* activity which can be continued after the school's influence is over should be a part of every child's education, instead of the select few.

In the same vein, perhaps, with the increased leisure promised in the future, it is time for the schools to promote an intensive campaign to develop an appreciation for the arts *in every student*. Present programs in art appreciation (where they exist) emphasize the role of the spectator, instead of the participant. A well-integrated program of personal *participation* in the arts, beginning in the elementary grades and continuing through high school, could produce this participation to such a degree that a lifelong activity, capable of producing great feelings of personal worth, might be developed. But as with athletics, our programs suggest that at the moment the area is only for a few, not for everyone. The band, because of its service function for athletic events (and the band seldom plays for swimming, track, or tennis meets), generally is over-enrolled, but how many students continue their interest after school is over? The symphony orchestra, the ballet, opera, chamber groups—in fact, the major musical forms of our culture—are seldom available in the public schools. *Spontaneous* singing and dancing occur seldom, if at all, among our youth. Many areas of personal competence, which could have a life-long significance and meaning, are thus simply not available in the high school program.

There is little doubt that such activities, promoting systems of status of a more worthwhile nature and of longer duration, could be developed into virtually universal activities, if our teaching staff had interests in these areas. The overwhelming force of the school faculty, devoted in word *and deed* to leisure interest in a wide range of sports and the arts, as participants as well as spectators, could well vanquish the ridiculous status system to which the American adolescent now seems to subscribe. But in truth, *do not many teachers agree with this system?* Do they not agree that the football player is important, while the boy who likes tennis, painting, or playing in a chamber group has something wrong with him? Studies by Coleman and others indicate that the adolescent subculture exists, but we do not know if it is immutable, because teachers have never really declared war on it, using their own lives as examples.

In a world of rapid change, the security which comes from

any sort of competence becomes a psychological necessity. It provides a stability which can transcend personal disruptions and—particularly through participation in the arts—can instill a feeling for order, permanence, and harmony which may be of great importance. However, it would seem that at the present time, the psychological values of the arts are more appreciated by therapists in mental hospitals than by teachers in the public schools.

These activities (and the reader can supply many more) have one additional merit, and that is through the chance for personal *self-judgments* of competence. That is, through practice a person can develop his own standards with which he can judge his own performance without being completely dependent on the status rewards of others. Great sources of personal satisfaction are available to the person who has the functional autonomy to evaluate his own performances. We are suggesting, then, that through the availability for *every* student of a wide range of activities of a meaningful and purposeful sort which can be continued into adult life, it may be possible for the school to add new dimensions of individual and social status. As a consequence, the school might reverse, to some degree, the trend (rooted in occupational, technological, and economic transformations and reinforced through the mass media) toward other-directed behavior and values. Also, such activities and status systems would help to reduce the overemphasis on prestige (which is the worth of a position) and would provide new areas for the status of esteem (which is the vitally important worth of a *person's* actions).

General Education

One of the most intriguing notions which is logically consistent with the material we have discussed in this and preceding chapters is that the strategy of general education programs, both in the schools and in the colleges, could well be reversed. That is, instead of being oriented primarily in the past, the program should center around the *present*, through utilization of the techniques of the social sciences in the examination of *contemporary* social institutions. The study of contemporary society generally has little status in the academic world because it does not have the reverential aura which surrounds the study of the past. (Also, statements regarding the past are safer than those regarding the present, as the former are more difficult to invalidate.)

The crucial assertion here is that the American heritage can be *deduced from* an analysis of contemporary American society, instead of from making generalizations based almost exclusively on the past, and ignoring present cultural and societal trends and issues. Many courses entitled Contemporary Society or Modern Social Problems start with prehistoric man and never get past the Civil War. Such courses seldom give students tools and insights to deepen their awareness of the present and the future; and these are, after all, the time dimensions they must live in. If the study of general education began with the present, the insights and methods developed would stand a much greater chance of being useful in the future. This does not mean, of course, that the study of the past should be eliminated, but it does mean that we should approach the past only after developing some understanding of the present.

Teachers feel more comfortable in the past because they have had a long time to study it, while the present represents problems which they themselves have not solved, changes which they have not yet accepted. Having lived longer than their students, teachers often recollect the past *as they lived it*, which the students cannot do. Today's high school students often think of Hitler as a rather comic figure who resembled Charlie Chaplin. This response horrifies teachers (and perhaps justifiably so), but how can one who lived through World War II communicate the experience to one who did not? Present events and experiences offer a much more fertile field for analysis, as the teacher and student approach them in somewhat the same terms.

Critics of this approach will say that our cultural heritage which forms the basis of general education cannot be discovered through an analysis of contemporary society and culture. Yet, if we cannot find our heritage in the present, to what extent is it *still* our heritage? The shift from Traditional to Emergent values, the evolution of bureaucracies and relativistic morality, the lack of personal autonomy—all suggest that certain assumptions which state that the present is caused *only* by the past need to be questioned. The student who approaches the present armed only with a collection of generalizations about the past (made, often, by other people) is going to view the present along only one dimension—how well it squares with judgments of the past. In the same vein, many teachers deal with their present classes only in terms of judgments made of previous classes. In both cases, historical judgments can render a person incapable of seeing the richness, complexity, and spontaneity of the present. We have shown many inadequacies in social science techniques; nevertheless, they represent profitable attempts at assessing the present. Certainly, they have produced a great deal of worthwhile and significant information.

Few schools offer courses in psychology, sociology, or anthropology at the present time, generally on the grounds that such study is too difficult. It is interesting to note that students can usually get advanced work of a high level in math, chemistry, and English, but not in the social sciences. Certainly any student who is believed to be capable of reading *Macbeth, Hamlet,* or *Lear* is capable of undertaking the social sciences. The same is clearly true of teachers as well.

The development of an interdisciplinary course in the social sciences which would actively study the present and the individual's place in it, fitting in historical concepts *around* this central theme, could be very useful in both secondary schools and colleges, but particularly as a way of accomplishing the objectives of general education for those whose education ends with high school. Without such a course, these students might not be capable of evaluating their lives or their culture, and thus may become the prisoners of those coercive forces within our society which claim to set them free.

NOTES

1. The Reconstructionist position is stated by T. Brameld. See his chapter in *Philosophies of Education*, P. Phenix, ed., (New York, 1961), 103-112. This book gives relatively clear treatments of some of the major philosophical problems in education. See also T. Brameld, *Toward a Reconstructed Philosophy of Education*, (New York, 1956), particularly the Epilogue entitled "Reconstructionism and Its Critics: A Dialogue."

2. Many publications have given some idea of the amazing growth of educational technology, as well as the lack of sound theory in its application. A good summary of the kind of project made possible by Title Seven of the National Defense Education Act can be found in *The New Media in Education,* edited by J. Edling (Sacramento, California, 1960).

3. H. Hullfish and P. Smith, *Reflective Thinking: The Method of Education,* (New York, 1961), 187-188.

4. G. Spindler, "Education in a Transforming American Culture," *Harvard Educational Review*, 25 (1955), 145-156.

5. Alexander Pope put it this way: He who builds a Church to God and not to Fame/Will never mark the Marble with his Name.

6. J. W. Getzels, "The Acquisition of Values in School and Society," *The High School in a New Era,* F. Chase and H. Anderson, eds., (Chicago, 1958), 146-161. This paper gives a good summary of analyses by Riesman, Spindler, Robert Lynd, and William H. Whyte, and interprets them in an educational framework. (Italics in original.)

7. See Getzels, *op. cit.* One of the best-known studies in the area is that of P. Jacobs, *Changing Values in College,* (New York, 1957). A penetrating analysis of this study, and the methodologies and conclusions of other studies of values has been done by David Riesman, "The Jacob Report," *American Sociological Review,* 23 (1958), 732-738. The major conclusion of these studies is that colleges generally fail to alter the students' values in any important way. However, the issues of big or small college, in big or small town, attitude of faculty, and purpose of attending make the generalizations very difficult to validate. As Riesman says, "The lack of specific impact of colleges today on many of their students is a tribute to their *general* effectiveness" (p. 737). Such studies need to be done at the high school level, both for the future collegian

and for the terminal student, in order to add to the meaning of the college studies. Some very exciting work will be done here; and ultimately, longitudinal studies, beginning with the very young child and extending throughout adulthood, may give us for the first time a picture of the developmental aspects of values. Other studies of college students which might be of interest are P. Lazarsfeld and W. Thielen, *The Academic Mind*, (Glencoe, Illinois, 1958); T. Newcomb, *Personality and Social Change*, (New York, 1958), a study of the impact of Bennington College; and J. Gillespie and G. Allport, *Youth's Outlook on the Future*, (New York, 1955), which offers some interesting comparative material. See also E. Eddy, *The College Influence on Student Character*, (Washington, D. C., 1959). Some of the methods of leapfrogging now available should be used in longitudinal studies which would provide us with a *developmental* knowledge of values, their acquisition, *and their extinction*.

Index

A

Acculturation, 76
Adelson, J., 108
Allport, G., 157, 169, 238
Amis, K., 109
Aristotle, 172
Aronson, E., 168
Authority in a democracy, 121-126

B

Baldwin, M., 169
Banks, T., 141
Bayles, E., 206
Beard, C., 144
Becker, C., 111, 137, 140, 141
Becker, H., 62, 109
Beilin, H., 108
Bendix, R., 59, 107, 108
Bensman, J., 60
Bergson, H., 157
Blalock, H., 60, 107
Blanshard, P., 227
Blau, P., 108
Bode, B., 135, 141, 187, 206
Boggs, S., 108
Brameld, T., 237
Bronfenbrenner, U., 61
Brown, M., 204
Brozek, J., 169
Bruner, J., 187, 205
Buckley, W., 59
Burke, K., 170

C

Campbell, D., 169
Cantril, H., 108, 168
Caplow, T., 140
Carpenter, D., 62
Caudill, W., 108
Centers, R., 16-18, 60
Chinoy, E., 107, 109, 167
Coleman, J., 62, 109, 162, 169
Combs, A., 207
Cooley, C., 144
Cranston, R., 169
Cultural homogeneity, 2
Cultural lag:
    definition of, 110-114
    technical culture—value culture,
        110-114
    value compatibility, 119-121
Cultural lag, social change, and education, 110-141
Cultural pluralism, 127-129
Culture, definition of, 3

D

Dalton, R., 167, 168
Darwin, C., 157
Davis, A., 16, 60, 61
Davis, K., 7, 59, 64, 140
Day, C., 55
Deese, J., 204
Descartes, R., 173
Dewey, J., 178, 189, 191, 205, 206

239